Seventeenth-Century English Poetry

The Borzoi Anthology of 17th-Century English Literature

GENERAL EDITOR

Joseph A. Mazzeo
Columbia University

Seventeenth-Century English Poetry (*Vols. I & II*)
EDITED BY *MIRIAM K. STARKMAN*
Queens College of The City University of New York

Seventeenth-Century English Prose (*Vol. III*)
EDITED BY *DAVID NOVARR*, *Cornell University*

Literary Criticism of Seventeenth-Century England (*Vol. IV*)
EDITED BY *EDWARD W. TAYLER*, *Columbia University*

Religious Prose of Seventeenth-Century England (*Vol. V*)
EDITED BY *ANNE DAVIDSON FERRY*, *Harvard University*

Seventeenth-Century English Poetry

EDITED BY

Miriam K. Starkman

QUEENS COLLEGE OF
THE CITY UNIVERSITY OF NEW YORK

ALFRED · A · KNOPF
NEW YORK
1967

THIS IS A BORZOI BOOK,
PUBLISHED BY ALFRED A. KNOPF, INC.

 Distributed by Random House, Inc. Published simultaneously in Toronto, Canada, by Random House of Canada Limited.

FIRST PRINTING

*Library of Congress
Catalog Card Number: 66–23228
Manufactured in the United States of America.*

Acknowledgments

Acknowledgments are due to the Clarendon Press for permission to use these standard editions:

John Donne. *John Donne: The Divine Poems.* 1952. Edited by Helen Gardner.
The Poems of John Donne. 1912. Edited by H. J. C. Grierson.

George Herbert. *The Works of George Herbert.* 1941. Edited by F. E. Hutchinson.

Henry Vaughan. *The Works of Henry Vaughan,* 2nd ed. 1957. Edited by L. C. Martin.

Thomas Traherne. *Thomas Traherne, Centuries, Poems, and Thanksgiving.* 1958. Edited by H. M. Margoliouth.

Richard Crashaw. *Poems English, Latin and Greek of Richard Crashaw,* 2nd ed. 1957. Edited by L. C. Martin.

Contents

John Donne (*cont.*)

George Herbert

FROM *The Temple*

Henry Vaughan

FROM *Silex Scintillans*

Thomas Traherne

Richard Crashaw

FROM *Steps to the Temple*

Seventeenth-Century English Poetry

Introduction

The division of these two volumes of the poetry of the seventeenth century (that anomalous term that encompasses the period from the 1590s to the 1660s) into one ushered in by John Donne and the other by Ben Jonson is not intended to perpetuate clichés about the "metaphysical" and "classical" schools of the period; it is intended, rather, to focus attention upon certain broad lines of poetic usage within the period and to provide representation of a maximum amount of the poetry of major figures. Each volume is intended to be self-sufficient, but both are not mutually exclusive. The first volume, in that it deals with the poetry of Donne, Herbert, Vaughan, Traherne, and Crashaw, may legitimately be labeled a volume of metaphysical poetry. By another series of assumptions, it may just as legitimately be labeled a volume of baroque poetry. For the second volume, terminology grows a little complex in that the Donnean manner no doubt influenced some of the "Sons of Ben": Carew and Suckling are cases in point. Donne was not anti-classical, and "The Expostulation," hitherto variously ascribed to either Donne or Jonson by responsible scholars, proves that Jonson was not untouched by metaphysics; his astute criticism of Donne proves no more than the fact that he was very sensitive to the work of a fellow poet. Remove the concept of classical genres from Donne and much of his work—his epigrams, elegies, satyres, and verse epistles—will be meaningless. Mr. Hugh Kenner's observation that Jonson and Donne are the Pound and Eliot of the seventeenth century[1] is very meaningful.

The term "metaphysical," as it describes the kind of poetry exemplified (though not innovated) and brought to its highest perfection in English in the work of John Donne, is not easily defined; nevertheless it is not expendable either. The critical preoccupation of the first half of our century with metaphysical poetry, one that attempted not so much to elucidate seventeenth-century poetry as to serve our own poetic and critical exigencies, is a fascinating and complex chapter in literary history. It left us, however, with a somewhat inflated awe of the metaphysical as if it were the final touchstone of taste in poetry. It also left us with some very complex and categorical definitions concerning the matter and method of metaphysical poetry. For the term may be used with an embarrassing hospitality to time and style: there have been at least two other metaphysical periods in English poetry besides the one at issue, the Medieval and our own; and as style the metaphysical may address itself in varying proportions to theme, or tone, or image, or diction, or versification. In our somewhat neo-classical idolatry of Donne, we have also tended to equate him with metaphysical poetry; in fact, however, there are many voices in metaphysical poetry, and members of the "school of Donne"—Lord Herbert of Cherbury and Bishop Henry King, for example—are relatively insignificant in contrast to the followers of Donne like George Herbert, or Henry Vaughan, who were less "influenced" by Donne than by their common historical and aesthetic determinants.

These common determinants relate primarily to a complex and changing world picture in which the hierarchical principle of the universe was in rapid flux; reformation and revolution were the staples of experience as well as of learning in church and state, in science, philosophy, and in poetics. The poets with whom we are concerned did not initiate the flux; they expressed it. They are "metaphysical" because they were occupied with philosophical reality, "the problem of the Many and the One," [2] because in this most transitional of transitional periods they

[1] Hugh Kenner, ed., *Seventeenth Century Poetry: The Schools of Donne and Jonson* (New York: Holt, Rinehart and Winston, 1964), p. xxx.

[2] James Smith, "On Metaphysical Poetry," *Scrutiny*, II, 3 (December 1933), 228.

straddled two worlds, heaven and earth, and one was as palpably real to them as the other. Their secular poetry, even in its moments of levity, has seriousness; their devotional poetry, even in its transcendental flights, has reality. They were colloquial and dramatic because they spoke the language of men and were deeply engaged. They were witty, subtle, and argumentative, learned and recondite, because they had taken all knowledge to be their province and were unimpressed by barriers among doctrines and disciplines. They were "strong" in their lines, rough in their accents, and original in their structures because they were in revolt against stale jingling tunes and wished to be heard in their authentic voices. They were reacting to a stale Petrarchism, a tarnished aureate diction, and classical allusions that had lost their savor. They were, in our terminology, psychologically serious. But they were not destructive and they did not reject that which was still viable in their inheritance. They were as concerned as any "classicist" with men and manners, the game of love, satire and panegyric, epistle and elegy, epigram and epitaph; their devotional poetry ran the whole gamut of prayer and praise. They had emotional as well as intellectual range, scepticism and passion. But they were not cultist or faddist in their innovations. They spoke in many voices, for metaphysical poetry has a broad spectrum.

Ironically, some of these characteristics for which we have most valued metaphysical poetry were considered "faults" in the seventeenth century. "For not being understood," Jonson said, Donne "would perish," "for not keeping of accent" he deserved hanging. Donne, Dryden complained, "affects the metaphysics, not only in his satires, but in his amorous verses, where nature only should reign; and perplexes the minds of the fair sex with nice speculations of philosophy, when he should engage their hearts, and entertain them with the softnesses of love." But in his own way Donne was trying to achieve "plainness" and logical urgency no less than Jonson and Dryden.

In his choice of genres Donne seldom strays outside the purlieus of the *genus humile*, the plain style—epigrams, epitaphs, satires, verse epistles, elegies. Only in the *Anniversary* poems does he move into the grand style, and for all their fascination they remain curiously unresolved as poems, no matter how accomplished they may be as meditations. Among his secular poems, however, it is for the *Songs and Sonets* that we value Donne primarily; they have been summoned to serve as arbiters of lyric taste because they have displayed the wit, irony, paradox, ambiguity, passion that, we have been told, should be the very stuff of poetry. But though we have come to a more temperate appraisal of Donne's lyricism lately, its true value has not been obscured. These poems are possessed of a timeless vigor and a desperate honesty. They ring every possible change on the theme of love, from outrageous cynicism to high passion, all deeply felt and believed. Written for a private audience when for any audience at all, most of them unpublished in Donne's lifetime, the songs and sonnets needed to accommodate themselves to nothing but their own realities. But to insist upon their anti-Petrarchism is inaccurate, for Petrarchism carries within it room enough for the stances of libertinism as well as Platonic worship of the lady. Donne's special quality is not that he plays the game of love differently so much as that he plays it so passionately and intellectually, and always honestly. His lyrics give the impression of being freshly minted though the whole complex history of the English lyric supports them, its native as well as its imported strains. There is no such religious an ecstasy in Donne's *Divine Poems* as in "The Extasie" of the *Songs and Sonets*. And the tension of the new and old astronomies is seldom so finely drawn as in the figures of "A Valediction; forbidding mourning." For such serious concern with the theme of love, philosophy, science, and theology were necessary referrents.

The characteristic image of metaphysical poetry, the "conceit," that is the "conception" as opposed to comment or observation, the primary ingredient of Donne's "wit," operates on many levels. It may depend upon subtle theological distinctions for its seriousness, as in "Aire and Angels":

> Then as an Angell, face, and wings
> Of aire, not pure as it, yet pure doth weare,
> So thy love may be my loves spheare;
> Just such disparitie
> As is twixt Aire and Angells puritie,
> 'Twixt womens love, and mens will ever bee.

or in "The Extasie":

On man heavens influence workes not so,
  But that it first imprints the ayre,
Soe soule into the soule may flow,
  Though it to body first repaire.

As our blood labours to beget
  Spirits, as like soules as it can,
Because such fingers need to knit
  That subtile knot, which makes us man:

So must pure lovers soules descend
  T' affections, and to faculties,
Which sense may reach and apprehend,
  Else a great Prince in prison lies.

Just as subtly, Donne can tune his conceit to achieve the air of a delicate libertinism, as in "The Funerall":

Who ever comes to shroud me, do not harme
  Nor question much
That subtile wreath of haire, which crowns my arme;
The mystery, the signe you must not touch,
  For 'tis my outward Soule,
Viceroy to that, which then to heaven being gone,
  Will leave this to controule,
And keepe these limbes, her Provinces, from dissolution.

or in "The Relique":

If this fall in a time, or land,
Where mis-devotion doth command,
Then, he that digges us up, will bring
Us, to the Bishop, and the King,
  To make us Reliques; then
Thou shalt be a Mary Magdalen, and I
  A something else thereby;

The distance between Donne's secular and his devotional poetry is short. As a category, devotional poetry has its own determinants, and Donne, like Jonson and Eliot after him, questioned its validity. In a letter to Sir Robert Carr, Donne wrote: "I did best when I had least truth for my subjects. In this present case there is so much truth as it defeats all Poetry." And certainly the balance between truth and poetry, between religious and poetic belief is a perilous one. The recognition of that balance, however, is crucial to an understanding of devotional poetry. Devotional poetry has a wide spectrum of usage, from the most discursive and didactic on the one hand to the most lyrical and ecstatic on the other. We cannot easily come to terms with Donne's "The Crosse" or "The Annunciation and Passion" unless we recognize them as meditations of a primarily didactic functioning. We may not be drawn to devotional meditation, but we cannot take exception to the poems for being themselves. With the exceptions of the "Holy Sonnets" and the three hymns, Donne's *Divine Poems* are occasional, discursive, and didactic. The "*La Corona*" sonnets approach ecclesiasticism. In the "Holy Sonnets," however, poetic and religious belief merge into a marvelous synthesis. Cast into the meditational mold, these sonnets possess a spiritual urgency and realism that makes them available to anyone sensitive to spiritual struggle. Here the metaphysical wit has a subject worthy of its steel. If in the secular songs and sonnets Donne sometimes worshipped the lady with a piety and learning appropriate to God, in the "Holy Sonnets" he worshipped God with a passion more usually accorded the lady:

> Yet dearely'I love you, and would be lov'd faine,
> But am betroth'd unto your enemie,
> Divorce mee,'untie, or breake that knot againe,
> Take mee to you, imprison mee, for I
> Except you'enthrall mee, never shall be free,
> Nor ever chast, except you ravish mee.

It was not Donne, however, but George Herbert who was the source and well-spring of devotional poetry for the seventeenth century. He gave it authority and range, and he served as model not only in his poetry but in his piety. Both poets worked within the inherited tradition of the divine poetry of the Middle Ages and the Renaissance as it was peculiarly the property of the Anglican preacher. And though Herbert was more single-mindedly the devotional poet, and the purer spirit, he had much the same sensibility as Donne. His symbolic usage, however, is richer than Donne's, his Old Testament typology more knowing and alive, his use of the meditation and the emblem more fully absorbed into the poetic necessity, his ear more musically tuned and subtle.

Born into the orthodox faith, and dead before the upheavals of either Laud or the Revolution, George Herbert remained a conservative formalist comfortable with the doctrine and ritual of the Anglican Church. He seems not to have been exercised much by dogma, but the inherited symbols of the Church, as they were available to him from the liturgy and iconography, he was able to put to brilliant use in his poetry. A professional rhetorician, he had a wide range of devices serving image and structure. He was gifted with an emblematic eye, by which he could turn his whole architectural edifice, as well as its component parts, into line and figure. But perhaps his greatest gift was his musical erudition as it served him for subject, image, and metrical guide. Born into a sophisticated level of society, and only by coincidence deprived of secular preferment, he renounced the Secular Muse of poetry and courted the Divine Muse with as much grace and concern for his *ars poetica* as ever did Sir Philip Sidney.

> Who sayes that fictions onely and false hair
>   Become a verse? Is there in truth no beautie?
> Is all good structure in a winding stair?
> May no lines passe, except they do their dutie
>   Not to a true, but painted chair?
>
> Is it no verse, except enchanted groves
> And sudden arbours shadow course-spunne lines?
> Must purling streams refresh a lovers loves?
> Must all be vail'd, while he that reades, divines,
>   Catching the sense at two removes?
>
> Shepherds are honest people; let them sing:
> Riddle who list, for me, and pull for Prime:
> I envie no mans nightingale or spring;
> Nor let them punish me with losse of rime,
>   Who plainly say, *My God, My King.*
>
> ("Jordan I")

And having decided for the Sacred Muse, he proceeded like Sidney to look in his heart and write:

> . . . *How wide is all this long pretence!*
> *There is in love a sweetnesse readie penn'd:*

Copie out onely that, and save expense.
(From "Jordan II")

In *The Temple* George Herbert raised a structure of great beauty and strength. Its order is beyond the order of simple narrative or the clustering of groups of poems, but of an essential unity of intention and effect. From the seventy-seven didactic verses of "The Church Porch," where we are urged to purge our hearts as Christ did the Temple (71), we pass under the lintel, "The *Superliminare*," and arrive at "The Altar," the first poem of "The Church" which is the central part of the edifice itself. After one hundred and seventy-three poems, we come to the last, "Love III":

> You must sit down, sayes Love, and taste my meat:
> So I did sit and eat.

The two hundred and seventy-nine lines, in rhyming couplets, of "The Church Militant," which follows "The Church," may be considered a coda to "The Temple" or a discrete work. Its subject is the history of the Church; it is entirely didactic.

The devotional range of *The Temple* is large. The subjects are drawn from the familiar phenomena of the Christian faith, taking in the whole drama of Christianity: the Church Calendar from Easter through Christmas, the feasts and festivals of the Church, the sacraments, the Church as *synagoga, ecclesia,* and structure. The manner is as generous as the matter. A random leafing of the pages takes us from the simple allusiveness of "The British Church" whose beauty Herbert spells out in contrast to the wanton painted one on the hill and the naked slovenly one in the valley:

> A fine aspect in fit aray
> Neither too mean, nor yet too gay,
> Shows who is best.
> Outlandish looks may not compare:
> For all they either painted are,
> Or else undrest.

to the dense eucharistic symbolism of "The Bunch of Grapes":

But can he want the grape, who hath the wine?
I have their fruit and more.
Blessed be God, who prosper'd *Noahs* vine,
And made it bring forth grapes good store.
But much more him I must adore,
Who of the Laws sowre juice sweet wine did make,
Ev'n God himself being pressed for my sake.

The neatest of hieroglyphs ("Aaron"), speaking emblems ("The Altar"), most musical of modulations ("Easter-Wings"), profound meditations ("The Sacrifice") follow one another with prodigal ease.

But Herbert's major themes are prayer and praise in the lyrical mode. The poet stands poised on the antithesis between God and Man, Sin and Salvation, Penitence and Thanksgiving, the Christian and the Congregation. He dwells comfortably at both ends, anguished by the sinfulness of man, but mindful of the everlasting goodness of God, and makes his peace with grace and skill, confident of salvation, which is his ultimate theme. Dogmatic and poetic realism meet in him on a level of universal spiritual awareness. Institutional and personal piety become one; piety and poetry become one. It is by the deepest irony that this sophisticated *dévot* should have become in the eighteenth and nineteenth centuries the "quaint" Mr. Herbert, that his subtle emblematic usage should have become an object lesson of "false wit," or that the singular purity of his faith should have been construed as parochialism. It is to the credit of modern scholarship that it restored Herbert to the eminence he enjoyed when Crashaw entitled his volume of devotion *Steps to the Temple*, and when Henry Vaughan prefaced his *Silex Scintillans* with homage to "the blessed man, Mr. George Herbert."

In the "author's Preface" to the 1655 edition of his *Silex Scintillans* (a re-issue of Part I, originally published in 1650, with the addition, for the first time, of Part II), Henry Vaughan violently renounced his Secular Muse and avowed his indebtedness to George Herbert:

The first, that with any effectual success attempted a *diversion* of this foul and overflowing *stream* [the "lascivious fictions" of secular poetry] was the blessed man, Mr. *George Herbert,* whose holy *life*

> and *verse* gained many pious *Converts*, (of whom I am the least) and gave the first check to a most flourishing and admired *wit* of his time.

Herbert thus becomes crucial not only to Vaughan's poetic but also to his religious conversion. Yet Vaughan's indebtedness to Herbert in the practice as well as the theory of his poetry is not, ultimately, crucial. Lines, images, titles are borrowed freely, but Vaughan's greatest poems are not Herbertian. Of all the poets represented in this volume, Henry Vaughan alone was not in holy orders, a point of some significance. Similarly, John Milton's "church-outing" by the prelates shaped his devotional poetry to a significant extent. Vaughan's lack of "orders," for all his doctrinal erudition, accounts for what may be called the "mechanick" touch in Vaughan's devotional poetry, vague intimations of John Bunyan. Lacking the blood and bone familiarity with the devotional tradition that is the natural property of the devotional poet in orders, he leans on Herbert, as he leans on the Bible and Nature, for his devotional matter. The situation, however, was not without its value; if it made Vaughan derivative and literalistic in some poems, in others it allowed him the freedom to assume his own authentic, original voice.

The majority of the poems in *Silex Scintillans* are traditional: homiletic and didactic poems, translations of the Psalms (that staple of devotional poetry), poems built on specific Biblical texts, and prayer and praise often derivative of Herbert. Some of these poems fall curiously flat, as if Vaughan were concerned with the letter rather than the spirit of devotion, as if the poet were speaking a foreign language. Vaughan's "The Passion," for example, in contrast to Herbert's "The Sacrifice" on the same theme, succeeds in supporting itself in only four lines of its fifty-six, and they are derived from Herbert's "The Agonie." After the first two lines: "I cannot reach it; and my striving eye/ Dazles at it, as at eternity," "Childe-hood" disintegrates into plain statement which is inadequate to its purposes. Essentially, however, these poems, numerous as they are, are not significant. For when Vaughan speaks in his own voice he is among the greatest of devotional poets. His proper position is at the transcendental point of the devotional spectrum, at vision. Some critics would label him a mystic, but their use of the term is so loose, so much qualified by limitations—he is a "nature" mystic, an "incomplete" mystic—that one does better to eschew it. But even a visionary quest is not entirely self-determined, and to a certain extent, at least, is determined by historical imperatives. Mr. Warnke suggests that by Vaughan's time (and the point is significant for Traherne too) "the new philosophy has triumphed, and the older view has become merely quaint." Only through magic and mysticism can the poet encompass his vision.[3]

The vision for Vaughan, though highly personal, is circumscribed by Christianity. Its major theme is Regeneration, conversion, or calling: the light of God shining suddenly upon the poet, the emptiness he felt before the call, the joys following it, the painful pilgrimage, the light that sparks only sporadically, the veil that obscures the light. Whether one interprets "Regeneration" as an Augustinian meditation on the Garden of the Soul, or as a mystical poem yearning for final consummation of the union of the soul with God, or more simply as a spiritual allegory of the soul's pilgrimage to God, is, finally, not more significant than that one recognize the transcendental voice of the poet, and the essential humanism of the poem; its painful pilgrimage is the privileged possession of every human being. Similarly, "The World" charters the difficulty of the spiritual quest and ends on the same note of uncertainty, beyond all effort the need for grace. The quest is attended by dejection: the Creatures are more safely housed than Man:

> He knocks at all doors, strays and roams,
> Nay hath not so much wit as some stones have
> Which in the darkest nights point to their homes,
> By some hid sense their Maker gave;
> Man is the shuttle, to whose winding quest
> And passage through these looms
> God order'd motion, but ordain'd no rest.
>
> (From "Man")

He looks back with nostalgia to the lost innocence of childhood:

> O how I long to travell back
> And tread again that ancient track!

[3] Frank J. Warnke, ed., *European Metaphysical Poetry* (New Haven: Yale University Press, 1961), p. 75.

That I might once more reach that plaine,
Where first I left my glorious traine,
From whence th'Inlightned spirit sees
That shady City of Palme trees;
(From "The Retreate")

Though Vaughan's biography tells us of the many losses he endured, his poems on death seem to have more than a biographical source; they are related to his quest for eternity, an urgency for assurances of eternity, glimpses of the heavenly city, a need, somehow, to tear away the veil between life and death.

They are all gone into the world of light!
And I alone sit lingring here;
Their very memory is fair and bright,
And my sad thoughts doth clear.

. . .

He that hath found some fledg'd birds nest, may know
At first sight, if the bird be flown;
But what fair Well, or Grove he sings in now,
That is to him unknown.

And yet, as Angels in some brighter dreams
Call to the soul, when man doth sleep:
So some strange thoughts transcend our wonted theams,
And into glory peep.

If a star were confin'd into a Tomb
Her captive flames must needs burn there;
But when the hand that lockt her up, gives room,
She'l shine through all the sphære.

O Father of eternal life, and all
Created glories under thee!
Resume thy spirit from this world of thrall
Into true liberty.

Either disperse these mists, which blot and fill
My perspective (still) as they pass,
Or else remove me hence unto that hill,
Where I shall need no glass.
(From "They are all gone")

With variations, Vaughan pursues the theme in "Come, come, what doe I here?" "I walkt the other day (to spend my hour)," "As time one day by me did pass," and "Fair and Yong light." The quest for eternity may, however, also be attended by joy anticipated, as in "Midnight," "The Morning-Watch," or, most simply, in "Peace."

The primary manifestation of Vaughan's vision is in Light: day and night; sun, star, and candle; streams, shoots, squibs, and seeds of light. The light may be reflected or refracted, obscured by veils or dust, but it is never completely hidden; even the dark is luminous. The garden of Nature, too, is divine: seed, bud, and flower, the Creatures, even inanimate nature as it worships dumbly, often hermetically, magnetically. For Nature is still allegorical for Vaughan, if not as systematically sacramental as it was for Herbert and Donne. We are still a long way from the secular transcendentalism of Romanticism, from Nature as landscape and teacher, but we can see the distant prospect of Romanticism in the future.

But for all our investigation of Vaughan's mind and art, his devotional antecedents, his formal usage, his Augustinian meditational structures and content, the emblematic control by which abstract concepts grow concrete and vivid on the page, his philosophical sources in Platonism and neo-Platonism, his Hermetic erudition by which all Nature turns magical and analogous of Creation, Vaughan remains, somehow, a difficult poet, a little obscure, a little elusive. Whatever may account for it—the fact that poets educated out of the formal framework of their time or art (like Browning) tend to speak a slightly foreign language; the fact that Vaughan was more a Welshman than the other devotional poets of his time (most of whom seem to have had some Welsh blood in them, as Miss White has noted); [4] the fact that he dwells in an already dying sacramental world; the fact that he often writes from a point in the devotional spectrum which is itself elusive—he exercises and teases the imagination, but our eyes dazzle. His philosophical erudition, Plato, Augustine, and Hermes, his inherited devotional tradition, all serve him as he needs them, for image and analogy, rather than for matter. For the visionary poet, his vision is sufficient subject. Divinity lies

[4] Helen C. White, *The Metaphysical Poets* (New York: Collier Books, 1962), p. 289.

all about Vaughan, immanent and transcendent. The vision is vouchsafed in glimpses, stray beams and squibs of light, the candle flickers, the veil becomes translucent, the seed grows secretly.

For Thomas Traherne the vision is a vision of Felicity:

> No empty Space; it is all full of Sight,
> All Soul and Life, an Ey most bright,
> All Light and Lov;
> Which doth at once all things possess and giv,
> Heven and Earth, with All that therin liv;
> It rests at quiet, and doth mov;
> Eternal is, yet Time includes;
> A Scene abov
> All Interludes.
>
> (From "Felicity")

The vision is a revelation of the extraordinary goodness, beauty, and generosity of God which lie all about us and need but to be apprehended to be possessed. By possessing the world we possess God, worship Him and become one with Him. The infant is born sinless, but his "content" and "innocence" are soon lost, and the child is left "alone and desolate," grieved and deprived:

> I wonder'd much to see
> That all my Wealth should be
> Confin'd in such a little Room,
> Yet hope for more I scarcely durst presume.
> It griev'd me sore
> That such a scanty Store
> Should be my All:
>
> (From "Poverty")

Childhood, however, is still relatively innocent and the lost vision may be recaptured, as the poet himself recaptured it (at the age of four) in a vision of blinding beauty. The theme is recurrent in Traherne's poetry, but nowhere is it presented so brilliantly as in the poetic prose of the *Centuries of Meditation:*

> The Corn was Orient and Immortal Wheat, which never should be reaped, nor was ever sown. I thought it had stood from everlasting to everlasting. The Dust and Stones of the Street were as Precious

> as GOLD. The Gates were at first the End of the World, The Green Trees when I saw them first through one of the Gates Transported and Ravished me; their Sweetness and unusual Beauty made my Heart to leap, and almost mad with Extasie, they were such strange and Wonderful Thing: The Men! O what Venerable and Reverend Creatures did the Aged seem! Immortal Cherubims! And yong Men Glittering and Sparkling Angels and Maids strange Seraphick Pieces of Life and Beauty! Boys and Girles Tumbling in the Street, and Playing, were moving Jewels. I knew not that they were Born or should Die. But all things abided Eternaly as they were in their Proper Places. Eternity was Manifest in the Light of the Day, and som thing infinit Behind evry thing appeared: which talked with my Expectation and moved my Desire. The Citie seemed to stand in Eden, or to be Built in Heaven. The Streets were mine, the Temple was mine, the People were mine, their Clothes and Gold and Silver was mine, as much as their Sparkling Eys Fair Skins and ruddy faces. The skies were mine, and so were the Sun and Moon and Stars, and all the World was mine, and I the only Spectator and Enjoyer of it. I knew no Churlish Proprieties, nor Bounds nor Divisions: but all Proprieties and Divisions were mine: all Treasures and the Possessors of them. So that with much adoe I was corrupted; and made to learn the Dirty Devices of this World. Which now I unlearn, and becom as it were a little Child again, that I may enter into the Kingdom of GOD.
>
> (From "The Third Century," Part III)

Life, in time, darkens the vision, and the poet's quest is a search for its recapture; his themes are recollections of Felicity, Felicity lost and found.

Unlike Vaughan, however, Traherne is as much preoccupied by the philosophy of his vision as by its experience. God is both the means and end of all our joy. He delights in giving, so that by taking of His world man may know and worship Him:

> The End in Him from Everlasting is
> The Fountain of all Bliss.
> From Everlasting it
> Efficient was, and Influence did Emit,
> That caused all. Before
> The World, we do Adore
> This Glorious End. Becaus all Benefit
> From it proceeds. Both are the very same.
> The End and Fountain differ but in Name.
>
> (From "The Anticipation," Stanza 4)

In our delight lies all His will:

For God enjoyed is all his End.
Himself he then doth Comprehend.
When He is Blessed, Magnified,
Extold, Exalted, Praisd and Glorified
Honord, Esteemd, Belovd, Enjoyd,
Admired, Sanctified, Obeyd,
That is receivd. For He
Doth place his Whole Felicitie
In that, who is despised and defied
Undeified almost if once denied.
(From "The Recovery," Stanza 2)

The system is a true "Circulation":

All things do first receiv, that giv.
Only tis God above,
That from, and in himself doth live,
Whose All sufficient Love
Without Original can flow
And all the Joys and Glories shew
Which Mortal Man can take Delight to know
He is the Primitive Eternal Spring
The Endless Ocean of each Glorious Thing.
The Soul a Vessel is
A Spacious Bosom to Contain
All the fair Treasures of his Bliss
Which run like Rivers from, into the Main,
And all it doth receiv returns again.
(From "The Circulation," Stanza 6)

Virtue is the delight in the world, the "Palace" built by the Bridegroom for the Bride ("The Recovery"); "Sin is a Deviation from the Way of God" ("Adam"). For reality is subjective; it lies in "Thoughts" ("Ideas"):

Thought! Surely *Thoughts* art tru;
They pleas as much as *Things* can do:
Nay Things are dead,
And in themselves are severed
From Souls; nor can they fill the Head
Without our Thoughts. Thoughts are the Reall things

From whence all Joy, from whence all Sorrow springs.
(From "Dreams")

Thoughts are superior to Matter, "Simple, like the Deitie" ("My Spirit"). And Memory and the Imagination are supreme:

My Child-hood is a Sphere
Wherein ten thousand hev'nly Joys appear:
Those *Thoughts* it doth include,
And those Affections, which review'd,
Again present to me
In better sort the *Things* which I did see.
Imaginations *Reall* are,
Unto my Mind again repair:
Which makes my Life a Circle of Delights;
A hidden Sphere of obvious Benefits:
An Earnest that the Actions of the Just
Shall still revive, and flourish in the Dust.
("The Review," II)

The ecstasy, however, is not very far from the speculative philosophy which supports it:

O Wondrous Self! O Sphere of Light,
O Sphere of Joy most fair;
O Act, O Power infinit;
O Subtile, and unbounded Air!
O Living Orb of Sight!
Thou which within me art, yet Me! Thou Ey,
And Temple of his Whole Infinitie!
(From "My Spirit")

The wonder, the Edenic joy, the Rapture are as much insisted on as figured forth:

O how Divine
Am I! To all this Sacred Wealth,
This Life and Health,
Who raisd? Who mine
Did make the same! What Hand Divine!
(From "The Rapture," Stanza 4)

We have traveled a long distance from the devotional tradition of Donne and Herbert, even from the vision of Vaughan.

Traherne has been called a mystic, but even with more qualifications and exceptions than Vaughan. He is, however, the most considerable poet in English before Blake to present a vision so carefully provided with its own philosophical justifications. The very necessity for the justifications, however, indicates the attenuation of the Metaphysical tradition. Image has given way to plain statement or simile, and insistence cannot rescue it; correspondence and symbol have given way to naturalism. His dogma lacks metaphor and symbol to embody it. Incantation takes the place of wit. Faintly in the distance we sense vague intimations of Whitman. For all that, Traherne's Felicity stands palpable and bright, a vision of great beauty.

In commenting upon Richard Crashaw last, we sacrifice chronological for genetic clarity. For though he stands in the tradition of seventeenth-century devotional poetry, he is, in a sense, atypical: extreme, sensuous, and decorative rather than logical and organic; synaesthetic, a little a-rational, unbalanced in his poetic usage, Baroque (or if the whole period is to be called Baroque, and the Metaphysical only one ingredient of it, High-Baroque). What links him to the devotional tradition, besides his fealty to Herbert, is first, his devotional range, the epigrams, the largely didactic occasional poems, the narrative poems, the translations of the Psalms, his great liturgical hymns and, second, his essentially symbolic usage (though he wears his symbols with a difference) and his emblematic and meditational quality. But thematic and formal distinctions are not easily pursued in Crashaw, for he tends to "deliquesce" into ardor, tone usurps theme and image, and he soon grows typical largely of himself. For the Baroque is hospitable to the kind of excess that offends some people in "On the wounds of our crucified Lord," or in "The Weeper," that *locus classicus* of "bad taste":

> Upwards thou dost weep.
> Heavn's bosome drinks the gentle stream.
> Where th'milky rivers creep,
> Thine floates above; & is the cream.
> Waters above th'Heavns, what they be
> We' are taught best by thy TEARES & thee.

But though this image is easy prey to such an accusation, and I cite a relatively restrained one, it is well to remember that it was intended to be read emblematically, that its literal level had long since been subsumed in the emblem. The poet does not attack gravity in these tears that flow upwards; only the tears of penitence as they move directly up to God are intended and made so vivid that there is no escaping the devotional point; they are intended to be read in the context of angelic, spiritual food, though the Cherub's song "Tasts of this Breakfast all day long."

The Baroque is also hospitable to mysticism. If the term "mystic" is to be used restrictively, referring to Christian mysticism in contrast to loose mysticisms of neo-Platonic or occult varieties of vision, ecstasy, apocalypse, or revelation, then a Christian mystical poet is a very rare phenomenon indeed. Somewhat more hospitably conceived, however, we may profitably use the term for Crashaw. In Crashaw's poetry, we speak more accurately of the mystical theme than of mysticism in general, for it is neither pervasive nor entirely sustained. More often we encounter ecstasy:

> Delicious DEATHS; soft exaltations
> Of soul; dear & divine annihilations;
>   A thousand unknown rites
> Of joyes & rarefy'd delights;
> A hundred thousand goods, glories, & graces,
>   And many a mystick thing
>   Which the divine embraces
> Of the deare spouse of spirits with them will bring
>   For which it is no shame
> That dull mortality must not know a name.
> (From "Prayer. An Ode")

Just as the context of these lines is outside the mystical way of Purgation, Illumination, and Contemplation that constitutes the pattern of orthodox Christian mysticism, Christ as a better lover than man, so the context of the following lines that conclude the "Description of A Religious House and Condition of Life" is specifically didactic, rising, however, to a flight of ecstasy:

> The self-remembring SOUL sweetly recovers
> Her kindred with the starrs; not basely hovers
> Below: But meditates her immortall way
> Home to the originall sourse of LIGHT & intellectuall Day.

It is in the Teresian poems that Crashaw approaches mysticism most explicitly, and there more often speculatively than otherwise. "In memory of the Vertuous and Learned Lady Madre de Teresa that sought an early Martyrdome" is, as the title suggests, more about martyrdom than about mysticism, the martyrdom that St. Teresa is denied so that she may "embrace a milder Martyrdome":

> Thou art Loves victim, and must dye
> A death more misticall and high.
> Into Loves hand thou shalt let fall,
> A still surving funerall.

"The Flaming Heart Upon The Book and Picture of the seraphicall saint Teresa (As She is Usually Expressed with a Seraphim biside her)" plays with epigram and emblem before it makes its final devotion, as in a litany, supplicating St. Teresa to be inspiration to him in a mystical death:

> Leave nothing of my SELF in me.
> Let me so read thy life, that I
> Unto all life of mine may dy.

It is, however, in his liturgical hymns that Crashaw's originality as a devotional poet most clearly lies. Their special quality is the baroque sensibility playing upon the theme of the sacred mysteries of Christianity. For all that they stem from the ecclesiastical end of the devotional range, they retain a humanistic relevance in their ardor, their odic quality. However much we are in the lap of a *Scala Meditationis*[5] in "To The Name Above Every Name, The Name of Jesus," we are less instructed than moved by it, hypnotized by its "witt of love." For ardor is the subject of all his hymns, though in varying degrees, whether it is Nativity, Assumption, or Epiphany that are the occasions. Even "In The Glorious Epiphanie of Our Lord God, A Hymn. Sung As By The Three Kings," the most intellectually substantial of them, surrounds its didactic point (ll. 206–235) by ardor. These hymns revel more than they meditate. There is as much private as public symbolism in them. Red, white, nest, breast, blush,

[5] Louis Martz, *The Poetry of Meditation* (New Haven: Yale University Press, 1954), p. 62.

tear, wound, dart, sweet(s) become associative, ritualistic keys (even though they derive from inherited symbols) to open the floodgates of the poet's fervor. His "vocabulary" [6] of rhymes supports the incantatory quality of his poems. Music is not only pattern and allusion for Crashaw, but the "stuff" of his ardor. "It is literally through musical ecstasy that Crashaw lifts us into his theme [in "To The Name" and "In the Glorious Epiphanie"] as it is through the music that he lifts himself into his experience." [7]

Goe, SOUL, out of thy Self, & seek for More.
  Goe & request
Great NATURE for the KEY of her huge Chest
Of Heavns, the self involving Sett of Sphears
(Which dull mortality more Feeles then heares)
  Then rouse the nest
Of nimble ART, & traverse round
The Aiery Shop of soul-appeasing Sound:
And beat a summons in the Same
  All-soveraign Name
To warn each severall kind
And shape of sweetnes, Be they such
  As sigh with supple wind
  Or answer Artfull Touch,
That they convene & come away
To wait at the love-crowned Doores of
  This Illustrious DAY.
Shall we dare This, my Soul? we'l doe't and bring
No Other note for't, but the Name we sing
  Wake LUTE & HARP
  And every sweet-lipp't Thing
  That talkes with tunefull string;
Start into life, And leap with me
Into a hasty Fitt-tun'd Harmony.

(From "To The Name Above Every Name")

In these hymns we see the *dévot* on his knees, the poet striving for a maximum expressiveness, sometimes beyond the natural limits of his medium, attempting to contain both music and painting in his poetry. If Crashaw is to continue in history as a

[6] See Mary Ellen Rickey, *Rhyme and Meaning in Richard Crashaw* (Lexington: University of Kentucky Press, 1961).
[7] Ruth C. Wallerstein, *Richard Crashaw* (Madison: University of Wisconsin Press, 1959), p. 146.

minor poet, at least his major intentions should be given their due.

This, briefly, then, plots some of the main points in the line of "Metaphysical" poetry. Whether secular or devotional its "poetic [is] of Correspondences," "the poet's universe" is "a complex system of universal, analogical relationships."[8] The power of Donne's secular poetry, as occasionally of some of its imitators', is immediately apparent though we are sometimes exercised by its subtlety and complexity. The devotional line (the devotional poets other than Donne wrote no really significant secular poetry) is, however, more vulnerable; though its other-worldly relevance is clear enough, its humanistic significance is, occasionally, questionable. If the metaphysical equilibrium was difficult for secular poetry, how much more difficult for devotional poetry that could so easily bog down in dogma at one end of its spectrum and evanesce into vagaries on the other! Some few great devotional poets were to appear after the seventeenth century, a Hopkins or an Eliot, but they sang *solus cum solo*. In a real sense, the seventeenth-century devotional poets sang a swan song; they had many heirs, but the sturdiest of them, by an appropriate irony, were the secular transcendentalists of nineteenth-century Romanticism.

[8] Joseph A. Mazzeo, "Metaphysical Poetry and the Poetic of Correspondence," in *Renaissance and Seventeenth-Century Studies* (New York: Columbia University Press, 1964), pp. 57, 59.

John Donne

John Donne, descended of an eminent Catholic family, was born in London in 1572. He was tutored at home until 1584, when he was matriculated at Hart Hall, Oxford; in 1587 he transferred to Trinity College, Cambridge. There is no record of a degree from either university. In 1591 he began his legal studies. From 1594–96 he was probably traveling abroad. In 1596 and 1597 he was in foreign service with the Earl of Essex as a volunteer for the expeditions against Cadiz and the Azores. In 1598 he became Secretary to Sir Thomas Egerton, whom he served until 1602. In 1601 Donne and Anne More, a niece of Lady Egerton, were secretly married. Donne was dismissed from his post and imprisoned for a short while. The couple was disowned by Anne's father, but they were given a home by her kinsman, Francis Wooley, in Pyrford, where they remained until 1604. In 1605 they took a small house in Mitcham, and Donne assisted Thomas Morton, later Bishop of Durham, in his controversy with the Catholics. Refusing Morton's offer of clerical preferment, which would have necessitated Donne's taking orders, Donne earned a precarious living by his pen. Between 1610–12 Sir Robert Drury was his patron; the family moved to a small house in Drury Lane in London, while Donne traveled abroad with Sir Robert. In 1614 Donne's political hopes were shattered after a brief sojourn in a Parliament that was shortly dismissed. He finally decided to take Holy Orders; in 1615 he was ordained priest, and somewhat later became Doctor of Divinity. In 1616 he was appointed Reader in Divinity at Lincoln's Inn, where he was required to preach fifty sermons a year. Anne Donne, who had borne twelve children, died in 1617. In 1619 Donne was sent abroad on a political mission with Lord Doncaster from which he returned in 1620. He was appointed Dean of St. Paul's in 1621, where he achieved fame as a preacher. Subsequently he was also appointed to the vicarage of St. Dunstan's in the West. For three months in 1625, during the plague, he stayed in Chelsea at the home of the Lady Magdalen Danvers. He preached his last sermon, before the king, on February 12, 1631, and took formal leave of his congregation. He died on March 21, 1631.

By 1600 Donne had probably written most of his love poems, elegies, and satyres. In 1608 he wrote Biathanatos, *a defense of suicide; in 1610* Pseudo Martyr, *an attempt to persuade Catholics to take an oath of allegiance to the king, was published; and in 1611 followed* Ignatius His Conclave, *an attack on the Jesuits. By this time Donne had already written some of his* Divine Poems; *"La Corona" in 1607, at least the first six of the "Holy Sonnets," "The Litany," and "The Cross." In 1611 and 1612 he wrote the two Anniversary Poems, "An Anatomy of the World" and "The Second Anniversary or The Progress of the Soul," to commemorate the death of young Elizabeth Drury.*

The major biographical source for Donne is The Life of Dr. John Donne *by Izaak Walton, first published in 1640 along with the LXXX sermons; it was enlarged in 1658.*

The first collected edition of Donne's poems was published posthumously in 1633.

The text followed here is Grierson's Clarendon Press edition, except for the Divine Poems *which follow Helen Gardner's Clarendon Press edition. A new edition of the elegies and the songs and sonnets by Helen Gardner has just been published by the Clarendon Press.*

FROM

Songs and Sonets

The good-morrow

I wonder by my troth, what thou, and I
Did, till we lov'd? were we not wean'd till then?
But suck'd on countrey pleasures, childishly?

Or snorted we in the seaven sleepers den?
T'was so; But this, all pleasures fancies bee.
If ever any beauty I did see,
Which I desir'd, and got, t'was but a dreame of thee.

And now good morrow to our waking soules,
Which watch not one another out of feare;
For love, all love of other sights controules, *10*
And makes one little roome, an every where.
Let sea-discoverers to new worlds have gone,
Let Maps to other, worlds on worlds have showne,
Let us possesse one world, each hath one, and is one.

My face in thine eye, thine in mine appeares,
And true plaine hearts doe in the faces rest,
Where can we finde two better hemispheares
Without sharpe North, without declining West?
What ever dyes, was not mixt equally;
If our two loves be one, or, thou and I *20*
Love so alike, that none doe slacken, none can die.

Song

Goe, and catche a falling starre,
  Get with child a mandrake roote,
Tell me, where all past yeares are,
  Or who cleft the Divels foot,
Teach me to heare Mermaides singing,
  Or to keep off envies stinging,
      And finde
      What winde
Serves to advance an honest minde.

If thou beest borne to strange sights, *10*
  Things invisible to see,

l.4 seaven sleepers: Christian heroes of a Syriac legend translated by Gregory of Tours. To escape the persecutions of the Emperor Decius, they hid in a cave, were walled up, and miraculously survived their two-hundred-year sleep. They awoke, unaware of the passage of time, to find the persecutions of Christians over.
l.2 mandrake roote: a forked root resembling the shape of a human being.

Ride ten thousand daies and nights,
Till age snow white haires on thee,
Thou, when thou retorn'st, wilt tell mee
All strange wonders that befell thee,
And sweare
No where
Lives a woman true, and faire.

If thou findst one, let mee know,
Such a Pilgrimage were sweet; 20
Yet doe not, I would not goe,
Though at next doore wee might meet,
Though shee were true, when you met her,
And last, till you write your letter,
Yet shee
Will bee
False, ere I come, to two, or three.

Womans constancy

Now thou hast lov'd me one whole day,
To morrow when thou leav'st, what wilt thou say?
Wilt thou then Antedate some new made vow?
Or say that now
We are not just those persons, which we were?
Or, that oathes made in reverentiall feare
Of Love, and his wrath, any may forsweare?
Or, as true deaths, true maryages untie,
So lovers contracts, images of those,
Binde but till sleep, deaths image, them unloose? 10
Or, your owne end to Justifie,
For having purpos'd change, and falsehood; you
Can have no way but falsehood to be true?
Vaine lunatique, against these scapes I could
Dispute, and conquer, if I would,
Which I abstaine to doe,
For by to morrow, I may thinke so too.

The undertaking

I have done one braver thing
Then all the *Worthies* did,
And yet a braver thence doth spring,
Which is, to keepe that hid.

It were but madnes now t'impart
The skill of specular stone,
When he which can have learn'd the art
To cut it, can finde none.

So, if I now should utter this,
Others (because no more 10
Such stuffe to worke upon, there is,)
Would love but as before.

But he who lovelinesse within
Hath found, all outward loathes,
For he who colour loves, and skinne,
Loves but their oldest clothes.

If, as I have, you also doe
Vertue'attir'd in woman see,
And dare love that, and say so too,
And forget the Hee and Shee; 20

And if this love, though placed so,
From prophane men you hide,
Which will no faith on this bestow,
Or, if they doe, deride:

Then you have done a braver thing
Then all the *Worthies* did;

l.2 Worthies: The original nine Worthies included Hector, Alexander, Julius Caesar, Joshua, David, Judas Maccabeus, Arthur, Charlemagne, and Godfrey of Bouillon; the list, however, was variable, and "all the *Worthies*" could add up to a formidable number.

l.6 specular stone: "old selenite," cut up into thin strips and used for glazing by the Ancients; it was no longer available, and hence the skill to work it would be useless. See Theodore Redpath, ed., *Songs and Sonets of John Donne* (London: Methuen and Co., 1959), p. 9.

And a braver thence will spring,
Which is, to keepe that hid.

The Sunne Rising

Busie old foole, unruly Sunne,
Why dost thou thus,
Through windowes, and through curtaines call on us?
Must to thy motions lovers seasons run?
Sawcy pedantique wretch, goe chide
Late schoole boyes, and sowre prentices,
Goe tell Court-huntsmen, that the King will ride,
Call countrey ants to harvest offices;
Love, all alike, no season knowes, nor clyme,
Nor houres, dayes, moneths, which are the rags of time. *10*

Thy beames, so reverend, and strong
Why shouldst thou thinke?
I could eclipse and cloud them with a winke,
But that I would not lose her sight so long:
If her eyes have not blinded thine,
Looke, and to morrow late, tell mee,
Whether both the'India's of spice and Myne
Be where thou leftst them, or lie here with mee.
Aske for those Kings whom thou saw'st yesterday,
And thou shalt heare, All here in one bed lay. *20*

She'is all States, and all Princes, I,
Nothing else is.
Princes doe but play us; compar'd to this,
All honor's mimique; All wealth alchimie.
Thou sunne art halfe as happy'as wee,
In that the world's contracted thus;
Thine age askes ease, and since thy duties bee
To warme the world, that's done in warming us.
Shine here to us, and thou art every where;
This bed thy center is, these walls, thy spheare. *30*

The Indifferent

I can love both faire and browne,
Her whom abundance melts, and her whom want
    betraies,
Her who loves lonenesse best, and her who maskes
    and plaies,
Her whom the country form'd, and whom the town,
Her who beleeves, and her who tries,
Her who still weepes with spungie eyes,
And her who is dry corke, and never cries;
I can love her, and her, and you and you,
I can love any, so she be not true.

Will no other vice content you? *10*
Wil it not serve your turn to do, as did your mothers?
Or have you all old vices spent, and now would finde
    out others?
Or doth a feare, that men are true, torment you?
Oh we are not, be not you so,
Let mee, and doe you, twenty know.
Rob mee, but binde me not, and let me goe.
Must I, who came to travaile thorow you,
Grow your fixt subject, because you are true?

Venus heard me sigh this song,
And by Loves sweetest Part, Variety, she swore, *20*
She heard not this till now; and that it should be so
    no more.
She went, examin'd, and return'd ere long,
And said, alas, Some two or three
Poore Heretiques in love there bee,
Which thinke to stablish dangerous constancie.
But I have told them, since you will be true,
You shall be true to them, who'are false to you.

Loves Usury

For every houre that thou wilt spare mee now,
        I will allow,
Usurious God of Love, twenty to thee,

When with my browne, my gray haires equall bee;
Till then, Love, let my body raigne, and let
Mee travell, sojourne, snatch, plot, have, forget,
Resume my last yeares relict: thinke that yet
We'had never met.

Let mee thinke any rivalls letter mine,
And at next nine 10
Keepe midnights promise; mistake by the way
The maid, and tell the Lady of that delay;
Onely let mee love none, no, not the sport;
From country grasse, to comfitures of Court,
Or cities quelque choses, let report
My minde transport.

This bargaine's good; if when I'am old, I bee
Inflam'd by thee,
If thine owne honour, or my shame, or paine,
Thou covet most, at that age thou shalt gaine. 20
Doe thy will then, then subject and degree,
And fruit of love, Love I submit to thee,
Spare mee till then, I'll beare it, though she bee
One that loves mee.

The Canonization

For Godsake hold your tongue, and let me love,
Or chide my palsie, or my gout,
My five gray haires, or ruin'd fortune flout,
With wealth your state, your minde with Arts improve,
Take you a course, get you a place,
Observe his honour, or his grace,
Or the Kings reall, or his stamped face
Contemplate, what you will, approve,
So you will let me love.

Alas, alas, who's injur'd by my love? 10
What merchants ships have my sighs drown'd?
Who saies my teares have overflow'd his ground?

l.7 Kings . . . stamped face: The King's "stamped face" appears on the coin of the realm; to "observe" it would be to be occupied in making money.

When did my colds a forward spring remove?
  When did the heats which my veines fill
  Adde one more to the plaguie Bill?
Soldiers finde warres, and Lawyers finde out still
  Litigious men, which quarrels move,
  Though she and I do love.

Call us what you will, wee are made such by love;
  Call her one, mee another flye, 20
We'are Tapers too, and at our owne cost die,
  And wee in us finde the'Eagle and the Dove.
    The Phœnix ridle hath more wit
    By us, we two being one, are it.
So to one neutrall thing both sexes fit,
  Wee dye and rise the same, and prove
  Mysterious by this love.

Wee can dye by it, if not live by love,
  And if unfit for tombes and hearse
Our legend bee, it will be fit for verse; 30
  And if no peece of Chronicle wee prove,
    We'll build in sonnets pretty roomes;
    As well a well wrought urne becomes
The greatest ashes, as halfe-acre tombes,
  And by these hymnes, all shall approve
  Us *Canoniz'd* for Love:

And thus invoke us; You whom reverend love
  Made one anothers hermitage;
You, to whom love was peace, that now is rage;
  Who did the whole worlds soule contract, and drove 40
    Into the glasses of your eyes
    (So made such mirrors, and such spies,
That they did all to you epitomize,)
  Countries, Townes, Courts: Beg from above
  A patterne of your love!

l.15 plaguie Bill: the weekly lists of mortality issued during the plagues.
l.32 in sonnets pretty roomes: The pun implied turns on *Stanza* which in Italian means *room*.

The triple Foole

I am two fooles, I know,
For loving, and for saying so
In whining Poëtry;
But where's that wiseman, that would not be I,
If she would not deny?
Then as th'earths inward narrow crooked lanes
Do purge sea waters fretfull salt away,
I thought, if I could draw my paines,
Through Rimes vexation, I should them allay,
Griefe brought to numbers cannot be so fierce, *10*
For, he tames it, that fetters it in verse.

But when I have done so,
Some man, his art and voice to show,
Doth Set and sing my paine,
And, by delighting many, frees againe
Griefe, which verse did restraine.
To Love, and Griefe tribute of Verse belongs,
But not of such as pleases when 'tis read,
Both are increased by such songs:
For both their triumphs so are published, *20*
And I, which was two fooles, do so grow three;
Who are a little wise, the best fooles bee.

Lovers infinitenesse

If yet I have not all thy love,
Deare, I shall never have it all,
I cannot breath one other sigh, to move,
Nor can intreat one other teare to fall,
And all my treasure, which should purchase thee,
Sighs, teares, and oathes, and letters I have spent.
Yet no more can be due to mee,
Then at the bargaine made was ment,
If then thy gift of love were partiall,
That some to mee, some should to others fall, *10*
Deare, I shall never have Thee All.

Or if then thou gavest mee all,
All was but All, which thou hadst then;

But if in thy heart, since, there be or shall,
New Love created bee, by other men,
Which have their stocks intire, and can in teares,
In sighs, in oathes, and letters outbid mee,
This new love may beget new feares,
For, this love was not vowed by thee.
And yet it was, thy gift being generall, 20
The ground, thy heart is mine, what ever shall
Grow there, deare, I should have it all.

Yet I would not have all yet,
Hee that hath all can have no more,
And since my love doth every day admit
New growth, thou shouldst have new rewards in store;
Thou canst not every day give me thy heart,
If thou canst give it, then thou never gavest it:
Loves riddles are, that though thy heart depart,
It stayes at home, and thou with losing savest it: 30
But wee will have a way more liberall,
Then changing hearts, to joyne them, so wee shall
Be one, and one anothers All.

Song

Sweetest love, I do not goe,
For wearinesse of thee,
Nor in hope the world can show
A fitter Love for mee;
But since that I
Must dye at last, 'tis best,
To use my selfe in jest
Thus by fain'd deaths to dye;

Yesternight the Sunne went hence,
And yet is here to day, 10
He hath no desire nor sense,
Nor halfe so short a way:
Then feare not mee,
But beleeve that I shall make
Speedier journeyes, since I take
More wings and spurres then hee.

O how feeble is mans power,
  That if good fortune fall,
Cannot adde another houre,
  Nor a lost houre recall! 20
    But come bad chance,
And wee joyne to'it our strength,
And wee teach it art and length,
  It selfe o'r us to'advance.

When thou sigh'st, thou sigh'st not winde,
  But sigh'st my soule away,
When thou weep'st, unkindly kinde,
  My lifes blood doth decay.
    It cannot bee
That thou lov'st mee, as thou say'st,
If in thine my life thou waste,
  Thou art the best of mee.

Let not thy divining heart
  Forethinke me any ill,
Destiny may take thy part,
  And may thy feares fulfill;
    But thinke that wee
Are but turn'd aside to sleepe;
They who one another keepe
  Alive, ne'r parted bee.

A Feaver

Oh doe not die, for I shall hate
  All women so, when thou art gone,
That thee I shall not celebrate,
  When I remember, thou wast one.

But yet thou canst not die, I know;
  To leave this world behinde, is death,
But when thou from this world wilt goe,
  The whole world vapors with thy breath.

Or if, when thou, the worlds soule, goest,
  It stay, tis but thy carkasse then, 10

The fairest woman, but thy ghost,
But corrupt wormes, the worthyest men.

O wrangling schooles, that search what fire
Shall burne this world, had none the wit
Unto this knowledge to aspire,
That this her feaver might be it?

And yet she cannot wast by this,
Nor long beare this torturing wrong,
For much corruption needfull is
To fuell such a feaver long. *20*

These burning fits but meteors bee,
Whose matter in thee is soone spent.
Thy beauty, 'and all parts, which are thee,
Are unchangeable firmament.

Yet t'was of my minde, seising thee,
Though it in thee cannot persever.
For I had rather owner bee
Of thee one houre, then all else ever.

Aire and Angels

Twice or thrice had I loved thee,
Before I knew thy face or name;
So in a voice, so in a shapelesse flame,
Angells affect us oft, and worship'd bee;
Still when, to where thou wert, I came,
Some lovely glorious nothing I did see.
But since my soule, whose child love is,
Takes limmes of flesh, and else could nothing doe,
More subtile then the parent is,
Love must not be, but take a body too, *10*
And therefore what thou wert, and who,
I bid Love aske, and now

Aire and Angels: The poem hinges on the scholastic speculations concerning the nature of angels, their ability, though immaterial, to take on shape or quality either of air or fire, in order to communicate with men.

That it assume thy body, I allow,
And fixe it selfe in thy lip, eye, and brow.

Whilst thus to ballast love, I thought,
And so more steddily to have gone,
With wares which would sinke admiration,
I saw, I had loves pinnace overfraught,
Ev'ry thy haire for love to worke upon
Is much too much, some fitter must be sought; 20
For, nor in nothing, nor in things
Extreme, and scatt'ring bright, can love inhere;
Then as an Angell, face, and wings
Of aire, not pure as it, yet pure doth weare,
So thy love may be my loves spheare;
Just such disparitie
As is twixt Aire and Angells puritie,
'Twixt womens love, and mens will ever bee.

The Anniversarie

All Kings, and all their favorites,
All glory of honors, beauties, wits,
The Sun it selfe, which makes times, as they passe,
Is elder by a yeare, now, then it was
When thou and I first one another saw:
All other things, to their destruction draw,
Only our love hath no decay;
This, no to morrow hath, nor yesterday,
Running it never runs from us away,
But truly keepes his first, last, everlasting day. 10

Two graves must hide thine and my coarse,
If, one might, death were no divorce.
Alas, as well as other Princes, wee,
(Who Prince enough in one another bee,)
Must leave at last in death, these eyes, and eares,

ll.15–18 The distinction is made between a vessel's capsizing by reason of overloading and insufficient ballasting.
l.24 it: may refer back to "Angell" or "aire."
ll.26–28 It is difficult to determine whether the implication is that man's love is purer than woman's, or woman's than man's.
l.11 coarse: corpse.

Oft fed with true oathes, and with sweet salt teares;
  But soules where nothing dwells but love
(All other thoughts being inmates) then shall prove
This, or a love increased there above,
When bodies to their graves, soules from their graves
    remove. 20

  And then wee shall be throughly blest,
  But wee no more, then all the rest;
Here upon earth, we'are Kings, and none but wee
Can be such Kings, nor of such subjects bee.
Who is so safe as wee? where none can doe
Treason to us, except one of us two.
  True and false feares let us refraine,
Let us love nobly, and live, and adde againe
Yeares and yeares unto yeares, till we attaine
To write threescore: this is the second of our raigne. 30

A Valediction: of my name, in the window

I

    My name engrav'd herein,
Doth contribute my firmnesse to this glasse,
  Which, ever since that charme, hath beene
  As hard, as that which grav'd it, was;
Thine eye will give it price enough, to mock
    The diamonds of either rock.

II

    'Tis much that Glasse should bee
As all confessing, and through-shine as I,
  'Tis more, that it shewes thee to thee,
  And cleare reflects thee to thine eye. 10
But all such rules, loves magique can undoe,
    Here you see mee, and I am you.

III

    As no one point, nor dash,
Which are but accessaries to this name,
  The showers and tempests can outwash,
  So shall all times finde mee the same;

You this intirenesse better may fulfill,
Who have the patterne with you still.

IIII

Or, if too hard and deepe
This learning be, for a scratch'd name to teach, 20
It, as a given deaths head keepe,
Lovers mortalitie to preach,
Or thinke this ragged bony name to bee
My ruinous Anatomie.

V

Then, as all my soules bee,
Emparadis'd in you, (in whom alone
I understand, and grow and see,)
The rafters of my body, bone
Being still with you, the Muscle, Sinew, and Veine,
Which tile this house, will come againe. 30

VI

Till my returne, repaire
And recompact my scattered body so.
As all the vertuous powers which are
Fix'd in the starres, are said to flow
Into such characters, as graved bee
When these starres have supremacie:

VII

So, since this name was cut
When love and griefe their exaltation had,
No doore, 'gainst this names influence shut;
As much more loving, as more sad, 40
'Twill make thee; and thou shouldst, till I returne,
Since I die daily, daily mourne.

VIII

When thy inconsiderate hand
Flings ope this casement, with my trembling name,
To looke on one, whose wit or land,
New battry to thy heart may frame,
Then thinke this name alive, and that thou thus
In it offendst my Genius.

IX

And when thy melted maid,
Corrupted by thy Lover's gold, and page, 50
His letter at thy pillow'hath laid,
Disputed it, and tam'd thy rage,
And thou begin'st to thaw towards him, for this,
May my name step in, and hide his.

X

And if this treason goe
To an overt act, and that thou write againe;
In superscribing, this name flow
Into thy fancy, from the pane.
So, in forgetting thou remembrest right,
And unaware to mee shalt write. 60

XI

But glasse, and lines must bee,
No meanes our firme substantiall love to keepe;
Neere death inflicts this lethargie,
And this I murmure in my sleepe;
Impute this idle talke, to that I goe,
For dying men talke often so.

A Valediction: of the booke

I'll tell thee now (deare Love) what thou shalt doe
To anger destiny, as she doth us,
How I shall stay, though she Esloygne me thus
And how posterity shall know it too;
How thine may out-endure
Sybills glory, and obscure
Her who from Pindar could allure,
And her, through whose helpe *Lucan* is not lame,

l.3 *Esloygne:* take away; derived from the Old French.
ll.5–9 In the list of notable women, Donne cites: the Sybil famous for her prophetic powers; Corinna, who, according to legend, five times defeated Pindar; Lucan's wife, who was reputed to have helped him write his *Pharsalia;* and, probably, Phantasia of Memphis, from whom Homer was said to have taken the *Iliad* and the *Odyssey.*

And her, whose booke (they say) *Homer* did finde, and
name.

Study our manuscripts, those Myriades 10
Of letters, which have past twixt thee and mee,
Thence write our Annals, and in them will bee
To all whom loves subliming fire invades,
Rule and example found;
There, the faith of any ground
No schismatique will dare to wound,
That sees, how Love this grace to us affords,
To make, to keep, to use, to be these his Records.

This Booke, as long-liv'd as the elements,
Or as the worlds forme, this all-graved tome 20
In cypher writ, or new made Idiome,
Wee for loves clergie only'are instruments:
When this booke is made thus,
Should againe the ravenous
Vandals and Goths inundate us,
Learning were safe; in this our Universe
Schooles might learne Sciences, Spheares Musick, An-
gels Verse.

Here Loves Divines, (since all Divinity
Is love or wonder) may finde all they seeke,
Whether abstract spirituall love they like, 30
Their Soules exhal'd with what they do not see,
Or, loth so to amuze
Faiths infirmitie, they chuse
Something which they may see and use;
For, though minde be the heaven, where love doth sit,
Beauty a convenient type may be to figure it.

Here more then in their bookes may Lawyers finde,
Both by what titles Mistresses are ours,
And how prerogative these states devours,
Transferr'd from Love himselfe, to womankinde, 40
Who though from heart, and eyes,
They exact great subsidies,
Forsake him who on them relies,
And for the cause, honour, or conscience give,
Chimeraes, vaine as they, or their prerogative.

Here Statesmen, (or of them, they which can reade,)
May of their occupation finde the grounds:
Love and their art alike it deadly wounds,
If to consider what 'tis, one proceed,
In both they doe excell 50
Who the present governe well,
Whose weaknesse none doth, or dares tell;
In this thy booke, such will their nothing see,
As in the Bible some can finde out Alchimy.

Thus vent thy thoughts; abroad I'll studie thee,
As he removes farre off, that great heights takes;
How great love is, presence best tryall makes,
But absence tryes how long this love will bee;
To take a latitude
Sun, or starres, are fitliest view'd 60
At their brightest, but to conclude
Of longitudes, what other way have wee,
But to marke when, and where the darke eclipses bee?

Loves growth

I scarce beleeve my love to be so pure
As I had thought it was,
Because it doth endure
Vicissitude, and season, as the grasse;
Me thinkes I lyed all winter, when I swore,
My love was infinite, if spring make'it more.

But if this medicine, love, which cures all sorrow
With more, not onely bee no quintessence,
But mixt of all stuffes, paining soule, or sense,
And of the Sunne his working vigour borrow, 10
Love's not so pure, and abstract, as they use
To say, which have no Mistresse but their Muse,
But as all else, being elemented too,

ll.59–61 "The latitude of a spot may always be found by measuring the distance from the zenith of a star whose altitude, i.e., distance from the equator, is known. The words 'At their brightest' are only used to point the antithesis with the 'dark eclipses' used to measure longitude." (H. J. C. Grierson, ed., *Donne's Poetical Works*, Oxford: Clarendon Press, 1929, Vol. II, pp. 29–30.)
l.8 quintessence: This word as used by Paracelsus suggests a *fifth* essence, or the essential quality inhering in any substance.

Love sometimes would contemplate, sometimes do.

And yet no greater, but more eminent,
  Love by the spring is growne;
  As, in the firmament,
Starres by the Sunne are not inlarg'd, but showne.
Gentle love deeds, as blossomes on a bough,
From love awakened root do bud out now. 20
If, as in water stir'd more circles bee
Produc'd by one, love such additions take,
Those like so many spheares, but one heaven make,
For, they are all concentrique unto thee.
And though each spring doe adde to love new heate,
As princes doe in times of action get
New taxes, and remit them not in peace,
No winter shall abate the springs encrease.

The Dreame

Deare love, for nothing lesse then thee
Would I have broke this happy dreame,
    It was a theame
For reason, much too strong for phantasie,
Therefore thou wakd'st me wisely; yet
My Dreame thou brok'st not, but continued'st it,
Thou art so truth, that thoughts of thee suffice,
To make dreames truths; and fables histories;
Enter these armes, for since thou thoughtst it best,
Not to dreame all my dreame, let's act the rest. 10

As lightning, or a Tapers light,
Thine eyes, and not thy noise wak'd mee;
    Yet I thought thee
(For thou lovest truth) an Angell, at first sight,
But when I saw thou sawest my heart,
And knew'st my thoughts, beyond an Angels art,
When thou knew'st what I dreamt, when thou knew'st when
Excesse of joy would wake me, and cam'st then,
I must confesse, it could not chuse but bee
Prophane, to thinke thee any thing but thee. 20

Comming and staying show'd thee, thee,
But rising makes me doubt, that now,
Thou art not thou.
That love is weake, where feare's as strong as hee;
'Tis not all spirit, pure, and brave,
If mixture it of *Feare, Shame, Honor,* have.
Perchance as torches which must ready bee,
Men light and put out, so thou deal'st with mee,
Thou cam'st to kindle, goest to come; Then I
Will dreame that hope againe, but else would die. 30

A Valediction: of weeping

Let me powre forth
My teares before thy face, whil'st I stay here,
For thy face coines them, and thy stampe they beare,
And by this Mintage they are something worth,
For thus they bee
Pregnant of thee;
Fruits of much griefe they are, emblemes of more,
When a teare falls, that thou falst which it bore,
So thou and I are nothing then, when on a divers shore.

On a round ball 10
A workeman that hath copies by, can lay
An Europe, Afrique, and an Asia,
And quickly make that, which was nothing, *All,*
So doth each teare,
Which thee doth weare,
A globe, yea world by that impression grow,
Till thy teares mixt with mine doe overflow
This world, by waters sent from thee, my heaven dissolved so.

O more then Moone,
Draw not up seas to drowne me in thy spheare, 20
Weepe me not dead, in thine armes, but forbeare
To teach the sea, what it may doe too soone;
Let not the winde
Example finde,
To doe me more harme, then it purposeth;

Since thou and I sigh one anothers breath,
Who e'r sighes most, is cruellest, and hasts the others
death.

Loves Alchymie

Some that have deeper digg'd loves Myne then I,
Say, where his centrique happinesse doth lie:
I have lov'd and got, and told,
But should I love, get, tell, till I were old,
I should not finde that hidden mysterie;
Oh, 'tis imposture all:
And as no chymique yet th'Elixar got,
But glorifies his pregnant pot,
If by the way to him befall
Some odoriferous thing, or medicinall, *10*
So, lovers dreame a rich and long delight,
But get a winter-seeming summers night.

Our ease, our thrift, our honor, and our day,
Shall we, for this vaine Bubles shadow pay?
Ends love in this, that my man,
Can be as happy'as I can; If he can
Endure the short scorne of a Bridegroomes play?
That loving wretch that sweares,
'Tis not the bodies marry, but the mindes,
Which he in her Angelique findes, *20*
Would sweare as justly, that he heares,
In that dayes rude hoarse minstralsey, the spheares.
Hope not for minde in women; at their best
Sweetnesse and wit, they'are but *Mummy*, possest.

The Flea

Marke but this flea, and marke in this,
How little that which thou deny'st me is;
It suck'd me first, and now sucks thee,

l.15 man: man-servant.
l.24 Mummy: implies both dead flesh and the medicinal uses to which it was put.

And in this flea, our two bloods mingled bee;
Thou know'st that this cannot be said
A sinne, nor shame, nor losse of maidenhead,
  Yet this enjoyes before it wooe,
  And pamper'd swells with one blood made of two,
  And this, alas, is more then wee would doe.

Oh stay, three lives in one flea spare, *10*
Where wee almost, yea more then maryed are.
This flea is you and I, and this
Our mariage bed, and mariage temple is;
Though parents grudge, and you, w'are met,
And cloysterd in these living walls of Jet.
  Though use make you apt to kill mee,
  Let not to that, selfe murder added bee,
  And sacrilege, three sinnes in killing three.

Cruell and sodaine, hast thou since
Purpled thy naile, in blood of innocence? *20*
Wherein could this flea guilty bee,
Except in that drop which it suckt from thee?
Yet thou triumph'st, and saist that thou
Find'st not thy selfe, nor mee the weaker now;
  'Tis true, then learne how false, feares bee;
  Just so much honor, when thou yeeld'st to mee,
  Will wast, as this flea's death tooke life from thee.

The Curse

Who ever guesses, thinks, or dreames he knowes
Who is my mistris, wither by this curse;
    His only, and only his purse
    May some dull heart to love dispose,
And shee yeeld then to all that are his foes;
  May he be scorn'd by one, whom all else scorne,
  Forsweare to others, what to her he'hath sworne,
  With feare of missing, shame of getting, torne:

Madnesse his sorrow, gout his cramp, may hee
Make, by but thinking, who hath made him such: *10*
    And may he feele no touch
    Of conscience, but of fame, and bee

Anguish'd not that'twas sinne, but that'twas shee:
In early and long scarcenesse may he rot,
For land which had been his, if he had not
Himselfe incestuously an heire begot:

May he dreame Treason, and beleeve, that hee
Meant to performe it, and confesse, and die,
And no record tell why:
His sonnes, which none of his may bee, 20
Inherite nothing but his infamie:
Or may he so long Parasites have fed,
That he would faine be theirs, whom he hath bred,
And at the last be circumcis'd for bread:

The venom of all stepdames, gamsters gall,
What Tyrans, and their subjects interwish,
What Plants, Mynes, Beasts, Foule, Fish,
Can contribute, all ill which all
Prophets, or Poets spake; And all which shall
Be annex'd in schedules unto this by mee, 30
Fall on that man; For if it be a shee
Nature before hand hath out-cursed mee.

The Message

Send home my long strayd eyes to mee,
Which (Oh) too long have dwelt on thee;
Yet since there they have learn'd such ill,
Such forc'd fashions,
And false passions,
That they be
Made by thee
Fit for no good sight, keep them still.

Send home my harmlesse heart againe,
Which no unworthy thought could staine; 10
But if it be taught by thine
To make jestings
Of protestings
And crosse both
Word and oath,
Keepe it, for then 'tis none of mine.

Yet send me back my heart and eyes,
That I may know, and see thy lyes,
And may laugh and joy, when thou
Art in anguish 20
And dost languish
For some one
That will none,
Or prove as false as thou art now.

A nocturnall upon S. Lucies *day, Being the shortest day*

Tis the yeares midnight, and it is the dayes,
Lucies, who scarce seaven houres herself unmaskes,
The Sunne is spent, and now his flasks
Send forth light squibs, no constant rayes;
The worlds whole sap is sunke:
The generall balme th'hydroptique earth hath drunk,
Whither, as to the beds-feet, like is shrunke,
Dead and enterr'd; yet all these seeme to laugh,
Compar'd with mee, who am their Epitaph.

Study me then, you who shall lovers bee 10
At the next world, that is, at the next Spring:
For I am every dead thing,
In whom love wrought new Alchimie.
For his art did expresse
A quintessence even from nothingnesse,
From dull privations, and leane emptinesse:
He ruin'd mee, and I am re-begot
Of absence, darknesse, death; things which are not.

All others, from all things, draw all that's good,
Life, soule, forme, spirit, whence they beeing have; 20
I, by loves limbecke, am the grave
Of all, that's nothing. Oft a flood
Have wee two wept, and so
Drownd the whole world, us two; oft did we grow

A nocturnall . . . day: St. Lucy's day fell on December 13, in the old calendar taken to be the shortest day of the year.
l.3 flasks: powder horns.
l.4 squibs: half-charges of ammunition used in military training.

To be two Chaosses, when we did show
Care to ought else; and often absences
Withdrew our soules, and made us carcasses.

But I am by her death, (which word wrongs her)
Of the first nothing, the Elixer grown;
Were I a man, that I were one, 30
I needs must know; I should preferre,
If I were any beast,
Some ends, some means; Yea plants, yea stones detest,
And love; All, all some properties invest;
If I an ordinary nothing were,
As shadow, a light, and body must be here.

But I am None; nor will my Sunne renew.
You lovers, for whose sake, the lesser Sunne
At this time to the Goat is runne
To fetch new lust, and give it you, 40
Enjoy your summer all;
Since shee enjoyes her long nights festivall,
Let mee prepare towards her, and let mee call
This houre her Vigill, and her Eve, since this
Both the yeares, and the dayes deep midnight is.

The Baite

Come live with mee, and bee my love,
And wee will some new pleasures prove
Of golden sands, and christall brookes,
With silken lines, and silver hookes.

There will the river whispering runne
Warm'd by thy eyes, more then the Sunne.
And there the'inamor'd fish will stay,
Begging themselves they may betray.

When thou wilt swimme in that live bath,
Each fish, which every channell hath, 10

l.39 Goat: refers either to the Tropic of Capricorn or to the zodiac sign; in either case the Sun is shining at "the farthest limit of its journey into the Southern Hemisphere." (See Redpath, p. 74.)
The Baite: The poem is a sequel to Marlowe's "The Passionate Shepherd to his Love" and Raleigh's "The Nymph's Reply."

Will amorously to thee swimme,
Gladder to catch thee, then thou him.

If thou, to be so seene, beest loath,
By Sunne, or Moone, thou darknest both,
And if my selfe have leave to see,
I need not their light, having thee.

Let others freeze with angling reeds,
And cut their legges, with shells and weeds,
Or treacherously poore fish beset,
With strangling snare, or windowie net: *20*

Let coarse bold hands, from slimy nest
The bedded fish in banks out-wrest,
Or curious traitors, sleavesilke flies
Bewitch poore fishes wandring eyes.

For thee, thou needst no such deceit,
For thou thy selfe art thine owne bait;
That fish, that is not catch'd thereby,
Alas, is wiser farre then I.

The Apparition

When by thy scorne, O murdresse, I am dead,
And that thou thinkst thee free
From all solicitation from mee,
Then shall my ghost come to thy bed,
And thee, fain'd vestall, in worse armes shall see;
Then thy sicke taper will begin to winke,
And he, whose thou art then, being tyr'd before,
Will, if thou stirre, or pinch to wake him, thinke
        Thou call'st for more,
And in false sleepe will from thee shrinke, *10*
And then poore Aspen wretch, neglected thou
Bath'd in a cold quicksilver sweat wilt lye
        A veryer ghost then I;
What I will say, I will not tell thee now,
Lest that preserve thee'; and since my love is spent,
I'had rather thou shouldst painfully repent,
Then by my threatnings rest still innocent.

The broken heart

He is starke mad, who ever sayes,
That he hath beene in love an houre,
Yet not that love so soone decayes,
But that it can tenne in lesse space devour;
Who will beleeve mee, if I sweare
That I have had the plague a yeare?
Who would not laugh at mee, if I should say,
I saw a flaske of *powder burne a day*?

Ah, what a trifle is a heart,
If once into loves hands it come! 10
All other griefes allow a part
To other griefes, and aske themselves but some;
They come to us, but us Love draws,
Hee swallows us, and never chawes:
By him, as by chain'd shot, whole rankes doe dye,
He is the tyran Pike, our hearts the Frye.

If 'twere not so, what did become
Of my heart, when I first saw thee?
I brought a heart into the roome,
But from the roome, I carried none with mee: 20
If it had gone to thee, I know
Mine would have taught thine heart to show
More pitty unto mee: but Love, alas,
At one first blow did shiver it as glasse.

Yet nothing can to nothing fall,
Nor any place be empty quite,
Therefore I thinke my breast hath all
Those peeces still, though they be not unite;
And now as broken glasses show
A hundred lesser faces, so 30
My ragges of heart can like, wish, and adore,
But after one such love, can love no more.

A Valediction: forbidding mourning

As virtuous men passe mildly away,
And whisper to their soules, to goe,

Whilst some of their sad friends doe say,
  The breath goes now, and some say, no:

So let us melt, and make no noise,
  No teare-floods, nor sigh-tempests move,
T'were prophanation of our joyes
  To tell the layetie our love.

Moving of th'earth brings harmes and feares,
  Men reckon what it did and meant, *10*
But trepidation of the spheares,
  Though greater farre, is innocent.

Dull sublunary lovers love
  (Whose soule is sense) cannot admit
Absence, because it doth remove
  Those things which elemented it.

But we by a love, so much refin'd,
  That our selves know not what it is,
Inter-assured of the mind,
  Care lesse, eyes, lips, and hands to misse. *20*

Our two soules therefore, which are one,
  Though I must goe, endure not yet
A breach, but an expansion,
  Like gold to ayery thinnesse beate.

If they be two, they are two so
  As stiffe twin compasses are two,
Thy soule the fixt foot, makes no show
  To move, but doth, if the'other doe.

And though it in the center sit,
  Yet when the other far doth rome, *30*
It leanes, and hearkens after it,
  And growes erect, as that comes home.

Such wilt thou be to mee, who must
  Like th'other foot, obliquely runne;

_ll.9–12_ The Ptolemaic explanation of the movements of the spheres produced by the natural movement of the ninth sphere was accepted as harmless, in contrast to earthquakes which were considered indications of God's displeasure with man.

Thy firmnes makes my circle just,
  And makes me end, where I begunne.

The Extasie

Where, like a pillow on a bed,
  A Pregnant banke swel'd up, to rest
The violets reclining head,
  Sat we two, one anothers best.

Our hands were firmely cimented
  With a fast balme, which thence did spring,
Our eye-beames twisted, and did thred
  Our eyes, upon one double string;

So to'entergraft our hands, as yet
  Was all the meanes to make us one, *10*
And pictures in our eyes to get
  Was all our propagation.

As 'twixt two equall Armies, Fate
  Suspends uncertaine victorie,
Our soules, (which to advance their state,
  Were gone out,) hung 'twixt her, and mee.

And whil'st our soules negotiate there,
  Wee like sepulchrall statues lay;
All day, the same our postures were,
  And wee said nothing, all the day. *20*

If any, so by love refin'd,
  That he soules language understood,
And by good love were growen all minde,
  Within convenient distance stood,

He (though he knew not which soule spake,
  Because both meant, both spake the same)

ll.7–8 The current theory of vision posited the motion of a beam from the eye to the object and back to the eye of the perceiver.
ll.11–12 propagation: consists of the "babies" in the eyes, the images of one another reflected in the pupils of the eyes of two people looking closely at one another.

Might thence a new concoction take,
  And part farre purer then he came.

This Extasie doth unperplex
  (We said) and tell us what we love, 30
Wee see by this, it was not sexe,
  Wee see, we saw not what did move:

But as all severall soules containe
  Mixture of things, they know not what,
Love, these mixt soules, doth mixe againe,
  And makes both one, each this and that.

A single violet transplant,
  The strength, the colour, and the size,
(All which before was poore, and scant,)
  Redoubles still, and multiplies. 40

When love, with one another so
  Interinanimates two soules,
That abler soule, which thence doth flow,
  Defects of lonelinesse controules.

Wee then, who are this new soule, know,
  Of what we are compos'd, and made,
For, th'Atomies of which we grow,
  Are soules, whom no change can invade.

But O alas, so long, so farre
  Our bodies why doe wee forbeare? 50
They are ours, though they are not wee, Wee are
  The intelligences, they the spheare.

We owe them thankes, because they thus,
  Did us, to us, at first convay,
Yeelded their forces, sense, to us,
  Nor are drosse to us, but allay.

On man heavens influence workes not so,
  But that it first imprints the ayre,

l.27 concoction: purification or refinement.
ll.57–59 Heavenly bodies cannot affect man directly; hence they must first "imprint" the air; so souls must work indirectly through bodies.

Soe soule into the soule may flow,
  Though it to body first repaire. *60*

As our blood labours to beget
  Spirits, as like soules as it can,
Because such fingers need to knit
  That subtile knot, which makes us man:

So must pure lovers soules descend
  T'affections, and to faculties,
Which sense may reach and apprehend,
  Else a great Prince in prison lies.

To'our bodies turne wee then, that so
  Weake men on love reveal'd may looke; *70*
Loves mysteries in soules doe grow,
  But yet the body is his booke.

And if some lover, such as wee,
  Have heard this dialogue of one,
Let him still marke us, he shall see
  Small change, when we'are to bodies gone.

Loves Deitie

I long to talke with some old lovers ghost,
  Who dyed before the god of Love was borne:
I cannot thinke that hee, who then lov'd most,
  Sunke so low, as to love one which did scorne.
But since this god produc'd a destinie,
And that vice-nature, custome, lets it be;
  I must love her, that loves not mee.

Sure, they which made him god, meant not so much,
  Nor he, in his young godhead practis'd it;
But when an even flame two hearts did touch, *10*
  His office was indulgently to fit
Actives to passives. Correspondencie
Only his subject was; It cannot bee
  Love, till I love her, that loves mee.

But every moderne god will now extend
  His vast prerogative, as far as Jove.

To rage, to lust, to write to, to commend,
All is the purlewe of the God of Love.
Oh were wee wak'ned by this Tyrannie
To ungod this child againe, it could not bee 20
I should love her, who loves not mee.

Rebell and Atheist too, why murmure I,
As though I felt the worst that love could doe?
Love might make me leave loving, or might trie
A deeper plague, to make her love mee too,
Which, since she loves before, I'am loth to see;
Falshood is worse then hate; and that must bee,
If shee whom I love, should love mee.

Loves diet

To what a combersome unwieldinesse
And burdenous corpulence my love had growne,
But that I did, to make it lesse,
And keepe it in proportion,
Give it a diet, make it feed upon
That which love worst endures, *discretion.*

Above one sigh a day I'allow'd him not,
Of which my fortune, and my faults had part;
And if sometimes by stealth he got
A she sigh from my mistresse heart, 10
And thought to feast on that, I let him see
'Twas neither very sound, nor meant to mee.

If he wroung from mee'a teare, I brin'd it so
With scorne or shame, that him it nourish'd not;
If he suck'd hers, I let him know
'Twas not a teare, which hee had got,
His drinke was counterfeit, as was his meat;
For, eyes which rowle towards all, weepe not, but sweat.

What ever he would dictate, I writ that,
But burnt my letters; When she writ to me, 20
And that that favour made him fat,
I said, if any title bee

Convey'd by this, Ah, what doth it availe,
To be the fortieth name in an entaile?

Thus I reclaim'd my buzard love, to flye
At what, and when, and how, and where I chuse;
  Now negligent of sport I lye,
  And now as other Fawkners use,
I spring a mistresse, sweare, write, sigh and weepe:
And the game kill'd, or lost, goe talke, and sleepe. 30

The Will

Before I sigh my last gaspe, let me breath,
Great love, some Legacies; Here I bequeath
Mine eyes to *Argus,* if mine eyes can see,
If they be blinde, then Love, I give them thee;
My tongue to Fame; to'Embassadours mine eares;
  To women or the sea, my teares.
Thou, Love, hast taught mee heretofore
By making mee serve her who'had twenty more,
That I should give to none, but such, as had too much before.

My constancie I to the planets give; 10
My truth to them, who at the Court doe live;
Mine ingenuity and opennesse,
To Jesuites; to Buffones my pensivenesse;
My silence to'any, who abroad hath beene;
  My mony to a Capuchin.
Thou Love taught'st me, by appointing mee
To love there, where no love receiv'd can be,
Onely to give to such as have an incapacitie.

My faith I give to Roman Catholiques;
All my good works unto the Schismaticks 20
Of Amsterdam; my best civility
And Courtship, to an Universitie;
My modesty I give to souldiers bare;
  My patience let gamesters share.
Thou Love taughtst mee, by making mee
Love her that holds my love disparity,
Onely to give to those that count my gifts indignity.

I give my reputation to those
Which were my friends; Mine industrie to foes;
To Schoolemen I bequeath my doubtfulnesse; 30
My sicknesse to Physitians, or excesse;
To Nature, all that I in Ryme have writ;
And to my company my wit.
Thou Love, by making mee adore
Her, who begot this love in mee before,
Taughtst me to make, as though I gave, when I did but restore.

To him for whom the passing bell next tolls,
I give my physick bookes; my writen rowles
Of Morall counsels, I to Bedlam give;
My brazen medals, unto them which live 40
In want of bread; To them which passe among
All forrainers, mine English tongue.
Thou, Love, by making mee love one
Who thinkes her friendship a fit portion
For yonger lovers, dost my gifts thus disproportion.

Therefore I'll give no more; But I'll undoe
The world by dying; because love dies too.
Then all your beauties will bee no more worth
Then gold in Mines, where none doth draw it forth;
And all your graces no more use shall have 50
Then a Sun dyall in a grave.
Thou Love taughtst mee, by making mee
Love her, who doth neglect both mee and thee,
To'invent, and practise this one way, to'annihilate all three.

The Funerall

Who ever comes to shroud me, do not harme
Nor question much
That subtile wreath of haire, which crowns my arme;
The mystery, the signe you must not touch,
For 'tis my outward Soule,
Viceroy to that, which then to heaven being gone,
Will leave this to controule,
And keepe these limbes, her Provinces, from dissolution.

For if the sinewie thread my braine lets fall
Through every part, 10

Can tye those parts, and make mee one of all;
These haires which upward grew, and strength and art
    Have from a better braine,
Can better do'it; Except she meant that I
    By this should know my pain,
As prisoners then are manacled, when they'are condemn'd to die.

What ere shee meant by'it, bury it with me,
    For since I am
Loves martyr, it might breed idolatrie,
If into others hands these Reliques came; 20
    As 'twas humility
To afford to it all that a Soule can doe,
    So, 'tis some bravery,
That since you would save none of mee, I bury some of you.

The Blossome

Little think'st thou, poore flower,
Whom I have watch'd sixe or seaven dayes,
And seene thy birth, and seene what every houre
Gave to thy growth, thee to this height to raise,
And now dost laugh and triumph on this bough,
    Little think'st thou
That it will freeze anon, and that I shall
To morrow finde thee falne, or not at all.

Little think'st thou poore heart
That labour'st yet to nestle thee, 10
And think'st by hovering here to get a part
In a forbidden or forbidding tree,
And hop'st her stiffenesse by long siege to bow:
    Little think'st thou,
That thou to morrow, ere that Sunne doth wake,
Must with this Sunne, and mee a journey take.

But thou which lov'st to bee
Subtile to plague thy selfe, wilt say,
Alas, if you must goe, what's that to mee?
Here lyes my businesse, and here I will stay: 20
You goe to friends, whose love and meanes present
    Various content

To your eyes, eares, and tongue, and every part.
If then your body goe, what need you a heart?

Well then, stay here; but know,
When thou hast stayd and done thy most;
A naked thinking heart, that makes no show,
Is to a woman, but a kinde of Ghost;
How shall shee know my heart; or having none,
Know thee for one? *30*
Practise may make her know some other part,
But take my word, shee doth not know a Heart.

Meet mee at London, then,
Twenty dayes hence, and thou shalt see
Mee fresher, and more fat, by being with men,
Then if I had staid still with her and thee.
For Gods sake, if you can, be you so too:
I would give you
There, to another friend, whom wee shall finde
As glad to have my body, as my minde. *40*

The Primrose

Upon this Primrose hill,
Where, if Heav'n would distill
A shoure of raine, each severall drop might goe
To his owne primrose, and grow Manna so;
And where their forme, and their infinitie
Make a terrestriall Galaxie,
As the small starres doe in the skie:
I walke to finde a true Love; and I see
That 'tis not a mere woman, that is shee,
But must, or more, or lesse then woman bee. *10*

Yet know I not, which flower
I wish; a sixe, or foure;
For should my true-Love lesse then woman bee,
She were scarce any thing; and then, should she
Be more then woman, shee would get above

ll.8–12 The point hinges on the fact that a primrose, usually a five-petaled flower, was called a true-love when it had four petals.

All thought of sexe, and thinke to move
My heart to study her, and not to love;
Both these were monsters; Since there must reside
Falshood in women, I could more abide,
She were by art, then Nature falsify'd. 20

Live Primrose then, and thrive
With thy true number five;
And women, whom this flower doth represent,
With this mysterious number be content;
Ten is the farthest number; if halfe ten
Belonge unto each woman, then
Each woman may take halfe us men;
Or if this will not serve their turne, Since all
Numbers are odde, or even, and they fall
First into this, five, women may take us all. 30

The Relique

When my grave is broke up againe
Some second ghest to entertaine,
(For graves have learn'd that woman-head
To be to more then one a Bed)
And he that digs it, spies
A bracelet of bright haire about the bone,
Will he not let'us alone,
And thinke that there a loving couple lies,
Who thought that this device might be some way
To make their soules, at the last busie day, 10
Meet at this grave, and make a little stay?

If this fall in a time, or land,
Where mis-devotion doth command,
Then, he that digges us up, will bring
Us, to the Bishop, and the King,
To make us Reliques; then
Thou shalt be a Mary Magdalen, and I
A something else thereby;
All women shall adore us, and some men;
And since at such time, miracles are sought, 20
I would have that age by this paper taught
What miracles wee harmelesse lovers wrought.

First, we lov'd well and faithfully,
Yet knew not what wee lov'd, nor why,
Difference of sex no more wee knew,
Then our Guardian Angells doe;
Comming and going, wee
Perchance might kisse, but not between those meales;
Our hands ne'r toucht the seales,
Which nature, injur'd by late law, sets free: *30*
These miracles wee did; but now alas,
All measure, and all language, I should passe,
Should I tell what a miracle shee was.

The Dampe

When I am dead, and Doctors know not why,
And my friends curiositie
Will have me cut up to survay each part,
When they shall finde your Picture in my heart,
You thinke a sodaine dampe of love
Will through all their senses move,
And worke on them as mee, and so preferre
Your murder, to the name of Massacre.

Poore victories! But if you dare be brave,
And pleasure in your conquest have, *10*
First kill th'enormous Gyant, your *Disdaine*,
And let th'enchantresse *Honor*, next be slaine,
And like a Goth and Vandall rize,
Deface Records, and Histories
Of your owne arts and triumphs over men,
And without such advantage kill me then.

For I could muster up as well as you
My Gyants, and my Witches too,
Which are vast *Constancy*, and *Secretnesse*,
But these I neyther looke for, nor professe; *20*
Kill mee as Woman, let mee die
As a meere man; doe you but try
Your passive valor, and you shall finde than,
In that you'have odds enough of any man.

l.5 *dampe:* chill or sickly vapor.
l.7 *preferre:* promote or increase.

Negative love

I never stoop'd so low, as they
Which on an eye, cheeke, lip, can prey,
    Seldome to them, which soare no higher
    Then vertue or the minde to'admire,
For sense, and understanding may
    Know, what gives fuell to their fire:
My love, though silly, is more brave,
For may I misse, when ere I crave,
If I know yet, what I would have.

If that be simply perfectest   10
Which can by no way be exprest
    But *Negatives*, my love is so.
    To All, which all love, I say no.
If any who deciphers best,
    What we know not, our selves, can know,
Let him teach mee that nothing; This
As yet my ease, and comfort is,
Though I speed not, I cannot misse.

The Prohibition

        Take heed of loving mee,
At least remember, I forbade it thee;
Not that I shall repaire my'unthrifty wast
Of Breath and Blood, upon thy sighes, and teares,
By being to thee then what to me thou wast;
But, so great Joy, our life at once outweares,
Then, least thy love, by my death, frustrate bee,
If thou love mee, take heed of loving mee.

        Take heed of hating mee,
Or too much triumph in the Victorie.   10
Not that I shall be mine owne officer,
And hate with hate againe retaliate;
But thou wilt lose the stile of conquerour,
If I, thy conquest, perish by thy hate.
Then, least my being nothing lessen thee,
If thou hate mee, take heed of hating mee.

Yet, love and hate mee too,
So, these extreames shall neithers office doe;
Love mee, that I may die the gentler way;
Hate mee, because thy love is too great for mee; 20
Or let these two, themselves, not me decay;
So shall I, live, thy Stage, not triumph bee;
Lest thou thy love and hate and mee undoe,
To let mee live, O love and hate mee too.

The Expiration

So, so, breake off this last lamenting kisse,
Which sucks two soules, and vapors Both away,
Turne thou ghost that way, and let mee turne this,
And let our selves benight our happiest day,
We ask'd none leave to love; nor will we owe
Any, so cheape a death, as saying, Goe;

Goe; and if that word have not quite kil'd thee,
Ease mee with death, by bidding mee goe too.
Oh, if it have, let my word worke on mee,
And a just office on a murderer doe. 10
Except it be too late, to kill me so,
Being double dead, going, and bidding, goe.

The Paradox

No Lover faith, I love, nor any other
Can judge a perfect Lover;
Hee thinkes that else none can, nor will agree
That any loves but hee:
I cannot say I lov'd, for who can say
Hee was kill'd yesterday?
Love with excesse of heat, more yong then old,
Death kills with too much cold;
Wee dye but once, and who lov'd last did die,
Hee that faith twice, doth lye: 10
For though hee seeme to move, and stirre a while,
It doth the sense beguile.

Such life is like the light which bideth yet
When the lights life is set,
Or like the heat, which fire in solid matter
Leaves behinde, two houres after.
Once I lov'd and dy'd; and am now become
Mine Epitaph and Tombe.
Here dead men speake their last, and so do I;
Love-slaine, loe, here I lye. 20

A Lecture upon the Shadow

Stand still, and I will read to thee
A Lecture, Love, in loves philosophy.
These three houres that we have spent,
Walking here, Two shadowes went
Along with us, which we our selves produc'd;
But, now the Sunne is just above our head,
We doe those shadowes tread;
And to brave clearnesse all things are reduc'd.
So whilst our infant loves did grow,
Disguises did, and shadowes, flow, 10
From us, and our cares; but, now 'tis not so.

That love hath not attain'd the high'st degree,
Which is still diligent lest others see.

Except our loves at this noone stay,
We shall new shadowes make the other way.
As the first were made to blinde
Others; these which come behinde
Will worke upon our selves, and blind our eyes.
If our loves faint, and westwardly decline;
To me thou, falsly, thine, 20
And I to thee mine actions shall disguise.
The morning shadowes weare away,
But these grow longer all the day,
But oh, loves day is short, if love decay.

Love is a growing, or full constant light;
And his first minute, after noone, is night.

FROM

Elegies

The Autumnall

No *Spring,* nor *Summer* Beauty hath such grace,
As I have seen in one *Autumnall* face.
Yong *Beauties* force our love, and that's a *Rape,*
This doth but *counsaile,* yet you cannot scape.
If t'were a *shame* to love, here t'were no *shame,*
Affection here takes *Reverences* name.
Were her first yeares the *Golden Age;* That's true,
But now shee's *gold* oft tried, and ever new.
That was her torrid and inflaming time,
This is her tolerable *Tropique clyme.* 10
Faire eyes, who askes more heate then comes from hence,
He in a fever wishes pestilence.
Call not these wrinkles, *graves;* If *graves* they were,
They were *Loves graves;* for else he is no where.
Yet lies not Love *dead* here, but here doth sit
Vow'd to this trench, like an *Anachorit.*
And here, till hers, which must be his *death,* come,
He doth not digge a *Grave,* but build a *Tombe.*
Here dwells he, though sojourne ev'ry where,
In *Progresse,* yet his standing house is here. 20
Here, where still *Evening* is; not *noone,* nor *night;*
Where no *voluptuousnesse,* yet all *delight.*
In all her words, unto all hearers fit,
You may at *Revels,* you at *Counsaile,* sit.
This is loves timber, youth his under-wood;
There he, as wine in *June,* enrages blood,
Which then comes seasonabliest, when our tast
And appetite to other things, is past.
Xerxes strange *Lydian* love, the *Platane* tree,

The Autumnall: This elegy was written to the Lady Magdalen Herbert, mother of George Herbert and Edward Herbert, later Lord Herbert of Cherbury. The tender description of aging beauty is more conventional than factual.
ll.29–32 Xerxes: reputed to have become enamoured of a very large, though apparently barren, plane tree. The Lady Magdalen had, however, been blessed with many children.

Was lov'd for age, none being so large as shee, 30
Or else because, being yong, nature did blesse
Her youth with ages glory, *Barrennesse*.
If we love things long sought, *Age* is a thing
Which we are fifty yeares in compassing.
If transitory things, which soone decay,
Age must be lovelyest at the latest day.
But name not *Winter-faces,* whose skin's slacke;
Lanke, as an unthrifts purse; but a soules sacke;
Whose *Eyes* seeke light within, for all here's shade;
Whose *mouthes* are holes, rather worne out, then
made; 40
Whose every tooth to a severall place is gone,
To vexe their soules at *Resurrection;*
Name not these living *Deaths-heads* unto mee,
For these, not *Ancient,* but *Antique* be.
I hate extreames; yet I had rather stay
With *Tombs,* then *Cradles,* to weare out a day.
Since such loves naturall lation is, may still
My love descend, and journey downe the hill,
Not panting after growing beauties, so,
I shall ebbe out with them, who home-ward goe. 50

On his Mistris

By our first strange and fatall interview,
By all desires which thereof did ensue,
By our long starving hopes, by that remorse
Which my words masculine perswasive force
Begot in thee, and by the memory
Of hurts, which spies and rivals threatned me,
I calmly beg: But by thy fathers wrath,
By all paines, which want and divorcement hath,
I conjure thee, and all the oathes which I
And thou have sworne to seale joynt constancy, 10
Here I unsweare, and overswear them thus,
Thou shalt not love by wayes so dangerous.
Temper, ô faire Love, loves impetuous rage,

l.47 **lation:** **an astronomical term referring to the natural movement of heavenly bodies.**
ll.13–14 **The situation of the poem turns on the poet's plea to his mistress not to follow him abroad disguised as a page.**

Be my true Mistris still, not my faign'd Page;
I'll goe, and, by thy kinde leave, leave behinde
Thee, onely worthy to nurse in my minde,
Thirst to come backe; ô if thou die before,
My soule from other lands to thee shall soare.
Thy (else Almighty) beautie cannot move
Rage from the Seas, nor thy love teach them love, 20
Nor tame wilde Boreas harshnesse; Thou hast reade
How roughly hee in peeces shivered
Faire Orithea, whom he swore he lov'd.
Fall ill or good, 'tis madnesse to have prov'd
Dangers unurg'd; Feed on this flattery,
That absent Lovers one in th'other be.
Dissemble nothing, not a boy, nor change
Thy bodies habite, nor mindes; bee not strange
To thy selfe onely; All will spie in thy face
A blushing womanly discovering grace; 30
Richly cloath'd Apes, are call'd Apes, and as soone
Ecclips'd as bright we call the Moone the Moone.
Men of France, changeable Camelions,
Spittles of diseases, shops of fashions,
Loves fuellers, and the rightest company
Of Players, which upon the worlds stage be,
Will quickly know thee, and no lesse, alas!
Th'indifferent Italian, as we passe
His warme land, well content to thinke thee Page,
Will hunt thee with such lust, and hideous rage, 40
As *Lots* faire guests were vext. But none of these
Nor spungy hydroptique Dutch shall thee displease,
If thou stay here. O stay here, for, for thee
England is onely a worthy Gallerie,
To walke in expectation, till from thence
Our greatest King call thee to his presence.
When I am gone, dreame me some happinesse,
Nor let thy lookes our long hid love confesse,
Nor praise, nor dispraise me, nor blesse nor curse
Openly loves force, nor in bed fright thy Nurse 50
With midnights startings, crying out, oh, oh
Nurse, ô my love is slaine, I saw him goe
O'r the white Alpes alone; I saw him I,
Assail'd, fight, taken, stabb'd, bleed, fall, and die.

ll.21–23 According to Ovid, Orithea was abducted by Boreas, the North Wind.
l.44 Gallerie: entrance hall, or waiting-room.

Augure me better chance, except dread *Jove*
Thinke it enough for me to'have had thy love.

FROM

Satyres

Satyre III

Kinde pitty chokes my spleene; brave scorn forbids
Those teares to issue which swell my eye-lids;
I must not laugh, nor weepe sinnes, and be wise,
Can railing then cure these worne maladies?
Is not our Mistresse faire Religion,
As worthy of all our Soules devotion,
As vertue was to the first blinded age?
Are not heavens joyes as valiant to asswage
Lusts, as earths honour was to them? Alas,
As wee do them in meanes, shall they surpasse 10
Us in the end, and shall thy fathers spirit
Meete blinde Philosophers in heaven, whose merit
Of strict life may be imputed faith, and heare
Thee, whom hee taught so easie wayes and neare
To follow, damn'd? O if thou dar'st, feare this;
This feare great courage, and high valour is.
Dar'st thou ayd mutinous Dutch, and dar'st thou lay
Thee in ships woodden Sepulchers, a prey
To leaders rage, to stormes, to shot, to dearth?
Dar'st thou dive seas, and dungeons of the earth? 20
Hast thou couragious fire to thaw the ice
Of frozen North discoveries? and thrise
Colder then Salamanders, like divine
Children in th'oven, fires of Spaine, and the line,
Whose countries limbecks to our bodies bee,
Canst thou for gaine beare? and must every hee
Which cryes not, Goddesse, to thy Mistresse, draw,
Or eate thy poysonous words? courage of straw!

Satyre III: Donne's first formal poetic investigation into the nature of truth, wisdom and faith, later developed more fully in the *Anniversaries* and in the *Divine Poems*.

O desperate coward, wilt thou seeme bold, and
To thy foes and his (who made thee to stand 30
Sentinell in his worlds garrison) thus yeeld,
And for forbidden warres, leave th'appointed field?
Know thy foes: The foule Devill (whom thou
Strivest to please,) for hate, not love, would allow
Thee faine, his whole Realme to be quit; and as
The worlds all parts wither away and passe,
So the worlds selfe, thy other lov'd foe, is
In her decrepit wayne, and thou loving this,
Dost love a withered and worne strumpet; last,
Flesh (it selfes death) and joyes which flesh can taste, 40
Thou lovest, and thy faire goodly soule, which doth
Give this flesh power to taste joy, thou dost loath.
Seeke true religion. O where? Mirreus
Thinking her unhous'd here, and fled from us,
Seekes her at Rome; there, because hee doth know
That shee was there a thousand yeares agoe,
He loves her ragges so, as wee here obey
The statecloth where the Prince sate yesterday.
Crantz to such brave Loves will not be inthrall'd,
But loves her onely, who at Geneva is call'd 50
Religion, plaine, simple, sullen, yong,
Contemptuous, yet unhansome; As among
Lecherous humors, there is one that judges
No wenches wholsome, but course country drudges.
Graius stayes still at home here, and because
Some Preachers, vile ambitious bauds, and lawes
Still new like fashions, bid him thinke that shee
Which dwels with us, is onely perfect, hee
Imbraceth her, whom his Godfathers will
Tender to him, being tender, as Wards still 60
Take such wives as their Guardians offer, or
Pay valewes. Carelesse Phrygius doth abhorre
All, because all cannot be good, as one
Knowing some women whores, dares marry none.
Graccus loves all as one, and thinkes that so
As women do in divers countries goe
In divers habits, yet are still one kinde,
So doth, so is Religion; and this blind-
nesse too much light breeds; but unmoved thou
Of force must one, and forc'd but one allow; 70
And the right; aske thy father which is shee,
Let him aske his; though truth and falshood bee

Neare twins, yet truth a little elder is;
Be busie to seeke her, beleeve mee this,
Hee's not of none, nor worst, that seekes the best.
To adore, or scorne an image, or protest,
May all be bad; doubt wisely; in strange way
To stand inquiring right, is not to stray;
To sleepe, or runne wrong, is. On a huge hill,
Cragged, and steep, Truth stands, and hee that will 80
Reach her, about must, and about must goe;
And what the hills suddennes resists, winne so;
Yet strive so, that before age, deaths twilight,
Thy Soule rest, for none can worke in that night.
To will, implyes delay, therefore now doe:
Hard deeds, the bodies paines; hard knowledge too
The mindes indeavours reach, and mysteries
Are like the Sunne, dazling, yet plaine to all eyes.
Keepe the truth which thou hast found; men do not stand
In so ill case here, that God hath with his hand 90
Sign'd Kings blanck-charters to kill whom they hate,
Nor are they Vicars, but hangmen to Fate.
Foole and wretch, wilt thou let thy Soule be tyed
To mans lawes, by which she shall not be tryed
At the last day? Oh, will it then boot thee
To say a Philip, or a Gregory,
A Harry, or a Martin taught thee this?
Is not this excuse for mere contraries,
Equally strong? cannot both sides say so?
That thou mayest rightly obey power, her bounds know; 100
Those past, her nature, and name is chang'd; to be
Then humble to her is idolatrie.
As streames are, Power is; those blest flowers that dwell
At the rough streames calme head, thrive and do well,
But having left their roots, and themselves given
To the streames tyrannous rage, alas, are driven
Through mills, and rockes, and woods, and at last, almost
Consum'd in going, in the sea are lost:
So perish Soules, which more chuse mens unjust
Power from God claym'd, then God himselfe to trust. 110

FROM

Letters to Severall Personages

To *Sir Edward Herbert.* at *Julyers*

Man is a lumpe, where all beasts kneaded bee,
  Wisdome makes him an Arke where all agree;
The foole, in whom these beasts do live at jarre,
  Is sport to others, and a Theater;
Nor scapes hee so, but is himselfe their prey,
  All which was man in him, is eate away,
And now his beasts on one another feed,
  Yet couple'in anger, and new monsters breed.
How happy'is hee, which hath due place assign'd
  To'his beasts, and disaforested his minde! *10*
Empail'd himselfe to keepe them out, not in;
  Can sow, and dares trust corne, where they have bin;
Can use his horse, goate, wolfe, and every beast,
  And is not Asse himselfe to all the rest.
Else, man not onely is the heard of swine,
  But he's those devills too, which did incline
Them to a headlong rage, and made them worse:
  For man can adde weight to heavens heaviest curse.
As Soules (they say) by our first touch, take in
  The poysonous tincture of Originall sinne, *20*
So, to the punishments which God doth fling,
  Our apprehension contributes the sting.
To us, as to his chickins, he doth cast
  Hemlocke, and wee as men, his hemlocke taste;
We do infuse to what he meant for meat,
  Corrosivenesse, or intense cold or heat.
For, God no such specifique poyson hath
  As kills we know not how; his fiercest wrath

To Sir . . . Julyers: Sir Edward Herbert, later Lord Herbert of Cherbury, the Cambridge Platonist, was in Juliers, besieged by the Prince of Orange; the siege marked the formal beginning of the Thirty Years' War. Sir Edward was known for his interest in philosophy and for the difficulty of his verse.
ll.23–24 Chickens were said to thrive on hemlock, poisonous to man.

Hath no antipathy, but may be good
    At lest for physicke, if not for our food. 30
Thus man, that might be'his pleasure, is his rod,
    And is his devill, that might be his God.
Since then our businesse is, to rectifie
    Nature, to what she was, wee'are led awry
By them, who man to us in little show;
    Greater then due, no forme we can bestow
On him; for Man into himselfe can draw
    All; All his faith can swallow,'or reason chaw.
All that is fill'd, and all that which doth fill,
    All the round world, to man is but a pill, 40
In all it workes not, but it is in all
    Poysonous, or purgative, or cordiall,
For, knowledge kindles Calentures in some,
    And is to others icy *Opium*.
As brave as true, is that profession than
    Which you doe use to make; that you know man.
This makes it credible; you have dwelt upon
    All worthy bookes, and now are such an one.
Actions are authors, and of those in you
    Your friends finde every day a mart of new. 50

An Anatomie of the World

The first Anniversary

When that rich Soule which to her heaven is gone,
Whom all do celebrate, who know they have one,
(For who is sure he hath a Soule, unlesse

The entrie into the worke.

l.43 Calentures: a tropical fever; hence a burning or passion.
An Anatomie of the World: In the 1611 edition this title is followed by: "Wherein, By occasion of the untimely death of Mistris Elizabeth Drury, the frailty and the decay of this whole World is represented."
The first Anniversary: The first and second Anniversaries were written in 1611 and 1612 to commemorate Elizabeth Drury (who died at the age of fifteen), daughter of Sir Robert Drury, Donne's patron. They represent Donne's most ambitious and sustained poetry. Louis Martz sees them as "Donne's most elaborate examples of the art of sacred parody and his most extensive efforts in the art of poetical meditation." (*Poetry of Meditation*, New

It see, and judge, and follow worthinesse,
And by Deedes praise it? hee who doth not this,
May lodge an In-mate soule, but 'tis not his.)
When that Queene ended here her progresse time,
And, as t'her standing house to heaven did climbe,
Where loath to make the Saints attend her long,
She's now a part both of the Quire, and Song, *10*
This World, in that great earthquake languished;
For in a common bath of teares it bled,
Which drew the strongest vitall spirits out:
But succour'd then with a perplexed doubt,
Whether the world did lose, or gaine in this,
(Because since now no other way there is,
But goodnesse, to see her, whom all would see,
All must endeavour to be good as shee,)
This great consumption to a fever turn'd,
And so the world had fits; it joy'd, it mourn'd; *20*
And, as men thinke, that Agues physick are,
And th'Ague being spent, give over care,
So thou sicke World, mistak'st thy selfe to bee
Well, when alas, thou'rt in a Lethargie.
Her death did wound and tame thee than, and than
Thou might'st have better spar'd the Sunne, or Man.
That wound was deep, but 'tis more misery,
That thou hast lost thy sense and memory.
'Twas heavy then to heare thy voyce of mone,
But this is worse, that thou art speechlesse growne. *30*
Thou hast forgot thy name, thou hadst; thou wast
Nothing but shee, and her thou hast o'rpast.
For as a child kept from the Font, untill
A prince, expected long, come to fulfill
The ceremonies, thou unnam'd had'st laid,

Haven: Yale University Press, 1954, p. 220.) Marjorie Nicolson interprets the two poems as composites of "one of the greatest religious poems of the seventeenth century. . . . The first is a lament over the body—the body of man and the body of the world—a meditation upon death and mortality. The second is a vision of the release of the soul from its prison." (*Breaking of the Circle*, Evanston, Ill.: Northwestern University Press, 1950, pp. 65–66.) Frank Manley interprets the two poems "in terms of the tradition of Wisdom. . . . They detach our love from this world and direct it toward the next, toward the luminous 'Idea of Woman,' who represents the image of God in man. . . . they stand in the same relation to one another as *scientia* to *sapientia*." (Frank Manley, ed., *John Donne: The Anniversaries*, Baltimore: Johns Hopkins Press, 1963, pp. 40, 42, 47.)

For further significant commentary on the poems see Coffin, Frye, Hardison, and Williamson.

Had not her comming, thee her Palace made:
Her name defin'd thee, gave thee forme, and frame,
And thou forgett'st to celebrate thy name.
Some moneths she hath beene dead (but being dead,
Measures of times are all determined) 40
But long she'ath beene away, long, long, yet none
Offers to tell us who it is that's gone.
But as in states doubtfull of future heires,
When sicknesse without remedie empaires
The present Prince, they're loth it should be said,
The Prince doth languish, or the Prince is dead:
So mankinde feeling now a generall thaw,
A strong example gone, equall to law,
The Cyment which did faithfully compact,
And glue all vertues, now resolv'd, and slack'd, 50
Thought it some blasphemy to say sh'was dead,
Or that our weaknesse was discovered
In that confession; therefore spoke no more
Then tongues, the Soule being gone, the losse deplore.
But though it be too late to succour thee,
Sicke World, yea, dead, yea putrified, since shee
Thy'intrinsique balme, and thy preservative,
Can never be renew'd, thou never live,
I (since no man can make thee live) will try,
What wee may gaine by thy Anatomy. 60
Her death hath taught us dearely, that thou art
Corrupt and mortall in thy purest part.
Let no man say, the world it selfe being dead,
'Tis labour lost to have discovered
The worlds infirmities, since there is none
Alive to study this dissection;
For there's a kinde of World remaining still,
Though shee which did inanimate and fill
The world, be gone, yet in this last long night,
Her Ghost doth walke; that is, a glimmering light, 70
A faint weake love of vertue, and of good,
Reflects from her, on them which understood
Her worth; and though she have shut in all day,
The twilight of her memory doth stay;
Which, from the carcasse of the old world, free,
Creates a new world, and new creatures bee
Produc'd: the matter and the stuffe of this,
Her vertue, and the forme our practice is:
And though to be thus elemented, arme

What life the world hath stil.

These creatures, from home-borne intrinsique harme, *80*
(For all assum'd unto this dignitie,
So many weedlesse Paradises bee,
Which of themselves produce no venemous sinne,
Except some forraine Serpent bring it in)
Yet, because outward stormes the strongest breake,
And strength it selfe by confidence growes weake,
This new world may be safer, being told
The dangers and diseases of the old: *The sicknesses of the World*
For with due temper men doe then forgoe,
Or covet things, when they their true worth know. *90*
There is no health; Physitians say that wee, *Impossibility of health*
At best, enjoy but a neutralitie.
And can there bee worse sicknesse, then to know
That we are never well, nor can be so?
Wee are borne ruinous: poore mothers cry,
That children come not right, nor orderly;
Except they headlong come and fall upon
An ominous precipitation.
How witty's ruine! how importunate
Upon mankinde! it labour'd to frustrate *100*
Even Gods purpose; and made woman, sent
For mans reliefe, cause of his languishment.
They were to good ends, and they are so still,
But accessory, and principall in ill;
For that first marriage was our funerall:
One woman at one blow, then kill'd us all,
And singly, one by one, they kill us now.
We doe delightfully our selves allow
To that consumption; and profusely blinde,
Wee kill our selves to propagate our kinde. *110*
And yet we do not that; we are not men:
There is not now that mankinde, which was then,
When as, the Sunne and man did seeme to strive,
(Joynt tenants of the world) who should survive; *Shortnesse of life.*
When, Stagge, and Raven, and the long-liv'd tree,
Compar'd with man, dy'd in minoritie;
When, if a slow pac'd starre had stolne away
From the observers marking, he might stay
Two or three hundred yeares to see't againe,
And then make up his observation plaine; *120*
When, as the age was long, the sise was great;
Mans growth confess'd, and recompenc'd the meat;
So spacious and large, that every Soule

Did a faire Kingdome, and large Realme controule:
And when the very stature, thus erect,
Did that soule a good way towards heaven direct.
Where is this mankinde now? who lives to age,
Fit to be made *Methusalem* his page?
Alas, we scarce live long enough to try
Whether a true made clocke run right, or lie. 130
Old Grandsires talke of yesterday with sorrow,
And for our children wee reserve to morrow.
So short is life, that every peasant strives,
In a torne house, or field, to have three lives.
And as in lasting, so in length is man
Contracted to an inch, who was a spanne; *Smalnesse of stature.*
For had a man at first in forrests stray'd,
Or shipwrack'd in the Sea, one would have laid
A wager, that an Elephant, or Whale,
That met him, would not hastily assaile 140
A thing so equall to him: now alas,
The Fairies, and the Pigmies well may passe
As credible; mankinde decayes so soone,
We'are scarce our Fathers shadowes cast at noone:
Onely death addes t'our length: nor are wee growne
In stature to be men, till we are none.
But this were light, did our lesse volume hold
All the old Text; or had wee chang'd to gold
Their silver; or dispos'd into lesse glasse
Spirits of vertue, which then scatter'd was. 150
But 'tis not so: w'are not retir'd, but dampt;
And as our bodies, so our mindes are crampt:
'Tis shrinking, not close weaving that hath thus,
In minde, and body both bedwarfed us.
Wee seeme ambitious, Gods whole worke t'undoe;
Of nothing hee made us, and we strive too,
To bring our selves to nothing backe; and wee
Doe what wee can, to do't so soone as hee.
With new diseases on our selves we warre,
And with new Physicke, a worse Engin farre. 160
Thus man, this worlds Vice-Emperour, in whom
All faculties, all graces are at home;
And if in other creatures they appeare,
They're but mans Ministers, and Legats there,
To worke on their rebellions, and reduce
Them to Civility, and to mans use:
This man, whom God did wooe, and loth t'attend

Till man came up, did downe to man descend,
This man, so great, that all that is, is his,
Oh what a trifle, and poore thing he is! *170*
If man were any thing, he's nothing now:
Helpe, or at least some time to wast, allow
T'his other wants, yet when he did depart
With her whom we lament, hee lost his heart.
She, of whom th'Ancients seem'd to prophesie,
When they call'd vertues by the name of *shee;*
Shee in whom vertue was so much refin'd,
That for Allay unto so pure a minde
Shee tooke the weaker Sex; shee that could drive
The poysonous tincture, and the staine of *Eve,* *180*
Out of her thoughts, and deeds; and purifie
All, by a true religious Alchymie;
Shee, shee is dead; shee's dead: when thou knowest this,
Thou knowest how poore a trifling thing man is.
And learn'st thus much by our Anatomie,
The heart being perish'd, no part can be free.
And that except thou feed (not banquet) on
The supernaturall food, Religion,
Thy better Growth growes withered, and scant;
Be more then man, or thou'rt lesse then an Ant. *190*
Then, as mankinde, so is the worlds whole frame
Quite out of joynt, almost created lame:
For, before God had made up all the rest,
Corruption entred, and deprav'd the best:
It seis'd the Angels, and then first of all
The world did in her cradle take a fall,
And turn'd her braines, and tooke a generall maime,
Wronging each joynt of th'universall frame.
The noblest part, man, felt it first; and than
Both beasts and plants, curst in the curse of man. *200*
So did the world from the first houre decay, *Decay of nature in other parts.*
That evening was beginning of the day,
And now the Springs and Sommers which we see,
Like sonnes of women after fiftie bee.
And new Philosophy calls all in doubt,
The Element of fire is quite put out;
The Sun is lost, and th'earth, and no mans wit
Can well direct him where to looke for it.
And freely men confesse that this world's spent,
When in the Planets, and the Firmament *210*
They seeke so many new; they see that this

Is crumbled out againe to his Atomies.
'Tis all in peeces, all cohaerence gone;
All just supply, and all Relation:
Prince, Subject, Father, Sonne, are things forgot,
For every man alone thinkes he hath got
To be a Phœnix, and that then can bee
None of that kinde, of which he is, but hee.
This is the worlds condition now, and now
She that should all parts to reunion bow, 220
She that had all Magnetique force alone,
To draw, and fasten sundred parts in one;
She whom wise nature had invented then
When she observ'd that every sort of men
Did in their voyage in this worlds Sea stray,
And needed a new compasse for their way;
She that was best, and first originall
Of all faire copies, and the generall
Steward to Fate; she whose rich eyes, and brest
Guilt the West Indies, and perfum'd the East; 230
Whose having breath'd in this world, did bestow
Spice on those Iles, and bad them still smell so,
And that rich Indie which doth gold interre,
Is but as single money, coyn'd from her:
She to whom this world must it selfe refer,
As Suburbs, or the Microcosme of her,
Shee, shee is dead; shee's dead: when thou knowst this,
Thou knowst how lame a cripple this world is.
And learn'st thus much by our Anatomy,
That this worlds generall sickenesse doth not lie 240
In any humour, or one certaine part;
But as thou sawest it rotten at the heart,
Thou seest a Hectique feaver hath got hold
Of the whole substance, not to be contrould,
And that thou hast but one way, not t'admit
The worlds infection, to be none of it.
For the worlds subtilst immateriall parts
Feele this consuming wound, and ages darts.
For the worlds beauty is decai'd, or gone,
Beauty, that's colour, and proportion. 250
We thinke the heavens enjoy their Sphericall, *Disformity of parts.*
Their round proportion embracing all.
But yet their various and perplexed course,
Observ'd in divers ages, doth enforce
Men to finde out so many Eccentrique parts,

Such divers downe-right lines, such overthwarts,
As disproportion that pure forme: It teares
The Firmament in eight and forty sheires,
And in these Constellations then arise
New starres, and old doe vanish from our eyes: *260*
As though heav'n suffered earthquakes, peace or war,
When new Towers rise, and old demolish't are.
They have impal'd within a Zodiake
The free-borne Sun, and keepe twelve Signes awake
To watch his steps; the Goat and Crab controule,
And fright him backe, who else to either Pole
(Did not these Tropiques fetter him) might runne:
For his course is not round; nor can the Sunne
Perfit a Circle, or maintaine his way
One inch direct; but where he rose to-day *270*
He comes no more, but with a couzening line,
Steales by that point, and so is Serpentine:
And seeming weary with his reeling thus,
He meanes to sleepe, being now falne nearer us.
So, of the Starres which boast that they doe runne
In Circle still, none ends where he begun.
All their proportion's lame, it sinkes, it swels.
For of Meridians, and Parallels,
Man hath weav'd out a net, and this net throwne
Upon the Heavens, and now they are his owne. *280*
Loth to goe up the hill, or labour thus
To goe to heaven, we make heaven come to us.
We spur, we reine the starres, and in their race
They're diversly content t'obey our pace.
But keepes the earth her round proportion still?
Doth not a Tenarif, or higher Hill
Rise so high like a Rocke, that one might thinke
The floating Moone would shipwracke there, and
sinke?
Seas are so deepe, that Whales being strooke to day,
Perchance to morrow, scarse at middle way *290*
Of their wish'd journies end, the bottome, die.
And men, to sound depths, so much line untie,
As one might justly thinke, that there would rise
At end thereof, one of th'Antipodies:
If under all, a Vault infernall bee,
(Which sure is spacious, except that we
Invent another torment, that there must
Millions into a straight hot roome be thrust)

Then solidnesse, and roundnesse have no place.
Are these but warts, and pock-holes in the face 300
Of th'earth? Thinke so: but yet confesse, in this
The worlds proportion disfigured is;
That those two legges whereon it doth rely, *Disorder in the world.*
Reward and punishment are bent awry.
And, Oh, it can no more be questioned,
That beauties best, proportion, is dead,
Since even griefe it selfe, which now alone
Is left us, is without proportion.
Shee by whose lines proportion should bee
Examin'd, measure of all Symmetree, 310
Whom had that Ancient seen, who thought soules made
Of Harmony, he would at next have said
That Harmony was shee, and thence infer,
That soules were but Resultances from her,
And did from her into our bodies goe,
As to our eyes, the formes from objects flow:
Shee, who if those great Doctors truly said
That the Arke to mans proportions was made,
Had been a type for that, as that might be
A type of her in this, that contrary 320
Both Elements, and Passions liv'd at peace
In her, who caus'd all Civill war to cease.
Shee, after whom, what forme so'er we see,
Is discord, and rude incongruitie;
Shee, shee is dead, shee's dead; when thou knowst this
Thou knowst how ugly a monster this world is:
And learn'st thus much by our Anatomie,
That here is nothing to enamour thee:
And that, not only faults in inward parts,
Corruptions in our braines, or in our hearts, 330
Poysoning the fountaines, whence our actions spring,
Endanger us: but that if every thing
Be not done fitly'and in proportion,
To satisfie wise, and good lookers on,
(Since most men be such as most thinke they bee)
They're lothsome too, by this Deformitee.
For good, and well, must in our actions meete;
Wicked is not much worse than indiscreet.
But beauties other second Element,
Colour, and lustre now, is as neere spent. 340

And had the world his just proportion,
Were it a ring still, yet the stone is gone.
As a compassionate Turcoyse which doth tell
By looking pale, the wearer is not well,
As gold falls sicke being stung with Mercury,
All the worlds parts of such complexion bee.
When nature was most busie, the first weeke,
Swadling the new borne earth, God seem'd to like
That she should sport her selfe sometimes, and play,
To mingle, and vary colours every day: *350*
And then, as though shee could not make inow,
Himselfe his various Rainbow did allow.
Sight is the noblest sense of any one,
Yet sight hath only colour to feed on,
And colour is decai'd: summers robe growes
Duskie, and like an oft dyed garment showes.
Our blushing red, which us'd in cheekes to spred,
Is inward sunke, and only our soules are red.
Perchance the world might have recovered,
If she whom we lament had not beene dead: *360*
But shee, in whom all white, and red, and blew
(Beauties ingredients) voluntary grew,
As in an unvext Paradise; from whom
Did all things verdure, and their lustre come,
Whose composition was miraculous,
Being all colour, all Diaphanous,
(For Ayre, and Fire but thick grosse bodies were,
And liveliest stones but drowsie, and pale to her,)
Shee, shee, is dead; shee's dead: when thou know'st
this,
Thou knowst how wan a Ghost this our world is: *370*
And learn'st thus much by our Anatomie,
That is should more affright, then pleasure thee.
And that, since all faire colour then did sinke,
'Tis now but wicked vanitie, to thinke
To colour vicious deeds with good pretence,
Or with bought colors to illude mens sense.

Weaknesse in the want of correspondence of heaven and earth.

Nor in ought more this worlds decay appeares,
Then that her influence the heav'n forbeares,
Or that the Elements doe not feele this,
The father, or the mother barren is. *380*
The cloudes conceive not raine, or doe not powre,
In the due birth time, downe the balmy showre;
Th'Ayre doth not motherly sit on the earth,

To hatch her seasons, and give all things birth;
Spring-times were common cradles, but are tombes;
And false-conceptions fill the generall wombes;
Th'Ayre showes such Meteors, as none can see,
Not only what they meane, but what they bee;
Earth such new wormes, as would have troubled
much
Th'Ægyptian *Mages* to have made more such. 390
What Artist now dares boast that he can bring
Heaven hither, or constellate any thing,
So as the influence of those starres may bee
Imprison'd in an Hearbe, or Charme, or Tree,
And doe by touch, all which those stars could doe?
The art is lost, and correspondence too.
For heaven gives little, and the earth takes lesse,
And man least knowes their trade and purposes.
If this commerce twixt heaven and earth were not
Embarr'd, and all this traffique quite forgot, 400
She, for whose losse we have lamented thus,
Would worke more fully, and pow'rfully on us:
Since herbes, and roots, by dying lose not all,
But they, yea Ashes too, are medicinall,
Death could not quench her vertue so, but that
It would be (if not follow'd) wondred at:
And all the world would be one dying Swan,
To sing her funerall praise, and vanish than.
But as some Serpents poyson hurteth not,
Except it be from the live Serpent shot, 410
So doth her vertue need her here, to fit
That unto us; shee working more then it.
But shee, in whom to such maturity
Vertue was growne, past growth, that it must die;
She, from whose influence all Impressions came,
But, by Receivers impotencies, lame,
Who, though she could not transubstantiate
All states to gold, yet guilded every state,
So that some Princes have some temperance;
Some Counsellers some purpose to advance 420
The common profit; and some people have
Some stay, no more then Kings should give, to crave;
Some women have some taciturnity,
Some nunneries some graines of chastitie.
She that did thus much, and much more could doe,
But that our age was Iron, and rustie too,

Shee, shee is dead; shee's dead; when thou knowst
this,
Thou knowst how drie a Cinder this world is.
And learn'st thus much by our Anatomy,
That 'tis in vaine to dew, or mollifie 430
It with thy teares, or sweat, or blood: nothing
Is worth our travaile, griefe, or perishing,
But those rich joyes, which did possesse her heart,
Of which she's now partaker, and a part.
But as in cutting up a man that's dead, *Conclusion.*
The body will not last out, to have read
On every part, and therefore men direct
Their speech to parts, that are of most effect;
So the worlds carcasse would not last, if I
Were punctuall in this Anatomy; 440
Nor smels it well to hearers, if one tell
Them their disease, who faine would think they're
well.
Here therefore be the end: And, blessed maid,
Of whom is meant what ever hath been said,
Or shall be spoken well by any tongue,
Whose name refines course lines, and makes prose
song,
Accept this tribute, and his first yeares rent,
Who till his darke short tapers end be spent,
As oft as thy feast sees this widowed earth,
Will yearely celebrate thy second birth, 450
That is, thy death; for though the soule of man
Be got when man is made, 'tis borne but than
When man doth die; our body's as the wombe,
And, as a Mid-wife, death directs it home.
And you her creatures, whom she workes upon,
And have your last, and best concoction
From her example, and her vertue, if you
In reverence to her, do thinke it due,
That no one should her praises thus rehearse,
As matter fit for Chronicle, not verse; 460
Vouchsafe to call to minde that God did make
A last, and lasting'st peece, a song. He spake
To *Moses* to deliver unto all,
That song, because hee knew they would let fall
The Law, the Prophets, and the History,
But keepe the song still in their memory:
Such an opinion (in due measure) made

Me this great Office boldly to invade:
Nor could incomprehensiblenesse deterre
Mee, from thus trying to emprison her, 470
Which when I saw that a strict grave could doe,
I saw not why verse might not do so too.
Verse hath a middle nature: heaven keepes Soules,
The Grave keepes bodies, Verse the Fame enroules.

Of the Progresse Of The Soule

The second Anniversarie

Nothing could make me sooner to confesse
That this world had an everlastingnesse, *The entrance.*
Then to consider, that a yeare is runne,
Since both this lower world's, and the Sunnes Sunne,
The Lustre, and the vigor of this All,
Did set; 'twere blasphemie to say, did fall.
But as a ship which hath strooke saile, doth runne
By force of that force which before, it wonne:
Or as sometimes in a beheaded man,
Though at those two Red seas, which freely ranne, 10
One from the Trunke, another from the Head,
His soule be sail'd, to her eternall bed,
His eyes will twinckle, and his tongue will roll,
As though he beckned, and cal'd backe his soule,
He graspes his hands, and he pulls up his feet,
And seemes to reach, and to step forth to meet
His soule; when all these motions which we saw,

Of the . . . Soule: In the 1612 edition the title is followed by: "Wherein, By occasion of the Religious death of Mistris Elizabeth Drury, the incommodities of the Soule in this life, and her exaltation in the next, are contemplated."
The second Anniversarie: See the note to *The first Anniversary* on page 74.

Are but as Ice, which crackles at a thaw:
Or as a Lute, which in moist weather, rings
Her knell alone, by cracking of her strings: 20
So struggles this dead world, now shee is gone;
For there is motion in corruption.
As some daies are at the Creation nam'd,
Before the Sunne, the which fram'd daies, was
fram'd,
So after this Sunne's set, some shew appeares,
And orderly vicissitude of yeares.
Yet a new Deluge, and of *Lethe* flood,
Hath drown'd us all, All have forgot all good,
Forgetting her, the maine reserve of all.
Yet in this deluge, grosse and generall, 30
Thou seest me strive for life; my life shall bee,
To be hereafter prais'd, for praysing thee;
Immortall Maid, who though thou would'st refuse
The name of Mother, be unto my Muse
A Father, since her chast Ambition is,
Yearely to bring forth such a child as this.
These Hymnes may worke on future wits, and so
May great Grand children of thy prayses grow,
And so, though not revive, embalme and spice
The world, which else would putrifie with vice. 40
For thus, Man may extend thy progeny,
Untill man doe but vanish, and not die.
These Hymnes thy issue, may encrease so long,
As till Gods great *Venite* change the song.
Thirst for that time, O my insatiate soule,
And serve thy thirst, with Gods safe-sealing Bowle.
Be thirstie still, and drinke still till thou goe
To th'only Health, to be Hydroptique so.
Forget this rotten world; And unto thee
Let thine owne times as an old storie bee. 50
Be not concern'd: studie not why, nor when;
Doe not so much as not beleeve a man.
For though to erre, be worst, to try truths forth,
Is far more businesse, then this world is worth.
The world is but a carkasse; thou art fed
By it, but as a worme, that carkasse bred;
And why should'st thou, poore worme, consider more,
When this world will grow better than before,
Then those thy fellow wormes doe thinke upon
That carkasses last resurrection. 60

A just dis-estimation of this world.

Forget this world, and scarce thinke of it so,
As of old clothes, cast off a yeare agoe.
To be thus stupid is Alacritie;
Men thus Lethargique have best Memory.
Look upward; that's towards her, whose happy state
We now lament not, but congratulate.
Shee, to whom all this world was but a stage,
Where all sat harkning how her youthfull age
Should be emploi'd, because in all shee did,
Some Figure of the Golden times was hid. 70
Who could not lacke, what e'r this world could give,
Because shee was the forme, that made it live;
Nor could complaine, that this world was unfit
To be staid in, then when shee was in it;
Shee that first tried indifferent desires
By vertue, and vertue by religious fires,
Shee to whose person Paradise adher'd,
As Courts to Princes, shee whose eyes enspheardd
Star-light enough, t'have made the South controule,
(Had shee beene there) the Star-full Northerne Pole, 80
Shee, shee is gone; she is gone; when thou knowest
this,
What fragmentary rubbidge this world is
Thou knowest, and that it is not worth a thought;
He honors it too much that thinkes it nought.
Thinke then, my soule, that death is but a Groome,
Which brings a Taper to the outward roome,
Whence thou spiest first a little glimmering light,
And after brings it nearer to thy sight:
For such approaches doth heaven make in death.
Thinke thy selfe labouring now with broken breath, 90
And thinke those broken and soft Notes to bee
Division, and thy happyest Harmonie.
Thinke thee laid on thy death-bed, loose and slacke;
And thinke that, but unbinding of a packe,
To take one precious thing, thy soule from thence.
Thinke thy selfe parch'd with fevers violence,
Anger thine ague more, by calling it
Thy Physicke; chide the slacknesse of the fit.
Thinke that thou hear'st thy knell, and think no more,
But that, as Bels cal'd thee to Church before, 100
So this, to the Triumphant Church, calls thee.
Thinke Satans Sergeants round about thee bee,
And thinke that but for Legacies they thrust;

Contemplation of our state in our death-bed.

Give one thy Pride, to'another give thy Lust:
Give them those sinnes which they gave thee before,
And trust th'immaculate blood to wash thy score.
Thinke thy friends weeping round, and thinke that
 they
Weepe but because they goe not yet thy way.
Thinke that they close thine eyes, and thinke in this,
That they confesse much in the world, amisse, *110*
Who dare not trust a dead mans eye with that,
Which they from God, and Angels cover not.
Thinke that they shroud thee up, and think from
 thence
They reinvest thee in white innocence.
Thinke that thy body rots, and (if so low,
Thy soule exalted so, thy thoughts can goe,)
Think thee a Prince, who of themselves create
Wormes which insensibly devoure their State.
Thinke that they bury thee, and thinke that right
Laies thee to sleepe but a Saint Lucies night. *120*
Thinke these things cheerefully: and if thou bee
Drowsie or slacke, remember then that shee,
Shee whose Complexion was so even made,
That which of her Ingredients should invade
The other three, no Feare, no Art could guesse:
So far were all remov'd from more or lesse.
But as in Mithridate, or just perfumes,
Where all good things being met, no one presumes
To governe, or to triumph on the rest,
Only because all were, no part was best. *130*
And as, though all doe know, that quantities
Are made of lines, and lines from Points arise,
None can these lines or quantities unjoynt,
And say this is a line, or this a point,
So though the Elements and Humors were
In her, one could say, this governes there.
Whose even constitution might have wonne
Any disease to venter on the Sunne,
Rather then her: and make a spirit feare,
That hee to disuniting subject were. *140*
To whose proportions if we would compare
Cubes, th'are unstable; Circles, Angular;
She who was such a chaine as Fate employes
To bring mankinde all Fortunes it enjoyes;
So fast, so even wrought, as one would thinke,

No Accident could threaten any linke;
Shee, shee embrac'd a sicknesse, gave it meat,
The purest blood, and breath, that e'r it eate;
And hath taught us, that though a good man hath
Title to heaven, and plead it by his Faith, *150*
And though he may pretend a conquest, since
Heaven was content to suffer violence,
Yea though hee plead a long possession too,
(For they're in heaven on earth who heavens workes
do)
Though hee had right and power and place, before,
Yet Death must usher, and unlocke the doore.
Thinke further on thy selfe, my Soule, and thinke
How thou at first wast made but in a sinke;
Thinke that it argued some infirmitie,
That those two soules, which then thou foundst in me, *160*
Thou fedst upon, and drewst into thee, both
My second soule of sense, and first of growth.
Thinke but how poore thou wast, how obnoxious;
Whom a small lumpe of flesh could poyson thus.
This curded milke, this poore unlittered whelpe
My body, could, beyond escape or helpe,
Infect thee with Originall sinne, and thou
Couldst neither then refuse, nor leave it now.
Thinke that no stubborne sullen Anchorit,
Which fixt to a pillar, or a grave, doth sit *170*
Bedded, and bath'd in all his ordures, dwels
So fowly as our Soules in their first-built Cels.
Thinke in how poore a prison thou didst lie
After, enabled but to suck, and crie.
Thinke, when 'twas growne to most, 'twas a poore
Inne,
A Province pack'd up in two yards of skinne,
And that usurp'd or threatned with the rage
Of sicknesses, or their true mother, Age.
But thinke that Death hath now enfranchis'd thee,
Thou hast thy'expansion now, and libertie; *180*
Thinke that a rustie Peece, discharg'd, is flowne
In peeces, and the bullet is his owne,
And freely flies: This to thy Soule allow,
Thinke thy shell broke, thinke thy Soule hatch'd but
now.
And think this slow-pac'd soule, which late did cleave
To'a body, and went but by the bodies leave,

Incommodities of the Soule in the Body.

Her liberty by death.

Twenty, perchance, or thirty mile a day,
Dispatches in a minute all the way
Twixt heaven, and earth; she stayes not in the ayre,
To looke what Meteors there themselves prepare; *190*
She carries no desire to know, nor sense,
Whether th'ayres middle region be intense;
For th'Element of fire, she doth not know,
Whether she past by such a place or no;
She baits not at the Moone, nor cares to trie
Whether in that new world, men live, and die.
Venus retards her not, to'enquire, how shee
Can, (being one starre) *Hesper,* and *Vesper* bee;
Hee that charm'd *Argus* eyes, sweet *Mercury,*
Workes not on her, who now is growne all eye; *200*
Who, if she meet the body of the Sunne,
Goes through, not staying till his course be runne;
Who findes in *Mars* his Campe no corps of Guard;
Nor is by *Jove,* nor by his father barr'd;
But ere she can consider how she went,
At once is at, and through the Firmament.
And as these starres were but so many beads
Strung on one string, speed undistinguish'd leads
Her through those Spheares, as through the beads, a
string,
Whose quick succession makes it still one thing: *210*
As doth the pith, which, lest our bodies slacke,
Strings fast the little bones of necke, and backe;
So by the Soule doth death string Heaven and Earth;
For when our Soule enjoyes this her third birth,
(Creation gave her one, a second, grace,)
Heaven is as neare, and present to her face,
As colours are, and objects, in a roome
Where darknesse was before, when Tapers come.
This must, my Soule, thy long-short Progresse bee;
To'advance these thoughts, remember then, that she, *220*
She, whose faire body no such prison was,
But that a Soule might well be pleas'd to passe
An age in her; she whose rich beauty lent
Mintage to other beauties, for they went
But for so much as they were like to her;
Shee, in whose body (if we dare preferre
This low world, to so high a marke as shee,)
The Westerne treasure, Easterne spicerie,
Europe, and Afrique, and the unknowne rest

Were easily found, or what in them was best; 230
And when w'have made this large discoverie
Of all, in her some one part then will bee
Twenty such parts, whose plenty and riches is
Enough to make twenty such worlds as this;
Shee, whom had they knowne who did first betroth
The Tutelar Angels, and assign'd one, both
To Nations, Cities, and to Companies,
To Functions, Offices, and Dignities,
And to each severall man, to him, and him,
They would have given her one for every limbe; 240
She, of whose soule, if wee may say, 'twas Gold,
Her body was th'Electrum, and did hold
Many degrees of that; wee understood
Her by her sight; her pure, and eloquent blood
Spoke in her cheekes, and so distinctly wrought,
That one might almost say, her body thought;
Shee, shee, thus richly and largely hous'd, is gone:
And chides us slow-pac'd snailes who crawle upon
Our prisons prison, earth, nor thinke us well,
Longer, then whil'st wee beare our brittle shell. 250
But 'twere but little to have chang'd our roome,
If, as we were in this our living Tombe
Oppress'd with ignorance, wee still were so.
Poore soule, in this thy flesh what dost thou know?
Thou know'st thy selfe so little, as thou know'st not,
How thou didst die, nor how thou wast begot.
Thou neither know'st, how thou at first cam'st in,
Nor how thou took'st the poyson of mans sinne.
Nor dost thou, (though thou know'st, that thou art
so)
By what way thou art made immortall, know. 260
Thou art too narrow, wretch, to comprehend
Even thy selfe: yea though thou wouldst but bend
To know thy body. Have not all soules thought
For many ages, that our body'is wrought
Of Ayre, and Fire, and other Elements?
And now they thinke of new ingredients,
And one Soule thinkes one, and another way
Another thinkes, and 'tis an even lay.
Knowst thou but how the stone doth enter in
The bladders cave, and never breake the skinne? 270
Know'st thou how blood, which to the heart does flow,
Doth from one ventricle to th'other goe?

Her ignorance in this life and knowledge in the next.

And for the putrid stuffe, which thou dost spit,
Know'st thou how thy lungs have attracted it?
There are no passages, so that there is
(For ought thou know'st) piercing of substances.
And of those many opinions which men raise
Of Nailes and Haires, dost thou know which to praise?
What hope have wee to know our selves, when wee
Know not the least things, which for our use be? *280*
Wee see in Authors, too stiffe to recant,
A hundred controversies of an Ant;
And yet one watches, starves, freeses, and sweats,
To know but Catechismes and Alphabets
Of unconcerning things, matters of fact;
How others on our stage their parts did Act;
What *Cæsar* did, yea, and what *Cicero* said.
Why grasse is greene, or why our blood is red,
Are mysteries which none have reach'd unto.
In this low forme, poore soule, what wilt thou doe? *290*
When wilt thou shake off this Pedantery,
Of being taught by sense, and Fantasie?
Thou look'st through spectacles; small things seeme great
Below; But up unto the watch-towre get,
And see all things despoyl'd of fallacies:
Thou shalt not peepe through lattices of eyes,
Nor heare through Labyrinths of eares, nor learne
By circuit, or collections to discerne,
In heaven thou straight know'st all, concerning it,
And what concernes it not, shalt straight forget. *300*
There thou (but in no other schoole) maist bee
Perchance, as learned, and as full, as shee,
Shee who all libraries had throughly read
At home in her owne thoughts, and practised
So much good as would make as many more:
Shee whose example they must all implore,
Who would or doe, or thinke well, and confesse
That all the vertuous Actions they expresse,
Are but a new, and worse edition
Of her some one thought, or one action: *310*
She who in th'art of knowing Heaven, was growne
Here upon earth, to such perfection,
That she hath, ever since to Heaven she came,
(In a far fairer print,) but read the same:
Shee, shee not satisfied with all this waight,
(For so much knowledge, as would over-fraight

Another, did but ballast her) is gone
As well t'enjoy, as get perfection.
And cals us after her, in that shee tooke,
(Taking her selfe) our best, and worthiest booke. 320
Returne not, my Soule, from this extasie,
And meditation of what thou shalt bee,
To earthly thoughts, till it to thee appeare,
With whom thy conversation must be there.
With whom wilt thou converse? what station
Canst thou choose out, free from infection,
That will not give thee theirs, nor drinke in thine?
Shalt thou not finde a spungie slacke Divine
Drinke and sucke in th'instructions of Great men,
And for the word of God, vent them agen? 330
Are there not some Courts (and then, no things bee
So like as Courts) which, in this let us see,
That wits and tongues of Libellers are weake,
Because they do more ill, then these can speake?
The poyson's gone through all, poysons affect
Chiefly the chiefest parts, but some effect
In nailes, and haires, yea excrements, will show;
So lyes the poyson of sinne in the most low.
Up, up, my drowsie Soule, where thy new eare
Shall in the Angels songs no discord heare; 340
Where thou shalt see the blessed Mother-maid
Joy in not being that, which men have said.
Where she is exalted more for being good,
Then for her interest of Mother-hood.
Up to those Patriarchs, which did longer sit
Expecting Christ, then they'have enjoy'd him yet.
Up to those Prophets, which now gladly see
Their Prophecies growne to be Historie.
Up to th'Apostles, who did bravely runne
All the Suns course, with more light then the Sunne. 350
Up to those Martyrs, who did calmly bleed
Oyle to th'Apostles Lamps, dew to their seed.
Up to those Virgins, who thought, that almost
They made joyntenants with the Holy Ghost,
If they to any should his Temple give.
Up, up, for in that squadron there doth live
She, who hath carried thither new degrees
(As to their number) to their dignities.
Shee, who being to her selfe a State, injoy'd
All royalties which any State employ'd; 360

Of our company in this life, and in the next.

For shee made warres, and triumph'd; reason still
Did not o'rthrow, but rectifie her will:
And she made peace, for no peace is like this,
That beauty, and chastity together kisse:
She did high justice, for she crucified
Every first motion of rebellious pride:
And she gave pardons, and was liberall,
For, onely her selfe except, she pardon'd all:
Shee coy'nd, in this, that her impressions gave
To all our actions all the worth they have: *370*
She gave protections; the thoughts of her brest
Satans rude Officers could ne'r arrest.
As these prerogatives being met in one,
Made her a soveraigne State; religion
Made her a Church; and these two made her all.
She who was all this All, and could not fall
To worse, by company, (for she was still
More Antidote, then all the world was ill,)
Shee, shee doth leave it, and by Death, survive
All this, in Heaven; whither who doth not strive *380*
The more, because shees there, he doth not know
That accidentall joyes in Heaven doe grow.
But pause, my soule; And study, ere thou fall
On accidentall joyes, th'essentiall.
Still before Accessories doe abide
A triall, must the principall be tride.

Of essentiall joy in this life and in the next.

And what essentiall joy can'st thou expect
Here upon earth? what permanent effect
Of transitory causes? Dost thou love
Beauty? (And beauty worthy'st is to move) *390*
Poore cousened cousenor, *that* she, and *that* thou,
Which did begin to love, are neither now;
You are both fluid, chang'd since yesterday;
Next day repaires, (but ill) last dayes decay.
Nor are, (although the river keepe the name)
Yesterdaies waters, and to daies the same.
So flowes her face, and thine eyes, neither now
That Saint, nor Pilgrime, which your loving vow
Concern'd, remaines; but whil'st you thinke you bee
Constant, you'are hourely in inconstancie. *400*
Honour may have pretence unto our love,
Because that God did live so long above
Without this Honour, and then lov'd it so,
That he at last made Creatures to bestow

Honour on him; not that he needed it,
But that, to his hands, man might grow more fit.
But since all Honours from inferiours flow,
(For they doe give it; Princes doe but shew
Whom they would have so honor'd) and that this
On such opinions, and capacities 410
Is built, as rise and fall, to more and lesse:
Alas, 'tis but a casuall happinesse.
Hath ever any man to'himselfe assign'd
This or that happinesse to'arrest his minde,
But that another man which takes a worse,
Thinks him a foole for having tane that course?
They who did labour Babels tower to'erect,
Might have considered, that for that effect,
All this whole solid Earth could not allow
Nor furnish forth materialls enow; 420
And that this Center, to raise such a place,
Was farre too little, to have beene the Base;
No more affords this world, foundation
To erect true joy, were all the meanes in one.
But as the Heathen made them severall gods,
Of all Gods Benefits, and all his Rods,
(For as the Wine, and Corne, and Onions are
Gods unto them, so Agues bee, and Warre)
And as by changing that whole precious Gold
To such small Copper coynes, they lost the old, 430
And lost their only God, who ever must
Be sought alone, and not in such a thrust:
So much mankinde true happinesse mistakes;
No Joy enjoyes that man, that many makes.
Then, Soule, to thy first pitch worke up againe;
Know that all lines which circles doe containe,
For once that they the Center touch, doe touch
Twice the circumference; and be thou such;
Double on heaven thy thoughts on earth emploid;
All will not serve; Only who have enjoy'd 440
The sight of God, in fulnesse, can thinke it;
For it is both the object, and the wit.
This is essentiall joy, where neither hee
Can suffer diminution, nor wee;
'Tis such a full, and such a filling good;
Had th'Angels once look'd on him, they had stood.
To fill the place of one of them, or more,
Shee whom wee celebrate, is gone before.

She, who had Here so much essentiall joy,
As no chance could distract, much lesse destroy; *450*
Who with Gods presence was acquainted so,
(Hearing, and speaking to him) as to know
His face in any naturall Stone, or Tree,
Better then when in Images they bee:
Who kept by diligent devotion,
Gods Image, in such reparation,
Within her heart, that what decay was growne,
Was her first Parents fault, and not her owne:
Who being solicited to any act,
Still heard God pleading his safe precontract; *460*
Who by a faithfull confidence, was here
Betroth'd to God, and now is married there;
Whose twilights were more cleare, then our mid-day;
Who dreamt devoutlier, then most use to pray;
Who being here fil'd with grace, yet strove to bee,
Both where more grace, and more capacitie
At once is given: she to Heaven is gone,
Who made this world in some proportion
A heaven, and here, became unto us all,
Joy, (as our joyes admit) essentiall. *470*
But could this low world joyes essentiall touch,
Heavens accidentall joyes would passe them much.
How poore and lame, must then our casuall bee?
If thy Prince will his subjects to call thee
My Lord, and this doe swell thee, thou art than,
By being greater, growne to bee lesse Man.
When no Physitian of redresse can speake,
A joyfull casuall violence may breake
A dangerous Apostem in thy breast;
And whil'st thou joyest in this, the dangerous rest, *480*
The bag may rise up, and so strangle thee.
What e'r was casuall, may ever bee.
What should the nature change? Or make the same
Certaine, which was but casuall, when it came?
All casuall joy doth loud and plainly say,
Only by comming, that it can away.
Only in Heaven joyes strength is never spent;
And accidentall things are permanent.
Joy of a soules arrivall ne'r decaies;
For that soule ever joyes and ever staies. *490*
Joy that their last great Consummation
Approaches in the resurrection;

Of accidentall joys in both places.

When earthly bodies more celestiall
Shall be, then Angels were, for they could fall;
This kinde of joy doth every day admit
Degrees of growth, but none of losing it.
In this fresh joy, 'tis no small part, that shee,
Shee, in whose goodnesse, he that names degree,
Doth injure her; ('Tis losse to be cal'd best,
There where the stuffe is not such as the rest) *500*
Shee, who left such a bodie, as even shee
Only in Heaven could learne, how it can bee
Made better; for shee rather was two soules,
Or like to full on both sides written Rols,
Where eyes might reade upon the outward skin,
As strong Records for God, as mindes within;
Shee, who by making full perfection grow,
Peeces a Circle, and still keepes it so,
Long'd for, and longing for it, to heaven is gone,
Where shee receives, and gives addition. *510*
Here in a place, where mis-devotion frames *Conclusion.*
A thousand Prayers to Saints, whose very names
The ancient Church knew not, Heaven knows not yet:
And where, what lawes of Poetry admit,
Lawes of Religion have at least the same,
Immortall Maide, I might invoke thy name.
Could any Saint provoke that appetite,
Thou here should'st make me a French convertite.
But thou would'st not; nor would'st thou be content,
To take this, for my second yeares true Rent, *520*
Did this Coine beare any other stampe, then his,
That gave thee power to doe, me, to say this.
Since his will is, that to posteritie,
Thou should'st for life, and death, a patterne bee,
And that the world should notice have of this,
The purpose, and th'authoritie is his;
Thou art the Proclamation; and I am
The Trumpet, at whose voyce the people came.

FROM

Divine Poems

Holy Sonnets
(1633)
Divine Meditations

1

As due by many titles I resigne
My selfe to thee, O God, first I was made
By thee, and for thee, and when I was decay'd
Thy blood bought that, the which before was thine,
I am thy sonne, made with thy selfe to shine,
Thy servant, whose paines thou hast still repaid,
Thy sheepe, thine Image, and till I betray'd
My selfe, a temple of thy Spirit divine;
Why doth the devill then usurpe in mee?
Why doth he steale, nay ravish that's thy right? *10*
Except thou rise and for thine owne worke fight,
Oh I shall soone despaire, when I doe see
That thou lov'st mankind well, yet wilt'not chuse me,
And Satan hates mee, yet is loth to lose mee.

2

Oh my blacke Soule! now thou art summoned
By sicknesse, deaths herald, and champion;
Thou art like a pilgrim, which abroad hath done
Treason, and durst not turne to whence hee is fled,
Or like a thiefe, which till deaths doome be read,
Wisheth himselfe delivered from prison;
But damn'd and hal'd to execution,
Wisheth that still he might be imprisoned;
Yet grace, if thou repent, thou canst not lacke;
But who shall give thee that grace to beginne? *10*

Divine Poems: In this volume the poems follow Professor Helen Gardner's edition (*John Donne: The Divine Poems*, Oxford: Clarendon Press, 1952).
Holy Sonnets: Professor Gardner's editing of these sonnets provides a unity and ordering they do not otherwise possess. The first

Oh make thy selfe with holy mourning blacke,
And red with blushing, as thou art with sinne;
Or wash thee in Christs blood, which hath this might
That being red, it dyes red soules to white.

3

This is my playes last scene, here heavens appoint
My pilgrimages last mile; and my race
Idly, yet quickly runne, hath this last pace,
My spans last inch, my minutes last point,
And gluttonous death, will instantly unjoynt
My body, and soule, and I shall sleepe a space,
But my'ever-waking part shall see that face,
Whose feare already shakes my every joynt:
Then, as my soule, to'heaven her first seate, takes flight,
And earth-borne body, in the earth shall dwell, *10*
So, fall my sinnes, that all may have their right,
To where they'are bred, and would presse me, to hell.
Impute me righteous, thus purg'd of evill,
For thus I leave the world, the flesh, and devill.

4

At the round earths imagin'd corners, blow
Your trumpets, Angells, and arise, arise
From death, you numberlesse infinities
Of soules, and to your scattred bodies goe,
All whom the flood did, and fire shall o'erthrow,
All whom warre, dearth, age, agues, tyrannies,
Despaire, law, chance, hath slaine, and you whose eyes,
Shall behold God, and never tast deaths woe.
But let them sleepe, Lord, and mee mourne a space,
For, if above all these, my sinnes abound, *10*
'Tis late to aske abundance of thy grace,
When wee are there; here on this lowly ground,
Teach mee how to repent; for that's as good
As if thou'hadst seal'd my pardon, with thy blood.

---

twelve sonnets, taken from the 1633 edition, date from 1609; the first six are meditations on "death and judgment, or the Last Things;" the last six are on the theme of love between Man and God. The four sonnets taken from the 1635 edition were written between 1609 and 1611 and are penitential in theme. The *Westmoreland* sonnets are occasional. (Gardner, pp. xl–l.)

5

If poysonous mineralls, and if that tree,
Whose fruit threw death on else immortall us,
If lecherous goats, if serpents envious
Cannot be damn'd; Alas; why should I bee?
Why should intent or reason, borne in mee,
Make sinnes, else equall, in mee, more heinous?
And mercy being easie, and glorious
To God, in his sterne wrath, why threatens hee?
But who am I, that dare dispute with thee?
O God, Oh! of thine onely worthy blood, *10*
And my teares, make a heavenly Lethean flood,
And drowne in it my sinnes blacke memorie.
That thou remember them, some claime as debt,
I thinke it mercy, if thou wilt forget.

6

Death be not proud, though some have called thee
Mighty and dreadfull, for, thou art not soe,
For, those, whom thou think'st, thou dost overthrow,
Die not, poore death, not yet canst thou kill mee;
From rest and sleepe, which but thy pictures bee,
Much pleasure, then from thee, much more must flow,
And soonest our best men with thee doe goe,
Rest of their bones, and soules deliverie.
Thou art slave to Fate, chance, kings, and desperate men,
And dost with poyson, warre, and sicknesse dwell, *10*
And poppie, or charmes can make us sleepe as well,
And better then thy stroake; why swell'st thou then?
One short sleepe past, wee wake eternally,
And death shall be no more, Death thou shalt die.

7

Spit in my face yee Jewes, and pierce my side,
Buffet, and scoffe, scourge, and crucifie mee,
For I have sinn'd, and sinn'd, and onely hee,
Who could do no iniquitie, hath dyed:
But by my death can not be satisfied
My sinnes, which passe the Jewes impiety:
They kill'd once an inglorious man, but I
Crucifie him daily, being now glorified.
Oh let mee then, his strange love still admire:
Kings pardon, but he bore our punishment. *10*

And *Jacob* came cloth'd in vile harsh attire
But to supplant, and with gainfull intent:
God cloth'd himselfe in vile mans flesh, that so
Hee might be weake enough to suffer woe.

8

Why are wee by all creatures waited on?
Why doe the prodigall elements supply
Life and food to mee, being more pure then I,
Simple, and further from corruption?
Why brook'st thou, ignorant horse, subjection?
Why dost thou bull, and bore so seelily
Dissemble weaknesse, and by'one mans stroke die,
Whose whole kinde, you might swallow and feed upon?
Weaker I am, woe is mee, and worse then you,
You have not sinn'd, nor need be timorous. *10*
But wonder at a greater wonder, for to us
Created nature doth these things subdue,
But their Creator, whom sin, nor nature tyed,
For us, his Creatures, and his foes, hath dyed.

9

What if this present were the worlds last night?
Marke in my heart, O Soule, where thou dost dwell,
The picture of Christ crucified, and tell
Whether that countenance can thee affright,
Teares in his eyes quench the amasing light,
Blood fills his frownes, which from his pierc'd head fell,
And can that tongue adjudge thee unto hell,
Which pray'd forgivenesse for his foes fierce spight?
No, no; but as in my idolatrie
I said to all my profane mistresses, *10*
Beauty, of pitty, foulnesse onely is
A signe of rigour: so I say to thee,
To wicked spirits are horrid shapes assign'd,
This beauteous forme assures a pitious minde.

10

Batter my heart, three person'd God; for, you
As yet but knocke, breathe, shine, and seeke to mend;
That I may rise, and stand, o'erthrow mee,'and bend
Your force, to breake, blowe, burn and make me new.
I, like an usurpt towne, to'another due,
Labour to'admit you, but Oh, to no end,

Reason your viceroy in mee, mee should defend,
But is captiv'd, and proves weake or untrue,
Yet dearely'I love you, and would be lov'd faine,
But am betroth'd unto your enemie,
Divorce mee,'untie, or breake that knot againe,
Take mee to you, imprison mee, for I
Except you'enthrall mee, never shall be free,
Nor ever chast, except you ravish mee.

11

Wilt thou love God, as he thee! then digest,
My Soule, this wholsome meditation,
How God the Spirit, by Angels waited on
In heaven, doth make his Temple in thy brest,
The Father having begot a Sonne most blest,
And still begetting, (for he ne'r begonne)
Hath deign'd to chuse thee by adoption,
Coheire to'his glory,'and Sabbaths endlesse rest;
And as a robb'd man, which by search doth finde
His stolne stuffe sold, must lose or buy'it againe: *10*
The Sonne of glory came downe, and was slaine,
Us whom he'had made, and Satan stolne, to unbinde.
'Twas much, that man was made like God before,
But, that God should be made like man, much more.

12

Father, part of his double interest
Unto thy kingdome, thy Sonne gives to mee,
His joynture in the knottie Trinitie,
Hee keepes, and gives mee his deaths conquest.
This Lambe, whose death, with life the world hath blest,
Was from the worlds beginning slaine, and he
Hath made two Wills, which with the Legacie
Of his and thy kingdome, doe thy Sonnes invest,
Yet such are those laws, that men argue yet
Whether a man those statutes can fulfill; *10*
None doth, but all-healing grace and Spirit,
Revive againe what law and letter kill.
Thy lawes abridgement, and thy last command
Is all but love; Oh let that last Will stand!

Holy Sonnets

(added in 1635)

Divine Meditations

I

Thou hast made me, And shall thy worke decay?
Repaire me now, for now mine end doth haste,
I runne to death, and death meets me as fast,
And all my pleasures are like yesterday,
I dare not move my dimme eyes any way,
Despaire behind, and death before doth cast
Such terrour, and my feebled flesh doth waste
By sinne in it, which it t'wards hell doth weigh;
Onely thou are above, and when towards thee
By thy leave I can looke, I rise againe; *10*
But our old subtle foe so tempteth me,
That not one houre I can my selfe sustaine;
Thy Grace may wing me to prevent his art
And thou like Adamant draw mine iron heart.

2

I am a little world made cunningly
Of Elements, and an Angelike spright,
But black sinne hath betraid to endlesse night
My worlds both parts, and (oh) both parts must die.
You which beyond that heaven which was most high
Have found new sphears, and of new lands can write,
Powre new seas in mine eyes, that so I might
Drowne my world with my weeping earnestly,
Or wash it, if it must be drown'd no more:
But oh it must be burnt; alas the fire *10*
Of lust and envie have burnt it heretofore,
And made it fouler; Let their flames retire,
And burne me ô Lord, with a fiery zeale
Of thee and thy house, which doth in eating heale.

3

O might those sighes and teares returne againe
Into my breast and eyes, which I have spent,
That I might in this holy discontent
Mourne with some fruit, as I have mourn'd in vaine;

In my Idolatry what showres of raine
Mine eyes did waste? what griefs my heart did rent?
That sufferance was my sinne, now I repent;
Because I did suffer I must suffer paine.
Th'hydroptique drunkard, and night-scouting thiefe,
The itchy Lecher, and selfe tickling proud 10
Have the remembrance of past joyes, for reliefe
Of comming ills. To (poore) me is allow'd
No ease; for, long, yet vehement griefe hath beene
Th'effect and cause, the punishment and sinne.

4

If faithfull soules be alike glorifi'd
As Angels, then my fathers soule doth see,
And adds this even to full felicitie,
That valiantly I hels wide mouth o'rstride:
But if our mindes to these soules be descry'd
By circumstances, and by signes that be
Apparent in us, not immediately,
How shall my mindes white truth to them be try'd?
They see idolatrous lovers weepe and mourne,
And vile blasphemous Conjurers to call 10
On Jesus name, and Pharisaicall
Dissemblers feigne devotion. Then turne
O pensive soule, to God, for he knowes best
Thy true griefe, for he put it in my breast.

Holy Sonnets

(from the Westmoreland MS.)

I

Since she whome I lovd, hath payd her last debt
To Nature, and to hers, and my good is dead,
And her soule early into heaven ravished,
Wholy in heavenly things my mind is sett.
Here the admyring her my mind did whett
To seeke thee God; so streames do shew the head,
But though I have found thee, and thou my thirst hast fed,
A holy thirsty dropsy melts mee yett.
But why should I begg more love, when as thou
Dost wooe my soule, for hers offring all thine: 10

And dost not only feare least I allow
My love to saints and Angels, things divine,
But in thy tender jealosy dost doubt
Least the World, fleshe, yea Devill putt thee out.

2

Show me deare Christ, thy spouse, so bright and cleare.
What, is it she, which on the other shore
Goes righly painted? or which rob'd and tore
Laments and mournes in Germany and here?
Sleepes she a thousand, then peepes up one yeare?
Is she selfe truth and errs? now new, now outwore?
Doth she,'and did she, and shall she evermore
On one, on seaven, or on no hill appeare?
Dwells she with us, or like adventuring knights
First travaile we to seeke and then make love? *10*
Betray kind husband thy spouse to our sights,
And let myne amorous soule court thy mild Dove,
Who is most trew, and pleasing to thee, then
When she'is embrac'd and open to most men.

3

Oh, to vex me, contraryes meete in one:
Inconstancy unnaturally hath begott
A constant habit; that when I would not
I change in vowes, and in devotione.
As humorous is my contritione
As my prophane love, and as soone forgott:
As ridlingly distemperd, cold and hott,
As praying, as mute; as infinite, as none.
I durst not view heaven yesterday; and to day
In prayers, and flattering speaches I court God: *10*
To morrow I quake with true feare of his rod.
So my devout fitts come and go away
Like a fantastique Ague: save that here
Those are my best dayes, when I shake with feare.

from OCCASIONAL POEMS

Goodfriday, 1613. Riding Westward

Let mans Soule be a Spheare, and then, in this,
The intelligence that moves, devotion is,
And as the other Spheares, by being growne
Subject to forraigne motions, lose their owne,
And being by others hurried every day,
Scarce in a yeare their naturall forme obey:
Pleasure or businesse, so, our Soules admit
For their first mover, and are whirld by it.
Hence is't, that I am carryed towards the West
This day, when my Soules forme bends toward the East. *10*
There I should see a Sunne, by rising set,
And by that setting endlesse day beget;
But that Christ on this Crosse, did rise and fall,
Sinne had eternally benighted all.
Yet dare I'almost be glad, I do not see
That spectacle of too much weight for mee.
Who sees Gods face, that is selfe life, must dye;
What a death were it then to see God dye?
It made his owne Lieutenant Nature shrinke,
It made his footstoole crack, and the Sunne winke. *20*
Could I behold those hands which span the Poles,
And tune all spheares at once, peirc'd with those holes?
Could I behold that endlesse height which is
Zenith to us, and to'our Antipodes,
Humbled below us? or that blood which is
The seat of all our Soules, if not of his,
Make durt of dust, or that flesh which was worne
By God, for his apparell, rag'd, and torne?
If on these things I durst not looke, durst I
Upon his miserable mother cast mine eye, *30*
Who was Gods partner here, and furnish'd thus
Halfe of that Sacrifice, which ransom'd us?
Though these things, as I ride, be from mine eye,
They'are present yet unto my memory,
For that looks towards them; and thou look'st towards mee,
O Saviour, as thou hang'st upon the tree;
I turne my backe to thee, but to receive

Goodfriday . . . Westward: For an analysis of this poem as a formal meditation, see Martz, pp. 54–56.

Corrections, till thy mercies bid thee leave.
O thinke mee worth thine anger, punish mee,
Burne off my rusts, and my deformity, 40
Restore thine Image, so much, by thy grace,
That thou may'st know mee, and I'll turne my face.

HYMNS

A Hymne to Christ, at the Authors last going into Germany

In what torne ship soever I embarke,
That ship shall be my embleme of thy Arke;
What sea soever swallow mee, that flood
Shall be to mee an embleme of thy blood;
Though thou with clouds of anger do disguise
Thy face; yet through that maske I know those eyes,
Which, though they turne away sometimes,
They never will despise.

I sacrifice this Iland unto thee,
And all whom I lov'd there, and who lov'd mee; 10
When I have put our seas twixt them and mee,
Put thou thy sea betwixt my sinnes and thee.
As the trees sap doth seeke the root below
In winter, in my winter now I goe,
Where none but thee, th'Eternall root
Of true Love I may know.

Nor thou nor thy religion dost controule,
The amorousnesse of an harmonious Soule,
But thou would'st have that love thy selfe: As thou
Art jealous, Lord, so I am jealous now, 20
Thou lov'st not, till from loving more, thou free
My soule: Who ever gives, takes libertie:
O, if thou car'st not whom I love
Alas, thou lov'st not mee.

Seale then this bill of my Divorce to All,
On whom those fainter beames of love did fall;
Marry those loves, which in youth scattered bee
On Fame, Wit, Hopes (false mistresses) to thee.

Churches are best for Prayer, that have least light:
To see God only, I goe out of sight: 30
And to scape stormy dayes, I chuse
An Everlasting night.

Hymne to God my God, in my sicknesse

Since I am comming to that Holy roome,
Where, with thy Quire of Saints for evermore,
I shall be made thy Musique; As I come
I tune the Instrument here at the dore,
And what I must doe then, thinke now before.

Whilst my Physitians by their love are growne
Cosmographers, and I their Mapp, who lie
Flat on this bed, that by them may be showne
That this is my South-west discoverie
Per fretum febris, by these streights to die, 10

I joy, that in these straits, I see my West;
For, though theire currants yeeld returne to none,
What shall my West hurt me? As West and East
In all flatt Maps (and I am one) are one,
So death doth touch the Resurrection.

Is the Pacifique Sea my home? Or are
The Easterne riches? Is *Jerusalem*?
Anyan, and *Magellan,* and *Gibraltare,*
All streights, and none but streights, are wayes to them,
Whether where *Japhet* dwelt, or *Cham,* or *Sem.* 20

We thinke that *Paradise* and *Calvarie,*
Christs Crosse, and *Adams* tree, stood in one place;
Looke Lord, and finde both *Adams* met in me;
As the first *Adams* sweat surrounds my face,
May the last *Adams* blood my soule embrace.

So, in his purple wrapp'd receive mee Lord,
By these his thornes give me his other Crowne;
And as to others soules I preach'd thy word,
Be this my Text, my Sermon to mine owne,
Therfore that he may raise the Lord throws down.

A Hymne to God the Father

I

Wilt thou forgive that sinne where I begunne,
  Which is my sin, though it were done before?
Wilt thou forgive those sinnes through which I runne,
  And doe them still: though still I doe deplore?
    When thou hast done, thou hast not done,
        For, I have more.

II

Wilt thou forgive that sinne by which I wonne
  Others to sinne? and, made my sinne their doore?
Wilt thou forgive that sinne which I did shunne
  A yeare, or two: but wallowed in, a score? *10*
    When thou hast done, thou hast not done,
        For, I have more.

III

I have a sinne of feare, that when I have spunne
  My last thred, I shall perish on the shore;
Sweare by thy selfe, that at my death thy Sunne
  Shall shine as it shines now, and heretofore;
    And, having done that, Thou hast done,
        I have no more.

George Herbert

On April 3, 1593, George Herbert was born into an eminent family, the fifth son of Richard and Magdalen Herbert, younger brother to Edward (later Lord Herbert of Cherbury). Until the age of twelve he was educated at home, and in 1605 he was enrolled in the Westminster School, where he was thoroughly grounded in Latin and Greek. Awarded a scholarship in 1608, he was matriculated at Trinity College, Cambridge, in 1609. His career at the University was distinguished: in 1612 he received his B.A.; in 1614 he was elected minor fellow at Trinity and shortly thereafter major fellow; in 1616 he received his M.A. At this time he seems to have devoted himself seriously to the study of divinity. In 1618 he was elected Public Orator, "the finest place," as he said, "at the University." This office, which involved his officiating at public University functions, should have helped him achieve preferment, but the death of three potential patrons, among them King James, spelled the disappointment of his hopes. Like many another English poet, then, he turned all his attention to the Church. Some time before 1626 he was ordained deacon, which marked the end of his secular ambitions. For about a year thereafter he was in partial retirement, probably ill, possibly working on his poetry. The Lady Magdalen Herbert died in 1627. On March 5, 1628, Herbert married Jane Danvers, a kinswoman of his stepfather, who survived him by thirty years. In April, 1630, he was inducted at Bemerton Church into the Rectory of Fuggleston St. Peter and Bemerton St. Andrew; in September of the same year he was ordained priest. Barely three years later, on March 1, 1633, he died and was buried in Bemerton.

The Temple *was first published posthumously in 1633; in 1652,* A Priest to The Temple *subtitled "Or, The Countrey Parson His Character, and Rule of Holy Life" was published; Herbert's prefatory note to the reader is dated 1632. For the rest, Herbert's works include some letters, Latin poems, Latin orations, two volumes of proverbs, a brief translation of Cornaro's* Treatise on Temperance, *and* Briefe Notes on Valdesso's Considerations.

The text followed is F. E. Hutchinson's Clarendon Press edition.

FROM

The Temple

from THE CHURCH-PORCH

PERIRRHANTERIUM

1

Thou, whose sweet youth and early hopes inhance
Thy rate and price, and mark thee for a treasure;
Hearken unto a Verser, who may chance
Ryme thee to good, and make a bait of pleasure.
  A verse may finde him, who a sermon flies,
  And turn delight into a sacrifice.

2

Beware of lust: it doth pollute and foul
Whom God in Baptisme washt with his own blood.
It blots thy lesson written in thy soul;
The holy lines cannot be understood.
  How dare those eyes upon a Bible look,
  Much lesse towards God, whose lust is all their book?

76

Summe up at night, what thou hast done by day;
And in the morning, what thou hast to do.
Dresse and undresse thy soul: mark the decay
And growth of it: if with thy watch, that too
  Be down, then winde up both; since we shall be
  Most surely judg'd, make thy accounts agree.

Perirrhanterium: The Greek for Aspergill, a device used for sprinkling holy water.

77

In brief, acquit thee bravely; play the man.
Look not on pleasures as they come, but go.
Deferre not the least vertue: lifes poore span
Make not an ell, by trifling in thy wo.
  If thou do ill; the joy fades, not the pains:
  If well; the pain doth fade, the joy remains.

SUPERLIMINARE

Thou, whom the former precepts have
Sprinkled and taught, how to behave
Thy self in church; approach, and taste
The churches mysticall repast.

Avoid, Profanenesse; come not here:
Nothing but holy, pure, and cleare,
Or that which groneth to be so,
May at his perill further go.

from THE CHURCH

The Altar

A broken ALTAR, Lord, thy servant reares,
Made of a heart, and cemented with teares:
  Whose parts are as thy hand did frame;
  No workmans tool hath touch'd the same.
      A HEART alone
      Is such a stone,
      As nothing but
      Thy pow'r doth cut.
      Wherefore each part
      Of my hard heart 10
      Meets in this frame,
      To praise thy Name:
  That, if I chance to hold my peace,
  These stones to praise thee may not cease.
Oh let thy blessed SACRIFICE be mine,
And sanctifie this ALTAR to be thine.

Superliminare: The inscription on the lintel implied here refers better to the second stanza than to the first.

The Sacrifice

Oh all ye, who passe by, whose eyes and minde
To worldly things are sharp, but to me blinde;
To me, who took eyes that I might you finde:
Was ever grief like mine?

The Princes of my people make a head
Against their Maker: they do wish me dead,
Who cannot wish, except I give them bread:
Was ever grief like mine?

Without me each one, who doth now me brave,
Had to this day been an Egyptian slave. *10*
They use that power against me, which I gave:
Was ever grief like mine?

Mine own Apostle, who the bag did beare,
Though he had all I had, did not forbeare
To sell me also, and to put me there:
Was ever grief, &c.

For thirtie pence he did my death devise,
Who at three hundred did the ointment prize,
Not half so sweet as my sweet sacrifice:
Was ever grief, &c. *20*

Therefore my soul melts, and my hearts deare treasure
Drops bloud (the onely beads) my words to measure:
O let this cup passe, if it be thy pleasure:
Was ever grief, &c.

These drops being temper'd with a sinners tears
A Balsome are for both the Hemispheres:
Curing all wounds, but mine; all, but my fears:
Was ever grief, &c.

The Sacrifice: This poem derives from medieval lyrics based on the liturgy sung during Holy Week, specifically the *Improperia*, the Reproaches of Christ from the Cross. For a full analysis, see Rosemond Tuve, *A Reading of George Herbert* (Chicago: University of Chicago Press, 1952), pp. 19–99.

Yet my Disciples sleep: I cannot gain
One houre of watching; but their drowsie brain 30
Comforts not me, and doth my doctrine stain:
Was ever grief, &c.

Arise, arise, they come. Look how they runne!
Alas! what haste they make to be undone!
How with their lanterns do they seek the sunne!
Was ever grief, &c.

With clubs and staves they seek me, as a thief,
Who am the Way and Truth, the true relief;
Most true to those, who are my greatest grief:
Was ever grief, &c. 40

Judas, dost thou betray me with a kisse?
Canst thou finde hell about my lips? and misse
Of life, just at the gates of life and blisse?
Was ever grief like mine?

See, they lay hold on me, not with the hands
Of faith, but furie: yet at their commands
I suffer binding, who have loos'd their bands:
Was ever grief, &c.

All my Disciples flie; fear puts a barre
Betwixt my friends and me. They leave the starre, 50
That brought the wise men of the East from farre.
Was ever grief, &c.

Then from one ruler to another bound
They leade me; urging, that it was not sound
What I taught: Comments would the text confound.
Was ever grief, &c.

The Priest and rulers all false witnesse seek
'Gainst him, who seeks not life, but is the meek
And readie Paschal Lambe of this great week:
Was ever grief, &c. 60

Then they accuse me of great blasphemie,
That I did thrust into the Deitie,
Who never thought that any robberie:
Was ever grief, &c.

Some said, that I the Temple to the floore
In three dayes raz'd, and raised as before.
Why, he that built the world can do much more:
Was ever grief, &c.

Then they condemne me all with that same breath,
Which I do give them daily, unto death. 70
Thus *Adam* my first breathing rendereth:
Was ever grief, &c.

They binde, and leade me unto *Herod:* he
Sends me to *Pilate*. This makes them agree;
But yet their friendship is my enmitie:
Was ever grief like mine?

Herod and all his bands do set me light,
Who teach all hands to warre, fingers to fight,
And onely am the Lord of Hosts and might:
Was ever grief, &c. 80

Herod in judgement sits, while I do stand;
Examines me with a censorious hand:
I him obey, who all things else command:
Was ever grief, &c.

The *Jews* accuse me with despitefulnesse;
And vying malice with my gentlenesse,
Pick quarrels with their onely happinesse:
Was ever grief, &c.

I answer nothing, but with patience prove
If stonie hearts will melt with gentle love. 90
But who does hawk at eagles with a dove?
Was ever grief, &c.

My silence rather doth augment their crie;
My dove doth back into my bosome flie,
Because the raging waters still are high:
Was ever grief, &c.

Heark how they crie aloud still, *Crucifie:*
It is not fit he live a day, they crie,
Who cannot live lesse then eternally:
Was ever grief, &c. *100*

Pilate, a stranger, holdeth off; but they,
Mine owne deare people, cry, *Away, away,*
With noises confused frighting the day:
Was ever grief, &c.

Yet still they shout, and crie, and stop their eares,
Putting my life among their sinnes and fears,
And therefore wish *my bloud on them and theirs:*
Was ever grief like mine?

See how spite cankers things. These words aright
Used, and wished, are the whole worlds light: *110*
But hony is their gall, brightnesse their night:
Was ever grief, &c.

They choose a murderer, and all agree
In him to do themselves a courtesie:
For it was their own case who killed me:
Was ever grief, &c.

And a seditious murderer he was:
But I the Prince of peace; peace that doth passe
All understanding, more than heav'n doth glasse:
Was ever grief, &c. *120*

Why, Cæsar is their onely King, not I:
He clave the stonie rock, when they were drie;
But surely not their hearts, as I well trie:
Was ever grief, &c.

Ah! how they scourge me! yet my tendernesse
Doubles each lash: and yet their bitternesse
Windes up my grief to a mysteriousnesse:
Was ever grief, &c.

They buffet him, and box him as they list,
Who grasps the earth and heaven with his fist, *130*
And never yet, whom he would punish, miss'd:
Was ever grief, &c.

Behold, they spit on me in scornfull wise,
Who by my spittle gave the blinde man eies,
Leaving his blindnesse to my enemies:
Was ever grief like mine?

My face they cover, though it be divine.
As *Moses* face was vailed, so is mine,
Lest on their double-dark souls either shine:
Was ever grief, &c. 140

Servants and abjects flout me; they are wittie:
Now prophesie who strikes thee, is their dittie.
So they in me denie themselves all pitie:
Was ever grief, &c.

And now I am deliver'd unto death,
Which each one calls for so with utmost breath,
That he before me well nigh suffereth:
Was ever grief, &c.

Weep not, deare friends, since I for both have wept
When all my tears were bloud, the while you slept: 150
Your tears for your own fortunes should be kept:
Was ever grief, &c.

The souldiers lead me to the Common Hall;
There they deride me, they abuse me all:
Yet for twelve heav'nly legions I could call:
Was ever grief, &c.

Then with a scarlet robe they me aray;
Which shews my bloud to be the onely way
And cordiall left to repair mans decay:
Was ever grief, &c. 160

Then on my head a crown of thorns I wear:
For these are all the grapes *Sion* doth bear,
Though I my vine planted and watred there:
Was ever grief, &c.

So sits the earths great curse in *Adams* fall
Upon my head: so I remove it all
From th' earth unto my brows, and bear the thrall:
Was ever grief like mine?

Then with the reed they gave to me before,
They strike my head, the rock from whence all store 170
Of heav'nly blessings issue evermore:
Was ever grief, &c.

They bow their knees to me, and cry, *Hail king:*
What ever scoffes & scornfulnesse can bring,
I am the floore, the sink, where they it fling:
Was ever grief, &c.

Yet since mans scepters are as frail as reeds,
And thorny all their crowns, bloudie their weeds;
I, who am Truth, turn into truth their deeds:
Was ever grief, &c. 180

The souldiers also spit upon that face,
Which Angels did desire to have the grace,
And Prophets, once to see, but found no place:
Was ever grief, &c.

Thus trimmed, forth they bring me to the rout,
Who *Crucifie him,* crie with one strong shout.
God holds his peace at man, and man cries out:
Was ever grief, &c.

They leade me in once more, and putting then
Mine own clothes on, they leade me out agen. 190
Whom devils flie, thus is he toss'd of men:
Was ever grief, &c.

And now wearie of sport, glad to ingrosse
All spite in one, counting my life their losse,
They carrie me to my most bitter crosse:
Was ever grief like mine?

My crosse I bear my self, untill I faint:
Then Simon bears it for me by constraint,
The decreed burden of each mortall Saint:
Was ever grief, &c. 200

O all ye who passe by, behold and see;
Man stole the fruit, but I must climbe the tree;
The tree of life to all, but onely me:
Was ever grief, &c.

Lo, here I hang, charg'd with a world of sinne,
The greater world o' the' two; for that came in
By words, but this by sorrow I must win:
Was ever grief, &c.

Such sorrow as, if sinfull man could feel,
Or feel his part, he would not cease to kneel, *210*
Till all were melted, though he were all steel:
Was ever grief, &c.

But, *O my God, my God!* why leav'st thou me,
The sonne, in whom thou dost delight to be?
My God, my God——
Never was grief like mine.

Shame tears my soul, my bodie many a wound;
Sharp nails pierce this, but sharper that confound;
Reproches, which are free, while I am bound.
Was ever grief, &c. *220*

Now heal thy self, Physician; now come down.
Alas! I did so, when I left my crown
And fathers smile for you, to feel his frown:
Was ever grief like mine?

In healing not my self, there doth consist
All that salvation, which ye now resist;
Your safetie in my sicknesse doth subsist:
Was ever grief, &c.

Betwixt two theeves I spend my utmost breath,
As he that for some robberie suffereth. *230*
Alas! what have I stollen from you? Death.
Was ever grief, &c.

A king my title is, prefixt on high;
Yet by my subjects am condemn'd to die
A servile death in servile companie:
Was ever grief, &c.

They give me vineger mingled with gall,
But more with malice: yet, when they did call,
With Manna, Angels food, I fed them all:
Was ever grief, &c. *240*

They part my garments, and by lot dispose
My coat, the type of love, which once cur'd those
Who sought for help, never malicious foes:
Was ever grief, &c.

Nay, after death their spite shall further go;
For they will pierce my side, I full well know;
That as sinne came, so Sacraments might flow:
Was ever grief, &c.

But now I die; now all is finished.
My wo, mans weal: and now I bow my head. 250
Onely let others say, when I am dead,
Never was grief like mine.

The Thanksgiving

Oh King of grief! (a title strange, yet true,
To thee of all kings onely due)
Oh King of wounds! how shall I grieve for thee,
Who in all grief preventest me?
Shall I weep bloud? why, thou hast wept such store
That all thy body was one doore.
Shall I be scourged, flouted, boxed, sold?
'Tis but to tell the tale is told.
My God, my God, why dost thou part from me?
Was such a grief as cannot be. 10
Shall I then sing, skipping thy dolefull storie,
And side with thy triumphant glorie?
Shall thy strokes be my stroking? thorns, my flower?
Thy rod, my posie? crosse, my bower?
But how then shall I imitate thee, and
Copie thy fair, though bloudie hand?
Surely I will revenge me on thy love,
And trie who shall victorious prove.
It thou dost give me wealth, I will restore
All back unto thee by the poore. 20
If thou dost give me honour, men shall see,
The honour doth belong to thee.
I will not marry; or, if she be mine,
She and her children shall be thine.

My bosome friend, if he blaspheme thy Name,
I will tear thence his love and fame.
One half of me being gone, the rest I give
Unto some Chappell, die or live.
As for thy passion—But of that anon,
When with the other I have done. 30
For thy predestination I'le contrive,
That three yeares hence, if I survive,
I'le build a spittle, or mend common wayes,
But mend mine own without delayes.
Then I will use the works of thy creation,
As if I us'd them but for fashion.
The world and I will quarrell; and the yeare
Shall not perceive, that I am here.
My musick shall finde thee, and ev'ry string
Shall have his attribute to sing; 40
That all together may accord in thee,
And prove one God, one harmonie.
If thou shalt give me wit, it shall appeare,
If thou hast giv'n it me, 'tis here.
Nay, I will reade thy book, and never move
Till I have found therein thy love,
Thy art of love, which I'le turn back on thee:
O my deare Saviour, Victorie!
Then for thy passion—I will do for that—
Alas, my God, I know not what. 50

The Reprisall

I have consider'd it, and finde
There is no dealing with thy mighty passion:
For though I die for thee, I am behinde;
My sinnes deserve the condemnation.

O make me innocent, that I
May give a disentangled state and free:
And yet thy wounds still my attempts defie,
For by thy death I die for thee.

Ah! was it not enough that thou
By thy eternall glorie didst outgo me? 10

Couldst thou not griefs sad conquests me allow,
But in all vict'ries overthrow me?

Yet by confession will I come
Into thy conquest: though I can do nought
Against thee, in thee I will overcome
The man, who once against thee fought.

The Agonie

Philosophers have measur'd mountains,
Fathom'd the depths of seas, of states, and kings,
Walk'd with a staffe to heav'n, and traced fountains:
But there are two vast, spacious things,
The which to measure it doth more behove:
Yet few there are that sound them; Sinne and Love.

Who would know Sinne, let him repair
Unto Mount Olivet; there shall he see
A man so wrung with pains, that all his hair,
His skinne, his garments bloudie be. *10*
Sinne is that presse and vice, which forceth pain
To hunt his cruell food through ev'ry vein.

Who knows not Love, let him assay
And taste that juice, which on the crosse a pike
Did set again abroach; then let him say
If ever he did taste the like.
Love is that liquour sweet and most divine,
Which my God feels as bloud; but I, as wine.

The Sinner

Lord, how I am all ague, when I seek
What I have treasur'd in my memorie!
Since, if my soul make even with the week,
Each seventh note by right is due to thee.
I finde there quarries of pil'd vanities,
But shreds of holinesse, that dare not venture
To shew their face, since crosse to thy decrees:
There the circumference earth is, heav'n the centre.

In so much dregs the quintessence is small:
The spirit and good extract of my heart 10
Comes to about the many hundred part.
Yet Lord restore thine image, heare my call:
And though my hard heart scarce to thee can grone,
Remember that thou once didst write in stone.

Good Friday

O My chief good,
How shall I measure out thy bloud?
How shall I count what thee befell,
And each grief tell?

Shall I thy woes
Number according to thy foes?
Or, since one starre show'd thy first breath,
Shall all thy death?

Or shall each leaf,
Which falls in Autumne, score a grief? 10
Or can not leaves, but fruit, be signe
Of the true vine?

Then let each houre
Of my whole life one grief devoure;
That thy distresse through all may runne,
And be my sunne.

Or rather let
My severall sinnes their sorrows get;
That as each beast his cure doth know,
Each sinne may so. 20

Since bloud is fittest, Lord, to write
Thy sorrows in, and bloudie fight;
My heart hath store, write there, where in
One box doth lie both ink and sinne:

That when sinne spies so many foes,
Thy whips, thy nails, thy wounds, thy woes,

All come to lodge there, sinne may say,
No room for me, and flie away.

Sinne being gone, oh fill the place,
And keep possession with thy grace; 30
Lest sinne take courage and return,
And all the writings blot or burn.

Redemption

Having been tenant long to a rich Lord,
Not thriving, I resolved to be bold,
And make a suit unto him, to afford
A new small-rented lease, and cancell th' old.
In heaven at his manour I him sought:
They told me there, that he was lately gone
About some land, which he had dearly bought
Long since on earth, to take possession.
I straight return'd, and knowing his great birth,
Sought him accordingly in great resorts; 10
In cities, theatres, gardens, parks, and courts:
At length I heard a ragged noise and mirth
Of theeves and murderers: there I him espied,
Who straight, *Your suit is granted,* said, & died.

Sepulchre

O blessed bodie! Whither art thou thrown?
No lodging for thee, but a cold hard stone?
So many hearts on earth, and yet not one
Receive thee?
Sure there is room within our hearts good store;
For they can lodge transgressions by the score:
Thousands of toyes dwell there, yet out of doore
They leave thee.

But that which shews them large, shews them unfit.
What ever sinne did this pure rock commit, 10
Which holds thee now? Who hath indited it
Of murder?

Where our hard hearts have took up stones to brain thee,
And missing this, most falsly did arraigne thee;
Onely these stones in quiet entertain thee,
And order.

And as of old the Law by heav'nly art
Was writ in stone; so thou, which also art
The letter of the word, find'st no fit heart
To hold thee. 20
Yet do we still persist as we began,
And so should perish, but that nothing can,
Though it be cold, hard, foul, from loving man
Withhold thee.

Easter

Rise heart; thy Lord is risen. Sing his praise
Without delayes,
Who takes thee by the hand, that thou likewise
With him mayst rise:
That, as his death calcined thee to dust,
His life may make thee gold, and much more, just.

Awake, my lute, and struggle for thy part
With all thy art.
The crosse taught all wood to resound his name,
Who bore the same. 10
His stretched sinews taught all strings, what key
Is best to celebrate this most high day.

Consort both heart and lute, and twist a song
Pleasant and long:
Or, since all musick is but three parts vied
And multiplied,
O let thy blessed Spirit bear a part,
And make up our defects with his sweet art.

I got me flowers to straw thy way;
I got me boughs off many a tree: 20
But thou wast up by break of day,
And brought'st thy sweets along with thee.

The Sunne arising in the East,
Though he give light, & th' East perfume;
If they should offer to contest
With thy arising, they presume.

Can there be any day but this,
Though many sunnes to shine endeavour?
We count three hundred, but we misse:
There is but one, and that one ever. 30

Easter-wings

Lord, who createdst man in wealth and store,
Though foolishly he lost the same,
Decaying more and more,
Till he became
Most poore:
With thee
O let me rise
As larks, harmoniously,
And sing this day thy victories:
Then shall the fall further the flight in me. 10

My tender age in sorrow did beginne:
And still with sicknesses and shame
Thou didst so punish sinne,
That I became
Most thinne.
With thee
Let me combine
And feel this day thy victorie:
For, if I imp my wing on thine,
Affliction shall advance the flight in me. 20

H. Baptisme (I)

As he that sees a dark and shadie grove,
Stayes not, but looks beyond it on the skie;
So when I view my sinnes, mine eyes remove
More backward still, and to that water flie,

Which is above the heav'ns, whose spring and vent
Is in my deare Redeemers pierced side.
O blessed streams! either ye do prevent
And stop our sinnes from growing thick and wide,
Or else give tears to drown them, as they grow.
In you Redemption measures all my time, 10
And spreads the plaister equall to the crime.
You taught the Book of Life my name, that so
What ever future sinnes should me miscall,
Your first acquaintance might discredit all.

H. Baptisme (II)

Since, Lord, to thee
A narrow way and little gate
Is all the passage, on my infancie
Thou didst lay hold, and antedate
My faith in me.

O let me still
Write thee great God, and me a childe:
Let me be soft and supple to thy will,
Small to my self, to others milde,
Behither ill. 10

Although by stealth
My flesh get on, yet let her sister
My soul bid nothing, but preserve her wealth:
The growth of flesh is but a blister;
Childhood is health.

Sinne (I)

Lord, with what care hast thou begirt us round!
Parents first season us: then schoolmasters
Deliver us to laws; they send us bound
To rules of reason, holy messengers,
Pulpits and Sundayes, sorrow dogging sinne,
Afflictions sorted, anguish of all sizes,
Fine nets and stratagems to catch us in,

Bibles laid open, millions of surprises,
Blessings beforehand, tyes of gratefulnesse,
    The sound of glorie ringing in our eares: *10*
    Without, our shame; within, our consciences;
Angels and grace, eternall hopes and fears.
    Yet all these fences and their whole aray
    One cunning bosome-sinne blows quite away.

Affliction (I)

When first thou didst entice to thee my heart,
                I thought the service brave:
So many joyes I writ down for my part,
                Besides what I might have
Out of my stock of naturall delights,
Augmented with thy gracious benefits.

I looked on thy furniture so fine,
                And made it fine to me:
Thy glorious houshold-stuffe did me entwine,
                And 'tice me unto thee. *10*
Such starres I counted mine: both heav'n and earth
Payd me my wages in a world of mirth.

What pleasures could I want, whose King I served,
                Where joyes my fellows were?
Thus argu'd into hopes, my thought reserved
                No place for grief or fear.
Therefore my sudden soul caught at the place,
And made her youth and fiercenesse seek thy face.

At first thou gav'st me milk and sweetnesses;
                I had my wish and way: *20*
My dayes were straw'd with flow'rs and happinesse;
                There was no moneth but May.
But with my yeares sorrow did twist and grow,
And made a partie unawares for wo.

My flesh began unto my soul in pain,
                Sicknesses cleave my bones;
Consuming agues dwell in ev'ry vein,
                And tune my breath to grones.

Sorrow was all my soul; I scarce beleeved,
Till grief did tell me roundly, that I lived. 30

When I got health, thou took'st away my life,
And more; for my friends die:
My mirth and edge was lost; a blunted knife
Was of more use then I.
Thus thinne and lean without a fence or friend,
I was blown through with ev'ry storm and winde.

Whereas my birth and spirit rather took
The way that takes the town;
Thou didst betray me to a lingring book,
And wrap me in a gown. 40
I was entangled in the world of strife,
Before I had the power to change my life.

Yet, for I threatned oft the siege to raise,
Not simpring all mine age,
Thou often didst with Academick praise
Melt and dissolve my rage.
I took thy sweetned pill, till I came where
I could not go away, nor persevere.

Yet lest perchance I should too happie be
In my unhappinesse, 50
Turning my purge to food, thou throwest me
Into more sicknesses.
Thus doth thy power crosse-bias me, not making
Thine own gift good, yet me from my wayes taking.

Now I am here, what thou wilt do with me
None of my books will show:
I reade, and sigh, and wish I were a tree;
For sure then I should grow
To fruit or shade: at least some bird would trust
Her houshold to me, and I should be just. 60

Yet, though thou troublest me, I must be meek;
In weaknesse must be stout.
Well, I will change the service, and go seek
Some other master out.
Ah my deare God! though I am clean forgot,
Let me not love thee, if I love thee not.

Prayer (I)

Prayer the Churches banquet, Angels age,
Gods breath in man returning to his birth,
The soul in paraphrase, heart in pilgrimage,
The Christian plummet sounding heav'n and earth;
Engine against th' Almightie, sinners towre,
Reversed thunder, Christ-side-piercing spear,
The six-daies world transposing in an houre,
A kinde of tune, which all things heare and fear;
Softnesse, and peace, and joy, and love, and blisse,
Exalted Manna, gladnesse of the best, *10*
Heaven in ordinarie, man well drest,
The milkie way, the bird of Paradise,
Church-bels beyond the starres heard, the souls bloud,
The land of spices; something understood.

Love I

Immortall Love, authour of this great frame,
Sprung from that beautie which can never fade;
How hath man parcel'd out thy glorious name,
And thrown it on that dust which thou hast made,
While mortall love doth all the title gain!
Which siding with invention, they together
Bear all the sway, possessing heart and brain,
(Thy workmanship) and give thee share in neither.
Wit fancies beautie, beautie raiseth wit:
The world is theirs; they two play out the game, *10*
Thou standing by: and though thy glorious name
Wrought our deliverance from th' infernall pit,
Who sings thy praise? onely a skarf or glove
Doth warm our hands, and make them write of love.

II

Immortall Heat, O let thy greater flame
Attract the lesser to it: let those fires,
Which shall consume the world, first make it tame;
And kindle in our hearts such true desires,
As may consume our lusts, and make thee way.

Then shall our hearts pant thee; then shall our brain
All her invention on thine Altar lay,
And there in hymnes send back thy fire again:
Our eies shall see thee, which before saw dust;
Dust blown by wit, till that they both were blinde: *10*
Thou shalt recover all thy goods in kinde,
Who wert disseized by usurping lust:
All knees shall bow to thee; all wits shall rise,
And praise him who did make and mend our eies.

The Temper (I)

How should I praise thee, Lord! how should my rymes
Gladly engrave thy love in steel,
If what my soul doth feel sometimes,
My soul might ever feel!

Although there were some fourtie heav'ns, or more,
Sometimes I peere above them all;
Sometimes I hardly reach a score,
Sometimes to hell I fall.

O rack me not to such a vast extent;
Those distances belong to thee: *10*
The world's too little for thy tent,
A grave too big for me.

Wilt thou meet arms with man, that thou dost stretch
A crumme of dust from heav'n to hell?
Will great God measure with a wretch?
Shall he thy stature spell?

O let me, when thy roof my soul hath hid,
O let me roost and nestle there:
Then of a sinner thou art rid,
And I of hope and fear. *20*

Yet take thy way; for sure thy way is best:
Stretch or contract me, thy poore debter:

The Temper (I): "Tempering" denoted the tuning of instruments for the purposes of "practical harmony." (*O.E.D.*) John Hollander considers this poem as "perhaps the purest example of the image of devotional 'tuning.'" (*The Untuning of the Sky*, Princeton: Princeton University Press, 1961, p. 289.)

This is but tuning of my breast,
To make the musick better.

Whether I flie with angels, fall with dust,
Thy hands made both, and I am there:
Thy power and love, my love and trust
Make one place ev'ry where.

The Temper (II)

It cannot be. Where is that mightie joy,
Which just now took up all my heart?
Lord, if thou must needs use thy dart,
Save that, and me; or sin for both destroy.

The grosser world stands to thy word and art;
By thy diviner world of grace
Thou suddenly dost raise and race,
And ev'ry day a new Creatour art.

O fix thy chair of grace, that all my powers
May also fix their reverence: *10*
For when thou dost depart from hence,
They grow unruly, and sit in thy bowers.

Scatter, or binde them all to bend to thee:
Though elements change, and heaven move,
Let not thy higher Court remove,
But keep a standing Majestie in me.

Jordan (I)

Who sayes that fictions onely and false hair
Become a verse? Is there in truth no beautie?
Is all good structure in a winding stair?
May no lines passe, except they do their dutie
Not to a true, but painted chair?

Jordan (I): The reference is to baptism by which the poet chooses the Divine Muse in place of the Secular one. (See Tuve, pp. 182 ff.)

Is it no verse, except enchanted groves
And sudden arbours shadow course-spunne lines?
Must purling streams refresh a lovers loves?
Must all be vail'd, while he that reades, divines,
  Catching the sense at two removes? 10

Shepherds are honest people; let them sing:
Riddle who list, for me, and pull for Prime:
I envie no mans nightingale or spring;
Nor let them punish me with losse of rime,
  Who plainly say, *My God, My King*.

Employment (I)

  If as a flowre doth spread and die,
  Thou wouldst extend me to some good,
Before I were by frosts extremitie
    Nipt in the bud;

  The sweetnesse and the praise were thine;
  But the extension and the room,
Which in thy garland I should fill, were mine
    At thy great doom.

  For as thou dost impart thy grace,
  The greater shall our glorie be. 10
The measure of our joyes is in this place,
    The stuffe with thee.

  Let me not languish then, and spend
  A life as barren to thy praise,
As is the dust, to which that life doth tend,
    But with delaies.

  All things are busie; onely I
  Neither bring hony with the bees,
Nor flowres to make that, nor the husbandrie
    To water these. 20

  I am no link of thy great chain,
  But all my companie is a weed.

l.12 Prime: indicates a good hand in the card game of *primero*. (*O.E.D.*)

Lord place me in thy consort; give one strain
To my poore reed.

The H. Scriptures

I

Oh Book! infinite sweetnesse! let my heart
Suck ev'ry letter, and a hony gain,
Precious for any grief in any part;
To cleare the breast, to mollifie all pain.
Thou art all health, health thriving till it make
A full eternitie: thou art a masse
Of strange delights, where we may wish & take.
Ladies, look here; this is the thankfull glasse,
That mends the lookers eyes: this is the well
That washes what it shows. Who can indeare 10
Thy praise too much? thou art heav'ns Lidger here,
Working against the states of death and hell.
Thou art joyes handsell: heav'n lies flat in thee,
Subject to ev'ry mounters bended knee.

II

Oh that I knew how all thy lights combine,
And the configurations of their glorie!
Seeing not onely how each verse doth shine,
But all the constellations of the storie.
This verse marks that, and both do make a motion
Unto a third, that ten leaves off doth lie:
Then as dispersed herbs do watch a potion,
These three make up some Christians destinie:
Such are thy secrets, which my life makes good,
And comments on thee: for in ev'ry thing 10
Thy words do finde me out, & parallels bring,
And in another make me understood.
Starres are poore books, & oftentimes do misse:
This book of starres lights to eternall blisse.

l.11 (I) *Lidger:* a legate or ambassador.

Church-musick

Sweetest of sweets, I thank you: when displeasure
Did through my bodie wound my minde,
You took me thence, and in your house of pleasure
A daintie lodging me assign'd.

Now I in you without a bodie move,
Rising and falling with your wings:
We both together sweetly live and love,
Yet say sometimes, *God help poore Kings*.

Comfort, I'le die; for if you poste from me,
Sure I shall do so, and much more: 10
But if I travell in your companie,
You know the way to heavens doore.

The Quidditie

My God, a verse is not a crown,
No point of honour, or gay suit,
No hawk, or banquet, or renown,
Nor a good sword, nor yet a lute:

It cannot vault, or dance, or play;
It never was in *France* or *Spain;*
Nor can it entertain the day
With my great stable or demain:

It is no office, art, or news,
Nor the Exchange, or busie Hall; 10
But it is that which while I use
I am with thee, and *most take all*.

Sunday

Day most calm, most bright,
The fruit of this, the next worlds bud,

l.8 God help poore Kings: refers to Psalm 149. (See Tuve, pp. 180–182.)

Th' indorsement of supreme delight,
Writ by a friend, and with his bloud;
The couch of time; cares balm and bay:
The week were dark but for thy light:
Thy torch doth show the way.

The other dayes and thou
Make up one man; whose face thou art,
Knocking at heaven with thy brow: *10*
The worky-daies are the back-part;
The burden of the week lies there,
Making the whole to stoup and bow,
Till thy release appeare.

Man had straight forward gone
To endlesse death: but thou dost pull
And turn us round to look on one,
Whom, if we were not very dull,
We could not choose but look on still:
Since there is no place so alone, *20*
The which he doth not fill.

Sundaies the pillars are,
On which heav'ns palace arched lies:
The other dayes fill up the spare
And hollow room with vanities.
They are the fruitfull beds and borders
In Gods rich garden: that is bare,
Which parts their ranks and orders.

The Sundaies of mans life,
Thredded together on times string, *30*
Make bracelets to adorn the wife
Of the eternall glorious King.
On Sunday heavens gate stands ope;
Blessings are plentifull and rife,
More plentifull then hope.

This day my Saviour rose,
And did inclose this light for his:
That, as each beast his manger knows,
Man might not of his fodder misse.
Christ hath took in this piece of ground, *40*

And made a garden there for those
Who want herbs for their wound.

The rest of our Creation
Our great Redeemer did remove
With the same shake, which at his passion
Did th' earth and all things with it move.
As Sampson bore the doores away,
Christs hands, though nail'd, wrought our salvation,
And did unhinge that day.

The brightnesse of that day 50
We sullied by our foul offence:
Wherefore that robe we cast away,
Having a new at his expence,
Whose drops of bloud paid the full price,
That was requir'd to make us gay,
And fit for Paradise.

Thou art a day of mirth:
And where the week-dayes trail on ground,
Thy flight is higher, as thy birth.
O let me take thee at the bound, 60
Leaping with thee from sev'n to sev'n,
Till that we both, being toss'd from earth,
Flie hand in hand to heav'n!

Ana- {MARY / ARMY} *gram*

How well her name an *Army* doth present,
In whom the *Lord of Hosts* did pitch his tent!

Deniall

When my devotions could not pierce
Thy silent eares;

l.47 As Sampson . . . away: Samson carrying away the gates of Gaza (Judges xvi.3) is used as a prefiguration of Christ rising from the Tomb. (See Tuve, pp. 159 ff.)
Anagram: The point of the epigram lies in the fact that Mary and the Church Militant are both tabernacles of Jesus.

Then was my heart broken, as was my verse:
My breast was full of fears
And disorder:

My bent thoughts, like a brittle bow,
Did flie asunder:
Each took his way; some would to pleasures go,
Some to the warres and thunder
Of alarms. *10*

As good go any where, they say,
As to benumme
Both knees and heart, in crying night and day,
Come, come, my God, O come,
But no hearing.

O that thou shouldst give dust a tongue
To crie to thee,
And then not heare it crying! all day long
My heart was in my knee,
But no hearing. *20*

Therefore, my soul lay out of sight,
Untun'd, unstrung:
My feeble spirit, unable to look right,
Like a nipt blossome, hung
Discontented.

O cheer and tune my heartlesse breast,
Deferre no time;
That so thy favours granting my request,
They and my minde may chime,
And mend my ryme. *30*

Christmas

All after pleasures as I rid one day,
My horse and I, both tir'd, bodie and minde,
With full crie of affections, quite astray,
I took up in the next inne I could finde.
There when I came, whom found I but my deare,
My dearest Lord, expecting till the grief

Of pleasures brought me to him, readie there
To be all passengers most sweet relief?
O Thou, whose glorious, yet contracted light,
Wrapt in nights mantle, stole into a manger; 10
Since my dark soul and brutish is thy right,
To Man of all beasts be not thou a stranger:
Furnish & deck my soul, that thou mayst have
A better lodging then a rack or grave.

The shepherds sing; and shall I silent be?
My God, no hymne for thee?
My soul's a shepherd too; a flock it feeds
Of thoughts, and words, and deeds.
The pasture is thy word: the streams, thy grace
Enriching all the place. 20
Shepherd and flock shall sing, and all my powers
Out-sing the day-light houres.
Then we will chide the sunne for letting night
Take up his place and right:
We sing one common Lord; wherefore he should
Himself the candle hold.
I will go searching, till I finde a sunne
Shall stay, till we have done;
A willing shiner, that shall shine as gladly,
As frost-nipt sunnes look sadly. 30
Then we will sing, and shine all our own day,
And one another pay:
His beams shall cheer my breast, and both so twine,
Till ev'n his beams sing, and my musick shine.

The World

Love built a stately house; where *Fortune* came,
And spinning phansies, she was heard to say,
That her fine cobwebs did support the frame,
Whereas they were supported by the same:
But *Wisdome* quickly swept them all away.

Then *Pleasure* came, who, liking not the fashion,
Began to make *Balcones, Terraces,*
Till she had weakned all by alteration:

But rev'rend *laws*, and many a *proclamation*
Reformed all at length with menaces. 10

Then enter'd *Sinne*, and with that Sycomore,
Whose leaves first sheltred man from drought & dew,
Working and winding slily evermore,
The inward walls and sommers cleft and tore:
But *Grace* shor'd these, and cut that as it grew.

Then *Sinne* combin'd with *Death* in a firm band
To raze the building to the very floore:
Which they effected, none could them withstand.
But *Love* and *Grace* took *Glorie* by the hand,
And built a braver Palace then before. 20

Vanitie (I)

The fleet Astronomer can bore,
And thred the spheres with his quick-piercing minde:
He views their stations, walks from doore to doore,
Surveys, as if he had design'd
To make a purchase there: he sees their dances,
And knoweth long before
Both their full-ey'd aspects, and secret glances.

The nimble Diver with his side
Cuts through the working waves, that he may fetch
His dearely-earned pearl, which God did hide 10
On purpose from the ventrous wretch:
That he might save his life, and also hers,
Who with excessive pride
Her own destruction and his danger wears.

The subtil Chymick can devest
And strip the creature naked, till he finde
The callow principles within their nest:
There he imparts to them his minde,
Admitted to their bed-chamber, before
They appeare trim and drest 20
To ordinarie suitours at the doore.

What hath not man sought out and found,
But his deare God? who yet his glorious law

Embosomes in us, mellowing the ground
With showres and frosts, with love & aw,
So that we need not say, Where's this command?
Poore man, thou searchest round
To finde out *death,* but missest *life* at hand.

Vertue

Sweet day, so cool, so calm, so bright,
The bridall of the earth and skie:
The dew shall weep thy fall to night;
For thou must die.

Sweet rose, whose hue angrie and brave
Bids the rash gazer wipe his eye:
Thy root is ever in its grave,
And thou must die.

Sweet spring, full of sweet dayes and roses,
A box where sweets compacted lie; 10
My musick shows ye have your closes,
And all must die.

Onely a sweet and vertuous soul,
Like season'd timber, never gives;
But though the whole world turn to coal,
Then chiefly lives.

The Pearl. Matth. 13. 45

I know the wayes of Learning; both the head
And pipes that feed the presse, and make it runne;
What reason hath from nature borrowed,
Or of it self, like a good huswife, spunne
In laws and policie; what the starres conspire,
What willing nature speaks, what forc'd by fire;
Both th' old discoveries, and the new-found seas,
The stock and surplus, cause and historie:
All these stand open, or I have the keyes:
Yet I love thee. 10

I know the wayes of Honour, what maintains
The quick returns of courtesie and wit:
In vies of favours whether partie gains,
When glorie swells the heart, and moldeth it
To all expressions both of hand and eye,
Which on the world a true-love-knot may tie,
And bear the bundle, wheresoe're it goes:
How many drammes of spirit there must be
To sell my life unto my friends or foes:
Yet I love thee. *20*

I know the wayes of Pleasure, the sweet strains,
The lullings and the relishes of it;
The propositions of hot bloud and brains;
What mirth and musick mean; what love and wit
Have done these twentie hundred yeares, and more:
I know the projects of unbridled store:
My stuffe is flesh, not brasse; my senses live,
And grumble oft, that they have more in me
Then he that curbs them, being but one to five:
Yet I love thee. *30*

I know all these, and have them in my hand:
Therefore not sealed, but with open eyes
I flie to thee, and fully understand
Both the main sale, and the commodities;
And at what rate and price I have thy love;
With all the circumstances that may move:
Yet through these labyrinths, not my groveling wit,
But thy silk twist let down from heav'n to me,
Did both conduct and teach me, how by it
To climbe to thee. *40*

Man

My God, I heard this day,
That none doth build a stately habitation,
But he that means to dwell therein.
What house more stately hath there been,
Or can be, then is Man? to whose creation
All things are in decay.

For Man is ev'ry thing,
And more: He is a tree, yet bears more fruit;
A beast, yet is, or should be more:
Reason and speech we onely bring. 10
Parrats may thank us, if they are not mute,
They go upon the score.

Man is all symmetrie,
Full of proportions, one limbe to another,
And all to all the world besides:
Each part may call the furthest, brother:
For head with foot hath private amitie,
And both with moons and tides.

Nothing hath got so farre,
But Man hath caught and kept it, as his prey. 20
His eyes dismount the highest starre:
He is in little all the sphere.
Herbs gladly cure our flesh; because that they
Finde their acquaintance there.

For us the windes do blow,
The earth doth rest, heav'n move, and fountains flow.
Nothing we see, but means our good,
As our delight, or as our treasure:
The whole is, either our cupboard of food,
Or cabinet of pleasure. 30

The starres have us to bed;
Night draws the curtain, which the sunne withdraws;
Musick and light attend our head.
All things unto our flesh are kinde
In their descent and being; to our minde
In their ascent and cause.

Each thing is full of dutie:
Waters united are our navigation;
Distinguished, our habitation;
Below, our drink; above, our meat; 40
Both are our cleanlinesse. Hath one such beautie?
Then how are all things neat?

More servants wait on Man,
Then he'l take notice of: in ev'ry path

He treads down that which doth befriend him,
When sicknesse makes him pale and wan.
Oh mightie love! Man is one world, and hath
Another to attend him.

Since then, my God, thou hast
So brave a Palace built; O dwell in it, 50
That it may dwell with thee at last!
Till then, afford us so much wit;
That, as the world serves us, we may serve thee,
And both thy servants be.

Jordan (II)

When first my lines of heav'nly joyes made mention,
Such was their lustre, they did so excell,
That I sought out quaint words, and trim invention;
My thoughts began to burnish, sprout, and swell,
Curling with metaphors a plain intention,
Decking the sense, as if it were to sell.

Thousands of notions in my brain did runne,
Off'ring their service, if I were not sped:
I often blotted what I had begunne;
This was not quick enough, and that was dead. 10
Nothing could seem too rich to clothe the sunne,
Much lesse those joyes which trample on his head.

As flames do work and winde, when they ascend,
So did I weave my self into the sense.
But while I bustled, I might heare a friend
Whisper, *How wide is all this long pretence!*
There is in love a sweetnesse readie penn'd:
Copie out onely that, and save expense.

The Quip

The merrie world did on a day
With his train-bands and mates agree

To meet together, where I lay,
And all in sport to geere at me.

First, Beautie crept into a rose,
Which when I pluckt not, Sir, said she,
Tell me, I pray, Whose hands are those?
But thou shalt answer, Lord, for me.

Then Money came, and chinking still,
What tune is this, poore man? said he: 10
I heard in Musick you had skill.
But thou shalt answer, Lord, for me.

Then came brave Glorie puffing by
In silks that whistled, who but he?
He scarce allow'd me half an eie.
But thou shalt answer, Lord, for me.

Then came quick Wit and Conversation,
And he would needs a comfort be,
And, to be short, make an Oration.
But thou shalt answer, Lord, for me. 20

Yet when the houre of thy designe
To answer these fine things shall come;
Speak not at large; say, I am thine:
And then they have their answer home.

Dulnesse

Why do I languish thus, drooping and dull,
As if I were all earth?
O give me quicknesse, that I may with mirth
Praise thee brim-full!

The wanton lover in a curious strain
Can praise his fairest fair;
And with quaint metaphors her curled hair
Curl o're again.

Thou art my lovelinesse, my life, my light,
Beautie alone to me: 10

Thy bloudy death and undeserv'd, makes thee
Pure red and white.

When all perfections as but one appeare,
That those thy form doth show,
The very dust, where thou dost tread and go,
Makes beauties here.

Where are my lines then? my approaches? views?
Where are my window-songs?
Lovers are still pretending, & ev'n wrongs
Sharpen their Muse: 20

But I am lost in flesh, whose sugred lyes
Still mock me, and grow bold:
Sure thou didst put a minde there, if I could
Finde where it lies.

Lord, cleare thy gift, that with a constant wit
I may but look towards thee:
Look onely; for to *love* thee, who can be,
What angel fit?

Peace

Sweet Peace, where dost thou dwell? I humbly crave,
Let me once know.
I sought thee in a secret cave,
And ask'd, if Peace were there.
A hollow winde did seem to answer, No:
Go seek elsewhere.

I did; and going did a rainbow note:
Surely, thought I,
This is the lace of Peaces coat:
I will search out the matter. 10
But while I lookt, the clouds immediately
Did break and scatter.

Then went I to a garden, and did spy
A gallant flower,
The Crown Imperiall: Sure, said I,
Peace at the root must dwell.

But when I digg'd, I saw a worm devoure
What show'd so well.

At length I met a rev'rend good old man,
Whom when for Peace 20
I did demand, he thus began:
There was a Prince of old
At Salem dwelt, who liv'd with good increase
Of flock and fold.

He sweetly liv'd; yet sweetnesse did not save
His life from foes.
But after death out of his grave
There sprang twelve stalks of wheat:
Which many wondring at, got some of those
To plant and set. 30

It prosper'd strangely, and did soon disperse
Through all the earth:
For they that taste it do rehearse,
That vertue lies therein,
A secret vertue bringing peace and mirth
By flight of sinne.

Take of this grain, which in my garden grows,
And grows for you;
Make bread of it: and that repose
And peace, which ev'ry where 40
With so much earnestnesse you do pursue,
Is onely there.

The Bunch of Grapes

Joy, I did lock thee up: but some bad man
Hath let thee out again:
And now, me thinks, I am where I began
Sev'n yeares ago: one vogue and vein,
One aire of thoughts usurps my brain.
I did towards Canaan draw; but now I am
Brought back to the Red sea, the sea of shame.

The Bunch of Grapes: For an analysis of the symbol upon which the poem turns, Christ as the Bunch of Grapes, the God of the New Dispensation, the Passion and Communion, see Tuve, pp. 113 ff.

For as the Jews of old by Gods command
Travell'd, and saw no town;
So now each Christian hath his journeys spann'd: 10
Their storie pennes and sets us down.
A single deed is small renown.
Gods works are wide, and let in future times;
His ancient justice overflows our crimes.

Then have we too our guardian fires and clouds;
Our Scripture-dew drops fast:
We have our sands and serpents, tents and shrowds;
Alas! our murmurings come not last.
But where's the cluster? where's the taste
Of mine inheritance? Lord, if I must borrow, 20
Let me as well take up their joy, as sorrow.

But can he want the grape, who hath the wine?
I have their fruit and more.
Blessed be God, who prosper'd *Noahs* vine,
And made it bring forth grapes good store.
But much more him I must adore,
Who of the Laws sowre juice sweet wine did make,
Ev'n God himself being pressed for my sake.

Love unknown

Deare Friend, sit down, the tale is long and sad:
And in my faintings I presume your love
Will more complie then help. A Lord I had,
And have, of whom some grounds, which may improve,
I hold for two lives, and both lives in me.
To him I brought a dish of fruit one day,
And in the middle plac'd my heart. But he
(I sigh to say)
Lookt on a servant, who did know his eye
Better then you know me, or (which is one) 10
Then I my self. The servant instantly
Quitting the fruit, seiz'd on my heart alone,
And threw it in a font, wherein did fall
A stream of bloud, which issu'd from the side
Of a great rock: I well remember all,
And have good cause: there it was dipt and dy'd,

And washt, and wrung: the very wringing yet
Enforceth tears. *Your heart was foul, I fear.*
Indeed 'tis true. I did and do commit
Many a fault more then my lease will bear; 20
Yet still askt pardon, and was not deni'd.
But you shall heare. After my heart was well,
And clean and fair, as I one even-tide
(I sigh to tell)
Walkt by my self abroad, I saw a large
And spacious fornace flaming, and thereon
A boyling caldron, round about whose verge
Was in great letters set *AFFLICTION*.
The greatnesse shew'd the owner. So I went
To fetch a sacrifice out of my fold, 30
Thinking with that, which I did thus present,
To warm his love, which I did fear grew cold.
But as my heart did tender it, the man,
Who was to take it from me, slipt his hand,
And threw my heart into the scalding pan;
My heart, that brought it (do you understand?)
The offerers heart. *Your heart was hard, I fear.*
Indeed it's true. I found a callous matter
Began to spread and to expatiate there:
But with a richer drug then scalding water 40
I bath'd it often, ev'n with holy bloud,
Which at a board, while many drunk bare wine,
A friend did steal into my cup for good,
Ev'n taken inwardly, and most divine
To supple hardnesses. But at the length
Out of the caldron getting, soon I fled
Unto my house, where to repair the strength
Which I had lost, I hasted to my bed.
But when I thought to sleep out all these faults
(I sigh to speak) 50
I found that some had stuff'd the bed with thoughts,
I would say *thorns*. Deare, could my heart not break,
When with my pleasures ev'n my rest was gone?
Full well I understood, who had been there:
For I had giv'n the key to none, but one:
It must be he. *Your heart was dull, I fear.*
Indeed a slack and sleepie state of minde
Did oft possesse me, so that when I pray'd,
Though my lips went, my heart did stay behinde.
But all my scores were by another paid, 60

Who took the debt upon him. *Truly, Friend,*
For ought I heare, your Master shows to you
More favour then you wot of. Mark the end.
The Font did onely, what was old, renew:
The Caldron suppled, what was grown too hard:
The Thorns did quicken, what was grown too dull:
All did but strive to mend, what you had marr'd.
Wherefore be cheer'd, and praise him to the full
Each day, each houre, each moment of the week,
Who fain would have you be new, tender, quick. 70

The Bag

Away despair! my gracious Lord doth heare.
Though windes and waves assault my keel,
He doth preserve it: he doth steer,
Ev'n when the boat seems most to reel.
Storms are the triumph of his art:
Well may he close his eyes, but not his heart.

Hast thou not heard, that my Lord JESUS di'd?
Then let me tell thee a strange storie.
The God of power, as he did ride
In his majestick robes of glorie, 10
Resolv'd to light; and so one day
He did descend, undressing all the way.

The starres his tire of light and rings obtain'd,
The cloud his bow, the fire his spear,
The sky his azure mantle gain'd.
And when they ask'd, what he would wear;
He smil'd and said as he did go,
He had new clothes a making here below.

When he was come, as travellers are wont,
He did repair unto an inne. 20
Both then, and after, many a brunt
He did endure to cancell sinne:
And having giv'n the rest before,
Here he gave up his life to pay our score.

But as he was returning, there came one
That ran upon him with a spear.

He, who came hither all alone,
Bringing nor man, nor arms, nor fear,
Receiv'd the blow upon his side,
And straight he turn'd, and to his brethren cry'd, 30

If ye have any thing to send or write,
I have no bag, but here is room:
Unto my Fathers hands and sight,
Beleeve me, it shall safely come.
That I shall minde, what you impart,
Look, you may put it very neare my heart.

Or if hereafter any of my friends
Will use me in this kinde, the doore
Shall still be open; what he sends
I will present, and somewhat more, 40
Not to his hurt. Sighs will convey
Any thing to me. Harke, Despair away.

The Collar

I struck the board, and cry'd, No more.
I will abroad.
What? shall I ever sigh and pine?
My lines and life are free; free as the rode,
Loose as the winde, as large as store.
Shall I be still in suit?
Have I no harvest but a thorn
To let me bloud, and not restore
What I have lost with cordiall fruit?
Sure there was wine 10
Before my sighs did drie it: there was corn
Before my tears did drown it.
Is the yeare onely lost to me?
Have I no bayes to crown it?
No flowers, no garlands gay? all blasted?
All wasted?
Not so, my heart: but there is fruit,
And thou hast hands.
Recover all thy sigh-blown age
On double pleasures: leave thy cold dispute 20
Of what is fit, and not. Forsake thy cage,
Thy rope of sands,

Which pettie thoughts have made, and made to thee
Good cable, to enforce and draw,
And be thy law,
While thou didst wink and wouldst not see.
Away; take heed:
I will abroad.
Call in thy deaths head there: tie up thy fears.
He that forbears *30*
To suit and serve his need,
Deserves his load.
But as I rav'd and grew more fierce and wilde
At every word,
Me thoughts I heard one calling, *Child!*
And I reply'd, *My Lord.*

Josephs coat

Wounded I sing, tormented I indite,
Thrown down I fall into a bed, and rest:
Sorrow hath chang'd its note: such is his will,
Who changeth all things, as him pleaseth best.
For well he knows, if but one grief and smart
Among my many had his full career,
Sure it would carrie with it ev'n my heart,
And both would runne untill they found a biere
To fetch the bodie; both being due to grief.
But he hath spoil'd the race; and giv'n to anguish *10*
One of Joyes coats, ticing it with relief
To linger in me, and together languish.
I live to shew his power, who once did bring
My *joyes* to *weep*, and now my *griefs* to *sing.*

The Pulley

When God at first made man,
Having a glasse of blessings standing by;

Josephs coat: "The title serves to indicate a common Christian idea, 'Take up my Cross . . .'—i.e., the eternal repetition, in men, of Christ's struggle, in the coat of his flesh, with the anguish which is the other side of all human joy." (Tuve, p. 178.)

Let us (said he) poure on him all we can:
Let the worlds riches, which dispersed lie,
Contract into a span.

So strength first made a way;
Then beautie flow'd, then wisdome, honour, pleasure:
When almost all was out, God made a stay,
Perceiving that alone of all his treasure
Rest in the bottome lay. 10

For if I should (said he)
Bestow this jewell also on my creature,
He would adore my gifts in stead of me,
And rest in Nature, not the God of Nature:
So both should losers be.

Yet let him keep the rest,
But keep them with repining restlesnesse:
Let him be rich and wearie, that at least,
If goodnesse leade him not, yet wearinesse
May tosse him to my breast. 20

The Flower

How fresh, O Lord, how sweet and clean
Are thy returns! ev'n as the flowers in spring;
To which, besides their own demean,
The late-past frosts tributes of pleasure bring.
Grief melts away
Like snow in May,
As if there were no such cold thing.

Who would have thought my shrivel'd heart
Could have recover'd greennesse? It was gone
Quite under ground; as flowers depart 10
To see their mother-root, when they have blown;
Where they together
All the hard weather,
Dead to the world, keep house unknown.

These are thy wonders, Lord of power,
Killing and quickning, bringing down to hell
And up to heaven in an houre;

Making a chiming of a passing-bell.
We say amisse,
This or that is: 20
Thy word is all, if we could spell.

O that I once past changing were,
Fast in thy Paradise, where no flower can wither!
Many a spring I shoot up fair,
Offring at heav'n, growing and groning thither:
Nor doth my flower
Want a spring-showre,
My sinnes and I joining together.

But while I grow in a straight line,
Still upwards bent, as if heav'n were mine own, 30
Thy anger comes, and I decline:
What frost to that? what pole is not the zone,
Where all things burn,
When thou dost turn,
And the least frown of thine is shown?

And now in age I bud again,
After so many deaths I live and write;
I once more smell the dew and rain,
And relish versing: O my onely light,
It cannot be 40
That I am he
On whom thy tempests fell all night.

These are thy wonders, Lord of love,
To make us see we are but flowers that glide:
Which when we once can finde and prove,
Thou hast a garden for us, where to bide.
Who would be more,
Swelling through store,
Forfeit their Paradise by their pride.

Aaron

Holinesse on the head,
Light and perfections on the breast,

Harmonious bells below, raising the dead
To leade them unto life and rest:
Thus are true Aarons drest.

Profanenesse in my head,
Defects and darknesse in my breast,
A noise of passions ringing me for dead
Unto a place where is no rest:
Poore priest thus am I drest. *10*

Onely another head
I have, another heart and breast,
Another musick, making live not dead,
Without whom I could have no rest:
In him I am well drest.

Christ is my onely head,
My alone onely heart and breast,
My onely musick, striking me ev'n dead;
That to the old man I may rest,
And be in him new drest. *20*

So holy in my head,
Perfect and light in my deare breast,
My doctrine tun'd by Christ, (who is not dead,
But lives in me while I do rest)
Come people; Aaron's drest.

A Parodie

Souls joy, when thou art gone,
And I alone,
Which cannot be,
Because thou dost abide with me,
And I depend on thee;

A Parodie: For an interesting analysis, see Tuve, "Sacred 'Parody' of Love Poetry, and Herbert," *Studies in the Renaissance* (New York: Renaissance Society of America, 1961), vol. VIII, pp. 249–290. Herbert "parodies" a love poem, "Soules joy, now I am gone," attributed to the third Earl of Pembroke. The word "parody," however, implies not a satirical use of the original, but a formal imitation, possibly of a musical tune to which it was sung.

Yet when thou dost suppresse
The cheerfulnesse
Of thy abode,
And in my powers not stirre abroad,
But leave me to my load: 10

O what a damp and shade
Doth me invade!
No stormie night
Can so afflict or so affright,
As thy eclipsed light.

Ah Lord! do not withdraw,
Lest want of aw
Make Sinne appeare;
And when thou dost but shine lesse cleare,
Say, that thou art not here. 20

And then what life I have,
While Sinne doth rave,
And falsly boast,
That I may seek, but thou art lost;
Thou and alone thou know'st.

O what a deadly cold
Doth me infold!
I half beleeve,
That Sinne sayes true: but while I grieve,
Thou com'st and dost relieve. 30

A Wreath

A Wreathed garland of deserved praise,
Of praise deserved, unto thee I give,
I give to thee, who knowest all my wayes,
My crooked winding wayes, wherein I live,
Wherein I die; not live: for life is straight,
Straight as a line, and ever tends to thee,
To thee, who art more farre above deceit,
Then deceit seems above simplicitie.
Give me simplicitie, that I may live,
So live and like, that I may know, thy wayes, 10

Know them and practise them: then shall I give
For this poore wreath, give thee a crown of praise.

Death

Death, thou wast once an uncouth hideous thing,
Nothing but bones,
The sad effect of sadder grones:
Thy mouth was open, but thou couldst not sing.

For we consider'd thee as at some six
Or ten yeares hence,
After the losse of life and sense,
Flesh being turn'd to dust, and bones to sticks.

We lookt on this side of thee, shooting short;
Where we did finde 10
The shells of fledge souls left behinde,
Dry dust, which sheds no tears, but may extort.

But since our Saviours death did put some bloud
Into thy face;
Thou art grown fair and full of grace,
Much in request, much sought for as a good.

For we do now behold thee gay and glad,
As at dooms-day;
When souls shall wear their new aray,
And all thy bones with beautie shall be clad. 20

Therefore we can go die as sleep, and trust
Half that we have
Unto an honest faithfull grave;
Making our pillows either down, or dust.

Dooms-day

Come away,
Make no delay.
Summon all the dust to rise,

Till it stirre, and rubbe the eyes;
While this member jogs the other,
Each one whispring, *Live you brother*?

Come away,
Make this the day.
Dust, alas, no musick feels,
But thy trumpet: then it kneels, *10*
As peculiar notes and strains
Cure Tarantulas raging pains.

Come away,
O make no stay!
Let the graves make their confession,
Lest at length they plead possession:
Fleshes stubbornnesse may have
Read that lesson to the grave.

Come away,
Thy flock doth stray. *20*
Some to windes their bodie lend,
And in them may drown a friend:
Some in noisome vapours grow
To a plague and publick wo.

Come away,
Help our decay.
Man is out of order hurl'd,
Parcel'd out to all the world.
Lord, thy broken consort raise,
And the musick shall be praise. *30*

Love (III)

Love bade me welcome: yet my soul drew back,
Guiltie of dust and sinne.
But quick-ey'd Love, observing me grow slack
From my first entrance in,
Drew nearer to me, sweetly questioning,
If I lack'd any thing.

A guest, I answer'd, worthy to be here:
Love said, You shall be he.

I the unkinde, ungratefull? Ah my deare,
I cannot look on thee. 10
Love took my hand, and smiling did reply,
Who made the eyes but I?

Truth Lord, but I have marr'd them: let my shame
Go where it doth deserve.
And know you not, sayes Love, who bore the blame?
My deare, then I will serve.
You must sit down, sayes Love, and taste my meat:
So I did sit and eat.

from THE CHURCH MILITANT

L'Envoy

King of Glorie, King of Peace,
With the one make warre to cease;
With the other blesse thy sheep,
Thee to love, in thee to sleep.
Let not Sinne devoure thy fold,
Bragging that thy bloud is cold,
That thy death is also dead,
While his conquests dayly spread;
That thy flesh hath lost his food,
And thy Crosse is common wood. 10
Choke him, let him say no more,
But reserve his breath in store,
Till thy conquests and his fall
Make his sighs to use it all,
And then bargain with the winde
To discharge what is behinde.

Blessed be God *alone,*
Thrice blessed Three in One.

FINIS.

Henry Vaughan

Henry Vaughan, the Silurist, was born in Wales in 1621/1622. With his twin brother, Thomas, he was educated by Matthew Herbert, a local clergyman. Both brothers went on to Jesus College, Oxford, in 1638. In 1640 Henry left without a degree, and went to London to study law. He remained in London until 1642, when, at the outbreak of the war, he enlisted in the army on the King's side. By 1646 he had married Catherine Wise and settled in Newton on Usk. (Upon her death in 1653, he married her sister.) Precisely when Vaughan undertook his medical studies, or whether he took a medical degree, there are no records to tell us; for the last forty years of his life he practiced as a country doctor. He died in 1695.

His first book, Poems With the tenth Satyre of Juvenal Englished, *was published in 1646. Some time between 1647 and 1650, however, Vaughan appears to have experienced a spiritual upheaval more in the nature of a regeneration than of a conversion. He violently rejected secular poetry and turned to devotion. The causes can only be conjectured: a growing disillusionment with the political situation, personal illness and grief upon the death of his beloved brother William in 1648, the influence of George Herbert, a growing preoccupation with hermetical philosophy (his brother Thomas had become one of the most important hermetical philosophers of his day, Eugenius Philalethes). In 1650 he published his first volume of devotional poetry,* Silex Scintillans; *it was published again, with the addition of a second part, under the same title in 1655. In 1651 his second volume of secular verse,* Olor Iscanus, *written probably by 1647, was pub-*

lished though Vaughan tried, unsuccessfully, to withdraw it. An intense period of prose composition at about this time resulted in two volumes on the Hermetic doctrine, Hermetical Physick *in 1655, and* The Chymists Key *in 1657. In 1652 he published* The Mount of Olives: Or, Solitary Devotions. Flores Solitudinis, *including three translations of devotional works and a Life of Paulinus, Bishop of Nola, was published in 1654.* Thalia Rediviva, *published in 1678 without his consent, and written probably about five years earlier, contains some "learned remains" of Thomas Vaughan, and some poems written by Vaughan much earlier but left out of the* Olor Iscanus *volume. So far as we know, Vaughan wrote nothing during the last forty years of his life.*

Several letters written by Henry Vaughan to John Aubrey and Anthony Wood provide us with some first-hand biographical information concerning the poet and his brother.

The text generally follows that of the Clarendon edition prepared by L. C. Martin.

FROM

Silex Scintillans

from PART I

Regeneration

A Ward, and still in bonds, one day
I stole abroad,
It was high-spring, and all the way
Primros'd, and hung with shade;
Yet, was it frost within,
And surly winds
Blasted my infant buds, and sinne
Like Clouds ecclips'd my mind.

Silex Scintillans: The text follows the "second Edition, in two Books" of 1655; the first edition, under the same name, contained only Part I.
Regeneration: Crucial to the understanding of Vaughan, this poem has been variously interpreted as having a mystical, hermetic, or an Augustinian basis.

2

Storm'd thus; I straight perceiv'd my spring
Meere stage, and show, *10*
My walke a monstrous, mountain'd thing
Rough-cast with Rocks, and snow;
And as a Pilgrims Eye
Far from reliefe,
Measures the melancholy skye
Then drops, and rains for griefe,

3

So sigh'd I upwards still, at last
'Twixt steps, and falls
I reach'd the pinacle, where plac'd
I found a paire of scales, *20*
I tooke them up and layd
In th'one late paines,
The other smoake, and pleasures weigh'd
But prov'd the heavier graines;

4

With that, some cryed, *Away;* straight I
Obey'd, and led
Full East, a faire, fresh field could spy
Some call'd it, *Jacobs Bed;*
A Virgin-soile, which no
Rude feet ere trod, *30*
Where (since he stept there,) only go
Prophets, and friends of God.

5

Here, I repos'd; but scarse well set,
A grove descryed
Of stately height, whose branches met
And mixt on every side;
I entred, and once in
(Amaz'd to see't,)
Found all was chang'd, and a new spring
Did all my senses greet; *40*

6

The unthrift Sunne shot vitall gold
A thousand peeces,

And heaven its azure did unfold
Checqur'd with snowie fleeces,
The aire was all in spice
And every bush
A garland wore; Thus fed my Eyes
But all the Eare lay hush.

7

Only a little Fountain lent
Some use for Eares, 50
And on the dumbe shades language spent
The Musick of her teares;
I drew her neere, and found
The Cisterne full
Of divers stones, some bright, and round
Others ill-shap'd, and dull.

8

The first (pray marke,) as quick as light
Danc'd through the floud,
But, th'last more heavy then the night
Nail'd to the Center stood; 60
I wonder'd much, but tyr'd
At last with thought,
My restless Eye that still desir'd
As strange an object brought;

9

It was a banke of flowers, where I descried
(Though 'twas mid-day,)
Some fast asleepe, others broad-eyed
And taking in the Ray,
Here musing long, I heard
A rushing wind 70
Which still increas'd, but whence it stirr'd
No where I could not find;

10

I turn'd me round, and to each shade
Dispatch'd an Eye,
To see, if any leafe had made
Least motion, or Reply,
But while I listning sought
My mind to ease

By knowing, where 'twas, or where not,
It whisper'd; *Where I please.* 80

Lord, then said I, *On me one breath,*
And let me dye before my death!

Cant. Cap. 5. ver. 17

Arise O North, and come thou South-wind, and blow upon my garden, that the spices thereof may flow out.

The Search

'Tis now cleare day: I see a Rose
Bud in the bright East, and disclose
The Pilgrim-Sunne; all night have I
Spent in a roving Extasie
To find my Saviour; I have been
As far as *Bethlem,* and have seen
His Inne, and Cradle; Being there
I met the *Wise-men,* askt them where
He might be found, or what starre can
Now point him out, grown up a Man? 10
To *Egypt* hence I fled, ran o're
All her parcht bosome to *Nile's* shore
Her yearly nurse; came back, enquir'd
Amongst the *Doctors,* and desir'd
To see the *Temple,* but was shown
A little dust, and for the Town
A heap of ashes, where some sed
A small bright sparkle was a bed,
Which would one day (beneath the pole,)
Awake, and then refine the whole. 20
Tyr'd here, I come to *Sychar;* thence
To *Jacobs wel,* bequeathed since
Unto his sonnes, (where often they
In those calme, golden Evenings lay
Watring their flocks, and having spent
Those white dayes, drove home to the Tent

The Search: For an analysis of this poem as a meditation on the Life of Christ, see Louis Martz, *The Poetry of Meditation* (New Haven: Yale University Press, 1954), pp. 86 ff.
l.21 Sychar: see John 4:5–6.

Their *well-fleec'd* traine;) And here (O fate!)
I sit, where once my Saviour sate;
The angry Spring in bubbles swell'd
Which broke in sighes still, as they fill'd, 30
And whisper'd, *Jesus had been there*
But *Jacobs children would not heare.*
Loath hence to part, at last I rise
But with the fountain in my Eyes,
And here a fresh search is decreed
He must be found, where he did bleed;
I walke the garden, and there see
Idæa's of his Agonie,
And moving anguishments that set
His blest face in a bloudy sweat; 40
I climb'd the Hill, perus'd the Crosse
Hung with my gaine, and his great losse,
Never did tree beare fruit like this,
Balsam of Soules, the bodyes blisse;
But, O his grave! where I saw lent
(For he had none,) a Monument,
An undefil'd, and new-heaw'd one,
But there was not the *Corner-stone;*
Sure (then said I,) my Quest is vaine,
Hee'le not be found, where he was slaine, 50
So mild a Lamb can never be
'Midst so much bloud, and Crueltie;
I'le to the Wilderness, and can
Find beasts more mercifull then man,
He liv'd there safe, 'twas his retreat
From the fierce *Jew*, and *Herods* heat,
And forty dayes withstood the fell,
And high temptations of hell;
With Seraphins there talked he
His fathers flaming ministrie, 60
He heav'nd their *walks*, and with his eyes
Made those wild shades a Paradise,
Thus was the desert sanctified
To be the refuge of his bride;
I'le thither then; see, It is day,
The Sun's broke through to guide my way.
But as I urg'd thus, and writ down
What pleasures should my Journey crown,
What silent paths, what shades, and Cells,
Faire, virgin-flowers, and hallow'd *Wells* 70

I should rove in, and rest my head
Where my deare Lord did often tread,
Sugring all dangers with successe,
Me thought I heard one singing thus;

1

Leave, leave, thy gadding thoughts;
Who Pores
and spies
Still out of Doores
descries
Within them nought. *80*

2

The skinne, and shell of things
Though faire,
are not
Thy wish, nor pray'r
but got
By meer Despair
of wings.

3

To rack old Elements,
or Dust
and say *90*
Sure here he must
needs stay
Is not the way,
nor just.

Search well another world; who studies this,
Travels in Clouds, seeks *Manna*, where none is.

Acts Cap. 17. ver. 27, 28.

That they should seek the Lord, if happily they might feel after him, and finde him, though he be not far off from every one of us, for in him we live, and move, and have our being.

The Retreate

Happy those early dayes! when I
Shin'd in my Angell-infancy.
Before I understood this place
Appointed for my second race,
Or taught my soul to fancy ought
But a white, Celestiall thought,
When yet I had not walkt above
A mile, or two, from my first love,
And looking back (at that short space,)
Could see a glimpse of his bright-face; *10*
When on some *gilded Cloud,* or *flowre*
My gazing soul would dwell an houre,
And in those weaker glories spy
Some shadows of eternity;
Before I taught my tongue to wound
My Conscience with a sinfull sound,
Or had the black art to dispence
A sev'rall sinne to ev'ry sence,
But felt through all this fleshly dresse
Bright *shootes* of everlastingnesse. *20*
 O how I long to travell back
And tread again that ancient track!
That I might once more reach that plaine,
Where first I left my glorious traine,
From whence th' Inlightned spirit sees
That shady City of Palme trees;
But (ah!) my soul with too much stay
Is drunk, and staggers in the way.
Some men a forward motion love,
But I by backward steps would move, *30*
And when this dust falls to the urn
In that state I came return.

"Come, come, what doe I here?"

¶

Come, come, what doe I here?
Since he is gone

Each day is grown a dozen year,
And each houre, one;
Come, come!
Cut off the sum,
By these soil'd teares!
(Which only thou
Know'st to be true,)
Dayes are my feares. *10*

2

Ther's not a wind can stir,
Or beam passe by,
But strait I think (though far,)
Thy hand is nigh;
Come, come!
Strike these lips dumb:
This restles breath
That soiles thy name,
Will ne'r be tame
Untill in death. *20*

3

Perhaps some think a tombe
No house of store,
But a dark, and seal'd up wombe,
Which ne'r breeds more.
Come, come!
Such thoughts benum;
But I would be
With him I weep
A bed, and sleep
To wake in thee. *30*

¶ *Content*

Peace, peace! I know 'twas brave,
But this corse fleece
I shelter in, is slave
To no such peece.
When I am gone,
I shall no ward-robes leave
To friend, or sonne
But what their own homes weave,

2

Such, though not proud, nor full,
May make them weep, *10*
And mourn to see the wooll
Outlast the sheep:
Poore, Pious weare!
Hadst thou bin rich, or fine
Perhaps that teare
Had mourn'd thy losse, not mine.

3

Why then these curl'd, puff'd points,
Or a laced story?
Death sets all out of Joint
And scornes their glory; *20*
Some Love a *Rose*
In hand, some in the skin;
But crosse to those,
I would have mine *within*.

"*Joy of my life! while left me here*"

¶

Joy of my life! while left me here,
And still my Love!
How in thy absence thou dost steere
Me from above!
A life well lead
This truth commends,
With quick, or dead
It never ends.

2

Stars are of mighty use: The night
Is dark, and long; *10*
The Rode foul, and where one goes right,
Six may go wrong.
One twinkling ray

ll.17–18 The elaborate *points* and *laces*, used to adorn a costume, probably refer to secular poetry which Vaughan abandoned for the Divine Muse.

Shot o'r some cloud,
May clear much way
And guide a croud.

3

Gods Saints are shining lights: who stays
Here long must passe
O're dark hills, swift streames, and steep ways
As smooth as glasse; 20
But these all night
Like Candles, shed
Their beams, and light
Us into Bed.

4

They are (indeed,) our Pillar-fires
Seen as we go,
They are that Cities shining spires
We travell too;
A swordlike gleame
Kept man for sin 30
First *Out;* This beame
Will guide him *In.*

"*Silence, and stealth of dayes!*"

¶

Silence, and stealth of dayes! 'tis now
Since thou art gone,
Twelve hundred houres, and not a brow
But Clouds hang on.
As he that in some Caves thick damp
Lockt from the light,
Fixeth a solitary lamp,
To brave the night
And walking from his Sun, when past
The glim'ring Ray 10
Cuts through the heavy mists in haste
Back to his day,

l.3 Twelve hundred houres: assumed to be the fifty days since the death of the poet's brother William.

So o'r fled minutes I retreat
Unto that hour
Which shew'd thee last, but did defeat
Thy light, and pow'r,
I search, and rack my soul to see
Those beams again,
But nothing but the snuff to me
Appeareth plain; 20
That dark, and dead sleeps in its known,
And common urn,
But those fled to their Makers throne,
There shine, and burn;
O could I track them! but souls must
Track one the other,
And now the spirit, not the dust
Must be thy brother.
Yet I have one *Pearle* by whose light
All things I see, 30
And in the heart of Earth, and night
Find Heaven, and thee.

Peace

My Soul, there is a Countrie
Far beyond the stars,
Where stands a winged Centrie
All skilfull in the wars,
There above noise, and danger
Sweet peace sits crown'd with smiles,
And one born in a Manger
Commands the Beauteous files,
He is thy gracious friend,
And (O my Soul awake!) 10
Did in pure love descend
To die here for thy sake,
If thou canst get but thither,
There growes the flowre of peace,
The Rose that cannot wither,
Thy fortresse, and thy ease;
Leave then thy foolish ranges;
For none can thee secure,
But one, who never changes,
Thy God, thy life, thy Cure. 20

Rom. Cap. 8. ver. 19

Etenim res Creatæ exerto Capite observantes expectant revelationem Filiorum Dei.

And do they so? have they a Sense
Of ought but Influence?
Can they their heads lift, and expect,
And grone too? why th'Elect
Can do no more: my volumes sed
They were all dull, and dead,
They judg'd them senslesse, and their state
Wholly Inanimate.
Go, go; Seal up thy looks,
And burn thy books. 10

2

I would I were a stone, or tree,
Or flowre by pedigree,
Or some poor high-way herb, or Spring
To flow, or bird to sing!
Then should I (tyed to one sure state,)
All day expect my date;
But I am sadly loose, and stray
A giddy blast each way;
O let me not thus range!
Thou canst not change. 20

3

Sometimes I sit with thee, and tarry
An hour, or so, then vary.
Thy other Creatures in this Scene
Thee only aym, and mean;
Some rise to seek thee, and with heads
Erect peep from their beds;
Others, whose birth is in the tomb,
And cannot quit the womb,
Sigh there, and grone for thee,
Their liberty. 30

4

O let not me do lesse! shall they
Watch, while I sleep, or play?

Shall I thy mercies still abuse
With fancies, friends, or newes?
O brook it not! thy bloud is mine,
And my soul should be thine;
O brook it not! why wilt thou stop
After whole showres one drop?
Sure, thou wilt joy to see
Thy sheep with thee. 40

Corruption

Sure, It was so. Man in those early days
Was not all stone, and Earth,
He shin'd a little, and by those weak Rays
Had some glimpse of his birth.
He saw Heaven o'r his head, and knew from whence
He came (condemned,) hither,
And, as first Love draws strongest, so from hence
His mind sure progress'd thither.
Things here were strange unto him: Swet, and till
All was a thorn, or weed, 10
Nor did those last, but (like himself,) dyed still
As soon as they did *Seed,*
They seem'd to quarrel with him; for that Act
That fel him, foyl'd them all,
He drew the Curse upon the world, and Crackt
The whole frame with his fall.
This made him long for *home,* as loath to stay
With murmurers, and foes;
He sigh'd for *Eden,* and would often say
Ah! what bright days were those? 20
Nor was Heav'n cold unto him; for each day
The vally, or the Mountain
Afforded visits, and still *Paradise* lay
In some green shade, or fountain.
Angels lay *Leiger* here; Each Bush, and Cel,
Each Oke, and high-way knew them,
Walk but the fields, or sit down at some *wel,*
And he was sure to view them.
Almighty *Love!* where art thou now? mad man
Sits down, and freezeth on, 30

l.25 Angels: ambassadors or permanent agents here on earth.

He raves, and swears to stir nor fire, nor fan,
    But bids the thread be spun.
I see, thy Curtains are Close-drawn; Thy bow
    Looks dim too in the Cloud,
Sin triumphs still, and man is sunk below
    The Center, and his shrowd;
All's in deep sleep, and night; Thick darknes lyes
    And hatcheth o'r thy people;
But hark! what trumpets that? what Angel cries
    Arise! Thrust in thy sickle. 40

Unprofitablenes

How rich, O Lord! how fresh thy visits are!
'Twas but Just now my bleak leaves hopeles hung
    Sullyed with dust and mud;
Each snarling blast shot through me, and did share
Their Youth, and beauty, Cold showres nipt, and wrung
    Their spiciness, and bloud;
But since thou didst in one sweet glance survey
Their sad decays, I flourish, and once more
    Breath all perfumes, and spice;
I smell a dew like *Myrrh,* and all the day 10
Wear in my bosome a full Sun; such store
    Hath one beame from thy Eys.
But, ah, my God! what fruit hast thou of this?
What one poor leaf did ever I yet fall
    To wait upon thy wreath?
Thus thou all day a thankless weed doest dress,
And when th' hast done, a stench, or fog is all
    The odour I bequeath.

The World

I saw Eternity the other night
Like a great *Ring* of pure and endless light,
  All calm, as it was bright,

l.40 See Rev. 14:14–18.

And round beneath it, Time in hours, days, years
Driv'n by the spheres
Like a vast shadow mov'd, In which the world
And all her train were hurl'd;
The doting Lover in his queintest strain
Did their Complain,
Neer him, his Lute, his fancy, and his flights, 10
Wits sour delights,
With gloves, and knots the silly snares of pleasure
Yet his dear Treasure
All scatter'd lay, while he his eys did pour
Upon a flowr.

2

The darksome States-man hung with weights and woe
Like a thick midnight-fog mov'd there so slow
He did nor stay, nor go;
Condemning thoughts (like sad Ecclipses) scowl
Upon his soul, 20
And Clouds of crying witnesses without
Pursued him with one shout.
Yet dig'd the Mole, and lest his ways be found
Workt under ground,
Where he did Clutch his prey, but one did see
That policie,
Churches and altars fed him, Perjuries
Were gnats and flies,
It rain'd about him bloud and tears, but he
Drank them as free. 30

3

The fearfull miser on a heap of rust
Sate pining all his life there, did scarce trust
His own hands with the dust,
Yet would not place one peece above, but lives
In feare of theeves.
Thousands there were as frantick as himself
And hug'd each one his pelf,
The down-right Epicure plac'd heav'n in sense
And scornd pretence
While others slipt into a wide Excesse 40
Said little lesse;
The weaker sort slight, triviall wares Inslave
Who think them brave,

And poor, despised truth sate Counting by
Their victory.

4

Yet some, who all this while did weep and sing,
And sing, and weep, soar'd up into the *Ring*,
But most would use no wing.
O fools (said I,) thus to prefer dark night
Before true light, *50*
To live in grots, and caves, and hate the day
Because it shews the way,
The way which from this dead and dark abode
Leads up to God,
A way where you might tread the Sun, and be
More bright than he.
But as I did their madnes so discusse
One whisper'd thus,
This Ring the Bride-groome did for none provide
But for his bride. *60*

John Cap. 2. ver. 16, 17

All that is in the world, the lust of the flesh, the lust of the Eys, and the pride of life, is not of the father, but is of the world.

And the world passeth away, and the lusts thereof, but he that doth the will of God abideth for ever.

The Constellation

Fair, order'd lights (whose motion without noise
Resembles those true Joys
Whose spring is on that hil where you do grow
And we here tast sometimes below,)

With what exact obedience do you move
Now beneath, and now above,
And in your vast progressions overlook
The darkest night, and closest nook!

Some nights I see you in the gladsome East,
Some others neer the West, *10*
And when I cannot see, yet do you shine
And beat about your endles line.

Silence, and light, and watchfulnes with you
Attend and wind the Clue,
No sleep, nor sloth assailes you, but poor man
Still either sleeps, or slips his span.

He grops beneath here, and with restless Care
First makes, then hugs a snare,
Adores dead dust, sets heart on Corne and grass
But seldom doth make heav'n his glass. 20

Musick and mirth (if there be musick here)
Take up, and tune his year,
These things are Kin to him, and must be had,
Who kneels, or sighs a life is mad.

Perhaps some nights hee'l watch with you, and peep
When it were best to sleep,
Dares know Effects, and Judge them long before,
When th' herb he treads knows much, much more.

But seeks he your *Obedience, Order, Light,*
Your calm and wel-train'd flight, 30
Where, though the glory differ in each star,
Yet is there peace still, and no war?

Since plac'd by him who calls you by your names
And fixt there all your flames,
Without Command you never acted ought
And then you in your Courses fought.

But here Commission'd by a black self-wil
The sons the father kil,
The Children Chase the mother, and would heal
The wounds they give, by crying, zeale. 40

Then Cast her bloud, and tears upon thy book
Where they for fashion look,
And like that Lamb which had the Dragons voice
Seem mild, but are known by their noise.

l.31 See 1 Cor. 15:41.
l.33 See Ps. 147.4.
l.36 See Judg. 5:20.
l.43 See Rev. 13:11.

Thus by our lusts disorder'd into wars
Our guides prove wandring stars,
Which for these mists, and black days were reserv'd,
What time we from our first love swerv'd.

Yet O for his sake who sits now by thee
All crown'd with victory, 50
So guide us through this Darknes, that we may
Be more and more in love with day;

Settle, and fix our hearts, that we may move
In order, peace, and love,
And taught obedience by thy whole Creation,
Become an humble, holy nation.

Give to thy spouse her perfect, and pure dress,
Beauty and *holiness*,
And so repair these Rents, that men may see
And say, *Where God is, all agree.* 60

Man

Weighing the stedfastness and state
Of some mean things which here below reside,
Where birds like watchful Clocks the noiseless date
And Intercourse of times divide,
Where Bees at night get home and hive, and flowrs
Early, aswel as late,
Rise with the Sun, and set in the same bowrs;

2

I would (said I) my God would give
The staidness of these things to man! for these
To his divine appointments ever cleave, 10
And no new business breaks their peace;
The birds nor sow, nor reap, yet sup and dine,
The flowres without clothes live,
Yet *Solomon* was never drest so fine.

3

Man hath stil either toyes, or Care,
He hath no root, nor to one place is ty'd,

But ever restless and Irregular
About this Earth doth run and ride,
He knows he hath a home, but scarce knows where,
He sayes it is so far 20
That he hath quite forgot how to go there.

4

He knocks at all doors, strays and roams,
Nay hath not so much wit as some stones have
Which in the darkest nights point to their homes,
By some hid sense their Maker gave;
Man is the shuttle, to whose winding quest
And passage through these looms
God order'd motion, but ordain'd no rest.

"*I walkt the other day (to spend my hour)*"

¶

I walkt the other day (to spend my hour)
Into a field
Where I sometimes had seen the soil to yield
A gallant flowre,
But Winter now had ruffled all the bowre
And curious store
I knew there heretofore.

2

Yet I whose search lov'd not to peep and peer
I'th' face of things
Thought with my self, there might be other springs 10
Besides this here
Which, like cold friends, sees us but once a year,
And so the flowre
Might have some other bowre.

3

Then taking up what I could neerest spie
I digg'd about
That place where I had seen him to grow out,
And by and by

I saw the warm Recluse alone to lie
Where fresh and green *20*
He lived of us unseen.

4

Many a question Intricate and rare
Did I there strow,
But all I could extort was, that he now
Did there repair
Such losses as befel him in this air
And would e'r long
Come forth most fair and young.

5

This past, I threw the Clothes quite o'r his head,
And stung with fear *30*
Of my own frailty dropt down many a tear
Upon his bed,
Then sighing whisper'd, *Happy are the dead!*
What peace doth now
Rock him asleep below?

6

And yet, how few believe such doctrine springs
From a poor root
Which all the Winter sleeps here under foot
And hath no wings
To raise it to the truth and light of things, *40*
But is stil trod
By ev'ry wandring clod.

7

O thou! whose spirit did at first inflame
And warm the dead,
And by a sacred Incubation fed
With life this frame
Which once had neither being, forme, nor name,
Grant I may so
Thy steps track here below,

8

That in these Masques and shadows I may see *50*
Thy sacred way,

And by those hid ascents climb to that day
Which breaks from thee
Who art in all things, though invisibly;
Shew me thy peace,
Thy mercy, love, and ease,

9

And from this Care, where dreams and sorrows raign
Lead me above
Where Light, Joy, Leisure, and true Comforts move
Without all pain, 60
There, hid in thee, shew me his life again
At whose dumbe urn
Thus all the year I mourn.

from PART II

Ascension-Hymn

Dust and clay
Mans antient wear!
Here you must stay,
But I elsewhere;
Souls sojourn here, but may not rest;
Who will ascend, must be undrest.

And yet some
That know to die
Before death come,
Walk to the skie 10
Even in this life; but all such can
Leave behinde them the old Man.

If a star
Should leave the Sphære,
She must first mar
Her flaming wear,
And after fall, for in her dress
Of glory, she cannot transgress.

Man of old
Within the line 20
Of *Eden* could
Like the Sun shine

All naked, innocent and bright,
And intimate with Heav'n, as light;

But since he
That brightness soil'd,
His garments be
All dark and spoil'd,
And here are left as nothing worth,
Till the Refiners fire breaks forth. *30*

Then comes he!
Whose mighty light
Made his cloathes be
Like Heav'n, all bright;
The Fuller, whose pure blood did flow
To make stain'd man more white then snow.

Hee alone
And none else can
Bring bone to bone
And rebuild man, *40*
And by his all subduing might
Make clay ascend more quick then light.

"*They are all gone into the world of light!*"

They are all gone into the world of light!
And I alone sit lingring here;
Their very memory is fair and bright,
And my sad thoughts doth clear.

It glows and glitters in my cloudy brest
Like stars upon some gloomy grove,
Or those faint beams in which this hill is drest,
After the Sun's remove.

I see them walking in an Air of glory,
Whose light doth trample on my days: *10*
My days, which are at best but dull and hoary,
Meer glimering and decays.

ll.35–36 **The image is of Christ the Fuller, the cleanser of cloth, or of man's sins.**

O holy hope! and high humility,
High as the Heavens above!
These are your walks, and you have shew'd them me
To kindle my cold love,

Dear, beauteous death! the Jewel of the Just,
Shining nowhere, but in the dark;
What mysteries do lie beyond thy dust;
Could man outlook that mark! 20

He that hath found some fledg'd birds nest, may know
At first sight, if the bird be flown;
But what fair Well, or Grove he sings in now,
That is to him unknown.

And yet, as Angels in some brighter dreams
Call to the soul, when man doth sleep:
So some strange thoughts transcend our wonted theams,
And into glory peep.

If a star were confin'd into a Tomb
Her captive flames must needs burn there; 30
But when the hand that lockt her up, gives room,
She'l shine through all the sphære.

O Father of eternal life, and all
Created glories under thee!
Resume thy spirit from this world of thrall
Into true liberty.

Either disperse these mists, which blot and fill
My perspective (still) as they pass,
Or else remove me hence unto that hill,
Where I shall need no glass. 40

Cock-crowing

Father of lights! what Sunnie seed,
What glance of day hast thou confin'd

Cock-crowing: For a close analysis of this poem as a "minor metaphor in the three larger images that are the major centers of Vaughan's poetic theology" see: Don Cameron Allen, *Image and Meaning* (Baltimore: Johns Hopkins Press, 1960), pp. 157 ff; see also Elizabeth Holmes, *Henry Vaughan and the Hermetic Philosophy* (Oxford: Blackwell, 1932), pp. 38 ff.

Into this bird? To all the breed
This busie Ray thou hast assign'd;
　　Their magnetisme works all night,
　　And dreams of Paradise and light.

Their eyes watch for the morning hue,
Their little grain expelling night
So shines and sings, as if it knew
The path unto the house of light. *10*
　　It seems their candle, howe'r done,
　　Was tinn'd and lighted at the sunne.

If such a tincture, such a touch,
So firm a longing can impowre
Shall thy own image think it much
To watch for thy appearing hour?
　　If a meer blast so fill the sail,
　　Shall not the breath of God prevail?

O thou immortall light and heat!
Whose hand so shines through all this frame, *20*
That by the beauty of the seat,
We plainly see, who made the same.
　　Seeing thy seed abides in me,
　　Dwell thou in it, and I in thee.

To sleep without thee, is to die;
Yea, 'tis a death partakes of hell:
For where thou dost not close the eye
It never opens, I can tell.
　　In such a dark, Ægyptian border,
　　The shades of death dwell and disorder. *30*

If joyes, and hopes, and earnest throws,
And hearts, whose Pulse beats still for light
Are given to birds; who, but thee, knows
A love-sick souls exalted flight?
　　Can souls be track'd by any eye
　　But his, who gave them wings to flie?

Onely this Veyle which thou hast broke,
And must be broken yet in me,
This veyle, I say, is all the cloke
And cloud which shadows thee from me. *40*

This veyle thy full-ey'd love denies,
And onely gleams and fractions spies.

O take it off! make no delay,
But brush me with thy light, that I
May shine unto a perfect day,
And warme me at thy glorious Eye!
O take it off! or till it flee,
Though with no Lilie, stay with me!

The Bird

Hither thou com'st: the busie wind all night
Blew through thy lodging, where thy own warm wing
Thy pillow was. Many a sullen storm
(For which course man seems much the fitter born,)
Rain'd on thy bed
And harmless head.

And now as fresh and chearful as the light
Thy little heart in early hymns doth sing
Unto that *Providence*, whose unseen arm
Curb'd them, and cloath'd thee well and warm. 10
All things that be, praise him; and had
Their lesson taught them, when first made.

So hills and valleys into singing break,
And though poor stones have neither speech nor tongue,
While active winds and streams both run and speak,
Yet stones are deep in admiration.
Thus Praise and Prayer here beneath the Sun
Make lesser mornings, when the great are done.

For each inclosed Spirit is a star
Inlightning his own little sphære, 20
Whose light, though fetcht and borrowed from far,
Both mornings makes, and evenings there.

But as these Birds of light make a land glad,
Chirping their solemn Matins on each tree:
So in the shades of night some dark fowls be,
Whose heavy notes make all that hear them, sad.

The Turtle then in Palm-trees mourns,
While Owls and Satyrs howl;
The pleasant Land to brimstone turns
And all her streams grow foul. 30

Brightness and mirth, and love and faith, all flye,
Till the Day-spring breaks forth again from high.

The Timber

Sure thou didst flourish once! and many Springs,
Many bright mornings, much dew, many showers
Past ore thy head: many light *Hearts* and *Wings*
Which now are dead, lodg'd in thy living bowers.

And still a new succession sings and flies;
Fresh Groves grow up, and their green branches shoot
Towards the old and still enduring skies,
While the low *Violet* thrives at their root.

But thou beneath the sad and heavy *Line*
Of death, dost waste all senseless, cold and dark; 10
Where not so much as dreams of light may shine,
Nor any thought of greenness, leaf or bark.

And yet (as if some deep hate and dissent,
Bred in thy growth betwixt high winds and thee,
Were still alive) thou dost great storms resent
Before they come, and know'st how near they be.

Else all at rest thou lyest, and the fierce breath
Of tempests can no more disturb thy ease;
But this thy strange resentment after death
Means onely those, who broke (in life) thy peace. 20

So murthered man, when lovely life is done,
And his blood freez'd, keeps in the Center still
Some secret sense, which makes the dead blood run
At his approach, that did the body kill.

And is there any murth'rer worse then sin?
Or any storms more foul then a lewd life?

Or what *Resentient* can work more within,
Then true remorse, when with past sins at strife?

He that hath left lifes vain joys and vain care,
And truly hates to be detain'd on earth, *30*
Hath got an house where many mansions are,
And keeps his soul unto eternal mirth.

But though thus dead unto the world, and ceas'd
From sin, he walks a narrow, private way;
Yet grief and old wounds make him sore displeas'd,
And all his life a rainy, weeping day.

For though he should forsake the world, and live
As meer a stranger, as man long since dead;
Yet joy it self will make a right soul grieve
To think, he should be so long vainly lead. *40*

But as shades set off light, so tears and grief
(Though of themselves but a sad blubber'd story)
By shewing the sin great, shew the relief
Far greater, and so speak my Saviors glory.

If my way lies through deserts and wilde woods;
Where all the Land with scorching heat is curst;
Better, the pools should flow with rain and floods
To fill my bottle, than I die with thirst.

Blest showers they are, and streams sent from above
Begetting *Virgins* where they use to flow; *50*
And trees of life no other waters love,
These upper springs and none else make them grow.

But these chaste fountains flow not till we dye;
Some drops may fall before, but a clear spring
And ever running, till we leave to fling
Dirt in her way, will keep above the skie.

Rom. Cap. 6. ver. 7

He that is dead, is freed from sin.

l.27 Resentient: "That which causes a change of feeling." (*O.E.D.*)

ll.47–48 The reference, recurrent in Vaughan, is to the miraculous water created in the desert from which Hagar filled the *bottle* to assuage Ishmael's thirst. (Gen. 21:9–21.)

The Seed growing secretly

S. MARK 4. 26

If this worlds friends might see but once
What some poor man may often feel,
Glory, and gold, and Crowns and Thrones
They would soon quit and learn to kneel.

My dew, my dew! my early love,
My souls bright food, thy absence kills!
Hover not long, eternal Dove!
Life without thee is loose and spills.

Somthing I had, which long ago
Did learn to suck, and sip, and taste, 10
But now grown sickly, sad and slow,
Doth fret and wrangle, pine and waste.

O spred thy sacred wings and shake
One living drop! one drop life keeps!
If pious griefs Heavens joys awake,
O fill his bottle! thy childe weeps!

Slowly and sadly doth he grow,
And soon as left, shrinks back to ill;
O feed that life, which makes him blow
And spred and open to thy will! 20

For thy eternal, living wells
None stain'd or wither'd shall come near:
A fresh, immortal *green* there dwells,
And spotless *white* is all the wear.

Dear, secret *Greenness!* nurst below
Tempests and windes, and winter-nights,
Vex not, that but one sees thee grow,
That *One* made all these lesser lights.

If those bright joys he singly sheds
On thee, were all met in one Crown, 30
Both Sun and Stars would hide their heads;
And Moons, though full, would get them down.

Let glory be their bait, whose mindes
Are all too high for a low Cell:
Though Hawks can prey through storms and winds,
The poor Bee in her hive must dwel.

Glory, the Crouds cheap tinsel still
To what most takes them, is a drudge;
And they too oft take good for ill,
And thriving vice for vertue judge. 40

What needs a Conscience calm and bright
Within it self an outward test?
Who breaks his glass to take more light,
Makes way for storms into his rest.

Then bless thy secret growth, nor catch
At noise, but thrive unseen and dumb;
Keep clean, bear fruit, earn life and watch
Till the white winged Reapers come!

"*As time one day by me did pass*"

¶

As time one day by me did pass
 Through a large dusky glasse
 He held, I chanc'd to look
 And spyed his curious book
Of past days, where sad Heav'n did shed
A mourning light upon the dead.

Many disordered lives I saw
 And foul records which thaw
 My kinde eyes still, but in
 A fair, white page of thin 10
And ev'n, smooth lines, like the Suns rays,
Thy name was writ, and all thy days.

O bright and happy Kalendar!
 Where youth shines like a star
 All pearl'd with tears, and may
 Teach age, *The Holy way;*

Where through thick pangs, high agonies
Faith into life breaks, and death dies.

As some meek *night-piece* which day quails,
    To candle-light unveils: 20
    So by one beamy line
    From thy bright lamp did shine,
In the same page thy humble grave
Set with green herbs, glad hopes and brave.

Here slept my thoughts dear mark! which dust
    Seem'd to devour, like rust;
    But dust (I did observe)
    By hiding doth preserve,
As we for long and sure recruits,
Candy with sugar our choice fruits. 30

O calm and sacred bed where lies
    In deaths dark mysteries
    A beauty far more bright
    Then the noons cloudless light
For whose dry dust green branches bud
And robes are bleach'd in the *Lambs* blood.

Sleep happy ashes! (blessed sleep!)
    While haplesse I still weep;
    Weep that I have out-liv'd
    My life, and unreliev'd 40
Must (soul-lesse shadow!) so live on,
Though life be dead, and my joys gone.

Childe-hood

I cannot reach it; and my striving eye
Dazles at it, as at eternity.
        Were now that Chronicle alive,
Those white designs which children drive,
And the thoughts of each harmless hour,
With their content too in my pow'r,
Quickly would I make my path even,
And by meer playing go to Heaven.

Why should men love
A Wolf, more then a Lamb or Dove? 10
Or choose hell-fire and brimstone streams
Before bright stars, and Gods own beams?
Who kisseth thorns, will hurt his face,
But flowers do both refresh and grace,
And sweetly living (*fie on men!*)
Are when dead, medicinal then.
If seeing much should make staid eyes,
And long experience should make wise;
Since all that age doth teach, is ill,
Why should I not love childe-hood still? 20
Why if I see a rock or shelf,
Shall I from thence cast down my self,
Or by complying with the world,
From the same precipice be hurl'd?
Those observations are but foul
Which make me wise to lose my soul.

And yet the *Practice* worldlings call
Business and weighty action all,
Checking the poor childe for his play,
But gravely cast themselves away. 30

Dear, harmless age! the short, swift span,
Where weeping virtue parts with man;
Where love without lust dwells, and bends
What way we please, without self-ends.

An age of mysteries! which he
Must live twice, that would Gods face see;
Which *Angels* guard, and with it play,
Angels! which foul men drive away.

How do I study now, and scan
Thee, more then ere I studyed man, 40
And onely see through a long night
Thy edges, and thy bordering light!
O for thy Center and mid-day!
For sure that is the *narrow way*.

l.44 See Matt. 7:14.

The Night

JOHN 2. 3

Through that pure *Virgin-shrine*,
That sacred vail drawn o'r thy glorious noon
That men might look and live as Glo-worms shine,
And face the Moon:
Wise *Nicodemus* saw such light
As made him know his God by night.

Most blest believer he!
Who in that land of darkness and blinde eyes
Thy long expected healing wings could see,
When thou didst rise, *10*
And what can never more be done,
Did at mid-night speak with the Sun!

O who will tell me, where
He found thee at that dead and silent hour!
What hallow'd solitary ground did bear
So rare a flower,
Within whose sacred leafs did lie
The fulness of the Deity.

No mercy-seat of gold,
No dead and dusty *Cherub*, nor carv'd stone, *20*
But his own living works did my Lord hold
And lodge alone;
Where *trees* and *herbs* did watch and peep
And wonder, while the *Jews* did sleep.

Dear night! this worlds defeat;
The stop to busie fools; cares check and curb;
The day of Spirits; my souls calm retreat
Which none disturb!
*Christs** progress, and his prayer time;
The hours to which high Heaven doth chime. *30*

l.5 Nicodemus: the learned Jew who came to Jesus by night and heard of Christian rebirth. See John 3:1–21.
ll.19–20 See Exod. 25.17–21.
* *Mark, chap.* 1.35. *S. Luke, chap.* 21.37. (Vaughan's note)

Gods silent, searching flight:
When my Lords head is fill'd with dew, and all
His locks are wet with the clear drops of night;
His still, soft call;
His knocking time; The souls dumb watch,
When Spirits their fair kinred catch.

Were all my loud, evil days
Calm and unhaunted as is thy dark Tent,
Whose peace but by some *Angels* wing or voice
Is seldom rent; 40
Then I in Heaven all the long year
Would keep, and never wander here.

But living where the Sun
Doth all things wake, and where all mix and tyre
Themselves and others, I consent and run
To ev'ry myre,
And by this worlds ill-guiding light,
Erre more then I can do by night.

There is in God (some say)
A deep, but dazling darkness; As men here 50
Say it is late and dusky, because they
See not all clear;
O for that night! where I in him
Might live invisible and dim.

The Water-fall

With what deep murmurs through times silent stealth
Doth thy transparent, cool and watry wealth
Here flowing fall,
And chide, and call,
As if his liquid, loose Retinue staid
Lingring, and were of this steep place afraid,
The common pass
Where, clear as glass,
All must descend
Not to an end: 10
But quickned by this deep and rocky grave,
Rise to a longer course more bright and brave.

Dear stream! dear bank, where often I
Have sate, and pleas'd my pensive eye,
Why, since each drop of thy quick store
Runs thither, whence it flow'd before,
Should poor souls fear a shade or night,
Who came (sure) from a sea of light?
Or since those drops are all sent back
So sure to thee, that none doth lack, 20
Why should frail flesh doubt any more
That what God takes, hee'l not restore?
O useful Element and clear!
My sacred wash and cleanser here,
My first consigner unto those
Fountains of life, where the Lamb goes?
What sublime truths, and wholesome themes,
Lodge in thy mystical, deep streams!
Such as dull man can never finde
Unless that Spirit lead his minde, 30
Which first upon thy face did move,
And hatch'd all with his quickning love.
As this loud brooks incessant fall
In streaming rings restagnates all,
Which reach by course the bank, and then
Are no more seen, just so pass men.
O my invisible estate,
My glorious liberty, still late!
Thou art the Channel my soul seeks,
Not this with Cataracts and Creeks. 40

Quickness

False life! a foil and no more, when
Wilt thou be gone?
Thou foul deception of all men
That would not have the true come on.

Thou art a Moon-like toil; a blinde
Self-posing state;
A dark contest of waves and winde;
A meer tempestuous debate.

Life is a fix'd, discerning light,
A knowing Joy; 10

No chance, or fit: but ever bright,
And calm and full, yet doth not cloy.

'Tis such a blissful thing, that still
Doth vivifie,
And shine and smile, and hath the skill
To please without Eternity.

Thou art a toylsom Mole, or less
A moving mist
But life is, what none can express,
A quickness, which my God hath kist. 20

The Wreath

Since I in storms us'd most to be
And seldom yielded flowers,
How shall I get a wreath for thee
From those rude, barren hours?

The softer dressings of the Spring,
Or Summers later store
I will not for thy temples bring,
Which *Thorns*, not *Roses* wore.

But a twin'd wreath of *grief* and *praise*,
Praise soil'd with tears, and tears again 10
Shining with joy, like dewy days,
This day I bring for all thy pain,
Thy causless pain! and sad as death;
Which sadness breeds in the most vain,
(O not in vain!) now beg thy breath;
Thy quickning breath, which gladly bears
Through saddest clouds to that glad place,
Where cloudless Quires sing without tears,
Sing thy just praise, and see thy face.

The Book

Eternal God! maker of all
That have liv'd here, since the mans fall;

The Rock of ages! in whose shade
They live unseen, when here they fade.

Thou knew'st this *papyr,* when it was
Meer *seed,* and after that but *grass;*
Before 'twas *drest* or *spun,* and when
Made *linen,* who did *wear* it then:
What were their lifes, their thoughts & deeds
Whither good *corn,* or fruitless *weeds.* *10*

Thou knew'st this *Tree,* when a green *shade*
Cover'd it, since a *Cover* made,
And where it flourish'd, grew and spread,
As if it never should be dead.

Thou knew'st this harmless *beast,* when he
Did live and feed by thy decree
On each green thing; then slept (well fed)
Cloath'd with this *skin,* which now lies spred
A *Covering* o're this aged book,
Which makes me wisely weep and look *20*
On my own dust; meer dust it is,
But not so dry and clean as this.
Thou knew'st and saw'st them all and though
Now scatter'd thus, dost know them so.

O knowing, glorious spirit! when
Thou shalt restore trees, beasts and men,
When thou shalt make all new again,
Destroying onely death and pain,
Give him amongst thy works a place,
Who in them lov'd and sought thy face! *30*

Thomas Traherne

Thomas Traherne was born in 1637, son of a Hereford shoemaker. After the early death of their parents, Thomas and his brother Philip were reared by a prosperous relative, Philip Traherne. Thomas came to Brasenose College, Oxford in 1652, took his B.A. in 1656, was ordained in 1657, and was "created" M.A. in 1661. He was appointed to the living of Credenhill in 1657 but appears not to have taken up residence until 1661. He remained at Credenhill until 1669, in the meantime working on his Roman Forgeries *which occasioned periodic visits to the Bodleian at Oxford, some eighty miles away, and enjoying membership in Susanna Hopton's devotional circle at Kington. In 1669 he took his B.D. and was appointed chaplain to Sir Orlando Bridgman, Keeper of the Seals, whom he accompanied to London. In 1672 he retired with his patron to Teddington. He died, shortly after his patron, in 1674.*

The only work to appear in Traherne's lifetime was Roman Forgeries, *1673, a polemic against the Church of Rome. A year after Traherne's death,* Christian Ethics *was published, 1675. In 1699 the volume briefly called* The Thanksgivings *was published by the Rev. Dr. Hicks. Traherne's poems and* Centuries *remained in manuscript until their discovery by W. T. Brooke. The poems were published for the first time in 1903 by Bertram Dobell, and reprinted in 1906. The* Poems of Felicity, *found in the Burney MS., were published by H. I. Bell; these represent Thomas's poems as emended by his brother Philip. Gladys Wade's edition of 1932 separates Thomas's poems from*

Philip's changes. Centuries of Meditation *was first published by Dobell in 1908.*

The text follows that of the Clarendon edition prepared by H. M. Margoliouth.

The Salutation

1

These little Limmes,
These Eys and Hands which here I find,
These rosie Cheeks wherwith my Life begins,
Where have ye been,? Behind
What Curtain were ye from me hid so long!
Where was? in what Abyss, my Speaking Tongue?

2

When silent I,
So many thousand thousand yeers,
Beneath the Dust did in a Chaos lie,
How could I Smiles or Tears, *10*
Or Lips or Hands or Eys or Ears perceiv?
Welcom ye Treasures which I now receiv.

3

I that so long
Was Nothing from Eternitie,
Did little think such Joys as Ear or Tongue,
To Celebrat or See:
Such Sounds to hear, such Hands to feel, such Feet,
Beneath the Skies, on such a Ground to meet.

4

New Burnisht Joys!
Which yellow Gold and Pearl excell! *20*
Such Sacred Treasures are the Lims in Boys,
In which a Soul doth Dwell;
Their Organized Joynts, and Azure Veins
More Wealth include, then all the World contains.

5

From Dust I rise,
And out of Nothing now awake,

These Brighter Regions which salute mine Eys,
A Gift from God I take.
The Earth, the Seas, the Light, the Day, the Skies,
The Sun and Stars are mine; if those I prize. *30*

6

Long time before
I in my Mothers Womb was born,
A God preparing did this Glorious Store,
The World for me adorne.
Into this Eden so Divine and fair,
So Wide and Bright, I com his Son and Heir.

7

A Stranger here
Strange Things doth meet, Strange Glories See;
Strange Treasures lodg'd in this fair World appear,
Strange all, and New to me. *40*
But that they mine should be, who nothing was,
That Strangest is of all, yet brought to pass.

Wonder

1

How like an Angel came I down!
How Bright are all Things here!
When first among his Works I did appear
O how their Glory me did Crown?
The World resembled his *Eternitie*,
In which my Soul did Walk;
And evry Thing that I did see,
Did with me talk.

2

The Skies in their Magnificence,
The Lively, Lovely Air; *10*
Oh how Divine, how soft, how Sweet, how fair!
The Stars did entertain my Sence,
And all the Works of God so Bright and pure,
So Rich and Great did seem,
As if they ever must endure,
In my Esteem.

3

A Native Health and Innocence
Within my Bones did grow,
And while my God did all his Glories shew,
I felt a Vigour in my Sence 20
That was all Spirit. I within did flow
With Seas of Life, like Wine;
I nothing in the World did know,
But 'twas Divine.

4

Harsh ragged Objects were conceald,
Oppressions Tears and Cries,
Sins, Griefs, Complaints, Dissentions, Weeping Eys,
Were hid: and only Things reveald,
Which Heav'nly Spirits, and the Angels prize.
The State of Innocence 30
And Bliss, not Trades and Poverties,
Did fill my Sence.

5

The Streets were pavd with Golden Stones,
The Boys and Girles were mine,
Oh how did all their Lovly faces shine!
The Sons of Men were Holy Ones.
Joy, Beauty, Welfare did appear to me,
And evry Thing which here I found,
While like an Angel I did see,
Adornd the Ground. 40

6

Rich Diamond and Pearl and Gold
In evry Place was seen;
Rare Splendors, Yellow, Blew, Red, White and Green,
Mine Eys did evrywhere behold,
Great Wonders clothd with Glory did appear,
Amazement was my Bliss.
That and my Wealth was evry where:
No Joy to this!

7

Cursd and Devisd Proprieties,
With Envy, Avarice 50

And Fraud, those Feinds that Spoyl even Paradice,
Fled from the Splendor of mine Eys.
And so did Hedges, Ditches, Limits, Bounds,
I dreamd not ought of those,
But wanderd over all mens Grounds,
And found Repose.

8

Proprieties themselvs were mine,
And Hedges Ornaments;
Walls, Boxes, Coffers, and their rich Contents
Did not Divide my Joys, but shine. *60*
Clothes, Ribbans, Jewels, Laces, I esteemd
My Joys by others worn;
For me they all to wear them seemd
When I was born.

Eden

I

A learned and a Happy Ignorance
Divided me,
From all the Vanitie,
From all the Sloth Care Pain and Sorrow that advance,
The madness and the Miserie
Of Men. No Error, no Distraction I
Saw soil the Earth, or overcloud the Skie.

2

I knew not that there was a Serpents Sting,
Whose Poyson shed
On Men, did overspread *10*
The World: nor did I Dream of such a Thing
As Sin; in which Mankind lay Dead.
They all were Brisk and Living Weights to me,
Yea Pure, and full of Immortalitie.

3

Joy, Pleasure, Beauty, Kindness, Glory, Lov,
Sleep, Day, Life, Light,
Peace, Melody, my Sight,

My Ears and Heart did fill, and freely mov.
All that I saw did me Delight.
The *Universe* was then a World of Treasure, 20
To me an Universal World of Pleasure.

4

Unwelcom Penitence was then unknown,
Vain Costly Toys,
Swearing and Roaring Boys,
Shops, Markets, Taverns, Coaches were unshewn;
So all things were that Drownd my Joys.
No Thorns choakt up my Path, nor hid the face
Of Bliss and Beauty, nor Ecclypst the Place.

5

Only what Adam in his first Estate,
Did I behold; 30
Hard Silver and Drie Gold
As yet lay under Ground; my Blessed Fate
Was more acquainted with the Old
And Innocent Delights, which he did see
In his Original Simplicitie.

6

Those Things which first his Eden did adorn,
My Infancy
Did crown. Simplicitie
Was my Protection when I first was born.
Mine Eys those Treasures first did see, 40
Which God first made. The first Effects of Lov
My first Enjoyments upon Earth did prov;

7

And were so Great, and so Divine, so Pure,
So fair and Sweet,
So True; when I did meet
Them here at first, they did my Soul allure,
And drew away my Infant feet
Quite from the Works of Men; that I might see
The Glorious Wonders of the DEITIE.

The Rapture

1

Sweet Infancy!
O fire of Heaven! O Sacred Light!
How Fair and Bright!
How Great am I,
Whom all the World doth magnifie!

2

O Heavenly Joy!
O Great and Sacred Blessedness,
Which I possess!
So great a Joy
Who did into my Armes convey! *10*

3

From God abov
Being sent, the Heavens me enflame,
To prais his Name.
The Stars do move!
The Burning Sun doth shew his Love.

4

O how Divine
Am I! To all this Sacred Wealth,
This Life and Health,
Who raisd? Who mine
Did make the same? What Hand Divine! *20*

My Spirit

1

My Naked Simple Life was I.
That Act so Strongly Shind
Upon the Earth, the Sea, the Skie,
That was the Substance of My Mind.
The Sence it self was I.
I felt no Dross nor Matter in my Soul,
No Brims nor Borders, such as in a Bowl

We see, My Essence was Capacitie.
That felt all Things,
The Thought that Springs 10
Therfrom's it self. It hath no other Wings
To Spread abroad, nor Eys to see,
Nor Hands Distinct to feel,
Nor Knees to Kneel:
But being Simple like the Deitie
In its own Centre is a Sphere
Not shut up here, but evry Where.

2

It Acts not from a Centre to
Its Object as remote,
But present is, when it doth view, 20
Being with the Being it doth note.
Whatever it doth do,
It doth not by another Engine work,
But by it self; which in the Act doth lurk.
Its Essence is Transformd into a true
And perfect Act.
And so Exact
Hath God appeard in this Mysterious Fact,
That tis all Ey, all Act, all Sight,
And what it pleas can be, 30
Not only see,
Or do; for tis more Voluble then Light:
Which can put on ten thousand Forms,
Being clothd with what it self adorns.

3

This made me present evermore
With whatso ere I saw.
An Object, if it were before
My Ey, was by Dame Natures Law,
Within my Soul. Her Store
Was all at once within me; all her Treasures 40
Were my Immediat and Internal Pleasures,
Substantial Joys, which did inform my Mind.
With all she wrought,
My Soul was fraught,
And evry Object in my Soul a Thought
Begot, or was; I could not tell,

Whether the Things did there
Themselvs appear,
Which in my Spirit *truly* seemd to dwell;
Or whether my conforming Mind 50
Were not alone even all that shind.

4

But yet of this I was most sure,
That at the utmost Length,
(so Worthy was it to endure)
My Soul could best Express its Strength.
It was so Indivisible, and so Pure,
That all my Mind was wholy Evry where
What ere it saw, twas ever wholy there;
The Sun ten thousand Legions off, was nigh:
The utmost Star, 60
Tho seen from far,
Was present in the Apple of my Eye.
There was my Sight, my Life, my Sence,
My Substance and my Mind
My Spirit Shind
Even there, not by a Transeunt Influence.
The Act was Immanent, yet there.
The Thing remote, yet felt even here.

5

O Joy! O Wonder, and Delight!
O Sacred Mysterie! 70
My Soul a Spirit infinit!
An Image of the Deitie!
A pure Substantiall Light!
That Being Greatest which doth Nothing seem!
Why twas my All, I nothing did esteem
But that alone. A Strange Mysterious Sphere!
A Deep Abyss
That sees and is
The only Proper Place or Bower of Bliss.
To its Creator tis so near 80
In Lov and Excellence
In Life and Sence,
In Greatness Worth and Nature; And so Dear;
In it, without Hyperbole,
The Son and friend of God we see.

6

A Strange Extended Orb of Joy,
Proceeding from within,
Which did on evry side convey
It self, and being nigh of Kin
To God did evry Way 90
Dilate it self even in an Instant, and
Like an Indivisible Centre Stand
At once Surrounding all Eternitie.
Twas not a Sphere
Yet did appear
One infinit. Twas somwhat evry where.
And tho it had a Power to see
Far more, yet still it shind
And was a Mind
Exerted for it saw Infinitie 100
Twas not a Sphere, but twas a Power
Invisible, and yet a Bower.

7

O Wondrous Self! O Sphere of Light,
O Sphere of Joy most fair;
O Act, O Power infinit;
O Subtile, and unbounded Air!
O Living Orb of Sight!
Thou which within me art, yet Me! Thou Ey,
And Temple of his Whole Infinitie!
O what a World art Thou! a World within! 110
All Things appear,
All Objects are
Alive in thee! Supersubstancial, Rare,
Abov them selvs, and nigh of Kin
To those pure Things we find
In his Great Mind
Who made the World! tho now Ecclypsd by Sin.
There they are Usefull and Divine,
Exalted there they ought to Shine.

An Infant-Ey

A simple Light from all Contagion free,
A Beam that's purely Spiritual, an Ey

That's altogether Virgin, Things doth see
    Ev'n like unto the Deity:
That is, it shineth in an hevenly Sence,
And round about (unmov'd) its Light dispence.

The visiv Rays are Beams of Light indeed,
Refined, subtil, piercing, quick and pure;
And as they do the sprightly Winds exceed,
    Are worthy longer to endure: *10*
They far out-shoot the Reach of Grosser Air,
Which with such Excellence may not compare.

But being once debas'd, they soon becom
Less activ than they were before; and then
After distracting Objects out they run,
    Which make us wretched Men.
A simple Infant's Ey is such a Treasure
That when 'tis lost, w' enjoy no reall Pleasure.

O that my Sight had ever simple been!
And never faln into a grosser state! *20*
Then might I evry Object still have seen
    (As now I see a golden Plate)
In such an hev'nly Light, as to descry
In it, or by it, my Felicity.

As easily might soar aloft as mov
On Earth; and things remote as well as nigh
My Joys should be; and could discern the Lov
    Of God in my Tranquility.
But Streams are heavy which the Winds can blow;
Whose grosser body must needs move below. *30*

The *East* was once my Joy; and so the Skies
And Stars at first I thought; the West was mine:
Then Praises from the Mountains did arise
    As well as Vapors: Evry Vine
Did bear me Fruit; the Fields my Gardens were;
My larger Store-house all the Hemisphere.

But Wantonness and Avarice got in
And spoil'd my Wealth; (I never can complain
Enough, till I am purged from my Sin
    And made an Infant once again:) *40*

So that my feeble and disabled Sense
Reacht only Near Things with its Influence.

A House, a Woman's Hand, a piece of Gold,
A Feast, a costly Suit, a beauteous Skin
That vy'd with Ivory, I did behold;
And all my Pleasure was in Sin:
Who had at first with simple Infant-Eys
Beheld as mine ev'n all Eternities.

O dy! dy unto all that draws thine Ey
From its first Objects: let not fading Pleasures 50
Infect thy Mind; but see thou carefully
Bid them adieu. Return: Thy Treasures
Abide thee still, and in their places stand
Inviting yet, and waiting thy Command.

The Return

To Infancy, O Lord, again I com,
That I my Manhood may improv:
My early Tutor is the Womb;
I still my Cradle lov.
'Tis strange that I should Wisest be,
When least I could an Error see.

Till I gain strength against Temptation, I
Perceiv it safest to abide
An Infant still; and therfore fly
(A lowly State may hide 10
A man from Danger) to the Womb,
That I may yet New-born becom.

My God, thy Bounty then did ravish me!
Before I learned to be poor,
I always did thy Riches see,
And thankfully adore:
Thy Glory and thy Goodness were
My Sweet Companions all the Year.

News

News from a forein Country came,
As if my Treasures and my Joys lay there;
So much it did my Heart enflame,
'Twas wont to call my Soul into mine Ear;
Which thither went to meet
Th' approaching Sweet,
And on the Threshold stood
To entertain the secret Good;
It hover'd there
As if 'twould leav mine Ear, 10
And was so eager to embrace
Th' expected Tidings, as they came,
That it could change its dwelling-place
To meet the voice of Fame.

As if new Tidings were the Things
Which did comprise my wished unknown Treasure,
Or els did bear them on their wings,
With so much Joy they came, with so much Pleasure,
My Soul stood at the Gate
To recreäte 20
It self with Bliss, and woo
Its speedier Approach; a fuller view
It fain would take,
Yet Journeys back would make
Unto my Heart, as if 'twould fain
Go out to meet, yet stay within,
Fitting a place to entertain
And bring the Tidings in.

What Sacred Instinct did inspire
My Soul in Childhood with an hope so strong? 30
What secret Force mov'd my Desire
T' expect my Joys beyond the Seas, so yong?
Felicity I knew
Was out of view;
And being left alone,
I thought all Happiness was gon
From Earth: for this
I long'd-for absent Bliss,

Deeming that sure beyond the Seas,
Or els in somthing near at hand 40
Which I knew not, since nought did pleas
I knew, my Bliss did stand.

But little did the Infant dream
That all the Treasures of the World were by,
And that himself was so the Cream
And Crown of all which round about did ly.
Yet thus it was! The Gem,
The Diadem,
The Ring enclosing all
That stood upon this Earthen Ball; 50
The hev'nly Ey,
Much wider than the Sky,
Wherin they All included were;
The Lov, the Soul, that was the King
Made to possess them, did appear
A very little Thing.

Felicity

Prompted to seek my Bliss abov the Skies,
How often did I lift mine Eys
Beyond the Spheres!
Dame Nature told me there was endless Space
Within my Soul; I spy'd its very face:
Sure it not for nought appears.
What is there which a Man may see
Beyond the Spheres?
FELICITY.

There in the Mind of God, that Sphere of Lov, 10
(In nature, hight, extent, abov
All other Spheres,)
A Man may see Himself, the World, the Bride
Of God *His Church,* which as they there are ey'd
Strangely exalted each appears:
His Mind is higher than the Space
Above the Spheres,
Surmounts all Place.

No empty Space; it is all full of Sight,
    All Soul and Life, an Ey most bright, 20
        All Light and Lov;
Which doth at once all things possess and giv,
Heven and Earth, with All that therin liv;
    It rests at quiet, and doth mov;
    Eternal is, yet Time includes;
        A Scene abov
        All Interludes.

Shadows in the Water

In unexperienc'd Infancy
Many a sweet Mistake doth ly:
Mistake tho false, intending tru;
A *Seeming* somwhat more than *View;*
    That doth instruct the Mind
    In Things that ly behind,
And many Secrets to us show
Which afterwards we com to know.

Thus did I by the Water's brink
Another World beneath me think; 10
And while the lofty spacious Skies
Reversed there abus'd mine Eys,
    I fancy'd other Feet
    Came mine to touch and meet;
As by som Puddle I did play
Another World within it lay.

Beneath the Water Peeple drown'd.
Yet with another Hev'n crown'd,
In spacious Regions seem'd to go
Freely moving to and fro: 20
    In bright and open Space
    I saw their very face;
Eys, Hands, and Feet they had like mine;
Another Sun did with them shine.

'Twas strange that Peeple there should walk,
And yet I could not hear them talk:
That throu a little watry Chink,

Which one dry Ox or Horse might drink,
    We other Worlds should see,
    Yet not admitted be; *30*
And other Confines there behold
Of Light and Darkness, Heat and Cold.

I call'd them oft, but call'd in vain;
No Speeches we could entertain:
Yet did I there expect to find
Som other World, to pleas my Mind.
    I plainly saw by these
    A new *Antipodes*,
Whom, tho they were so plainly seen,
A Film kept off that stood between. *40*

By walking Men's reversed Feet
I chanc'd another World to meet;
Tho it did not to View exceed
A Phantasm, 'tis a World indeed,
    Where Skies beneath us shine,
    And Earth by Art divine
Another face presents below,
Where Peeple's feet against Ours go.

Within the Regions of the Air,
Compass'd about with Hev'ns fair, *50*
Great Tracts of Land there may be found
Enricht with Fields and fertil Ground;
    Where many num'rous Hosts,
    In those far distant Coasts,
For other great and glorious Ends,
Inhabit, my yet unknown Friends.

O ye that stand upon the Brink,
Whom I so near me, throu the Chink,
With Wonder see: What Faces there,
Whose Feet, whose Bodies, do ye wear? *60*
    I my Companions see
    In You, another Me.
They seemed Others, but are We;
Our second Selvs those Shadows be.

Look how far off those lower Skies
Extend themselvs! scarce with mine Eys

I can them reach. O ye my Friends,
What *Secret* borders on those Ends?
Are lofty Hevens hurl'd
'Bout your inferior World? 70
Are ye the Representatives
Of other Peopl's distant Lives?

Of all the Play-mates which I knew
That here I do the Image view
In other Selvs; what can it mean?
But that below the purling Stream
Som unknown Joys there be
Laid up in Store for me;
To which I shall, when that thin Skin
Is broken, be admitted in. 80

On Leaping over the Moon

I saw new Worlds beneath the Water ly,
New Peeple; and another Sky,
And Sun, which seen by Day
Might things more clear display.
Just such another
Of late my Brother
Did in his Travel see, and saw by Night
A much more strange and wondrous Sight:
Nor could the World exhibit such another,
So Great a Sight, but in a Brother. 10

Adventure strange! No such in Story we
New or old, tru or feigned, see.
On Earth he seem'd to mov
Yet Heven went abov;
Up in the Skies
His Body flies
In open, visible, yet Magick, sort:
As he along the Way did sport
Like Icarus over the Flood he soars
Without the help of Wings or Oars. 20

As he went tripping o'r the King's high-way,
A little pearly River lay

O'r which, without a Wing
Or Oar, he dar'd to swim,
Swim throu the Air
On Body fair;
He would not use nor trust *Icarian* Wings
Lest they should prov deceitful things;
For had he faln, it had been wondrous high,
Not from, but from abov, the Sky: 30

He might hav dropt throu that thin Element
Into a fathomless Descent;
Unto the nether Sky
That did beneath him ly,
And there might tell
What Wonders dwell
On Earth abov. Yet bold he briskly runs
And soon the Danger overcoms;
Who, as he leapt, with Joy related soon
How *happy he* o'r-leapt the Moon. 40

What wondrous things upon the Earth are don
Beneath, and yet abov, the Sun?
Deeds all appear again
In higher Spheres; remain
In Clouds as yet:
But there they get
Another Light, and in another way
Themselvs to us *abov* display.
The Skies themselves this earthly Globe surround;
W'are even here within them found. 50

On hev'nly Ground within the Skies we walk,
And in this middle Center talk:
Did we but wisely mov,
On Earth in Hev'n abov,
We then should be
Exalted high
Abov the Sky: from whence whoever falls,
Through a long dismall Precipice,
Sinks to the deep Abyss where *Satan* crawls
Where horrid Death and Despair lies. 60

As much as others thought themselvs to ly
Beneath the Moon, so much more high

Himself he thought to fly
Above the starry Sky,
As *that* he spy'd
Below the Tide.
Thus did he yield me in the shady Night
A wondrous and instructiv Light,
Which taught me that under our Feet there is
As o'r our Heads, a Place of Bliss. 70

"*To the same purpos; he, not long before*"

To the same purpos; he, not long before
Brought home from Nurse, went to the door
To do som little thing
He must not do within,
With Wonder cries,
As in the Skies
He saw the Moon, *O yonder is the Moon*
Newly com after me to Town,
That shin'd at Lugwardin but yesternight,
Where I enjoy'd the self-same Light. 10

As if it had ev'n twenty thousand faces,
It shines at once in many places;
To all the Earth so wide
God doth the Stars divide
With so much Art
The Moon impart,
They serve us all; serv wholy ev'ry One
As if they served him alone.
While evry single Person hath such Store,
'Tis want of Sense that makes us poor. 20

Consummation

The Thoughts of Men appear
Freely to mov within a Sphere
Of endless Reach; and run,

l.9 Lugwardin: a village near Hereford where Philip Traherne the younger may have been taken after the death of his parents.

Tho in the Soul, beyond the Sun.
The Ground on which they acted be
Is unobserv'd Infinity.

Extended throu the Sky,
Tho here, beyond it far they fly:
Abiding in the Mind
An endless Liberty they find: 10
Throu-out all Spaces can extend,
Nor ever meet or know an End.

They, in their native Sphere,
At boundless Distances appear:
Eternity can measure;
Its no Beginning see with Pleasure.
Thus in the Mind an endless Space
Doth nat'rally display its face.

Wherin becaus we no
Object distinctly find or know; 20
We sundry Things invent,
That may our Fancy giv content;
See Points of Space beyond the Sky,
And in those Points see Creatures ly.

Spy Fishes in the Seas,
Conceit them swimming there with Eas;
The Dolphins and the Whales,
Their very Finns, their very Scales,
As there within the briny Deep
Their Tails the flowing Waters sweep. 30

Can see the very Skies,
As if the same were in our Eys;
The Sun, tho in the Night,
As if it mov'd within our Sight;
One Space beyond another still
Discovered; think while ye will.

Which, tho we don't descry,
(Much like by night an Idle Ey,
Not shaded with a Lid,
But in a darksom Dungeon hid) 40

At last shall in a glorious Day
Be made its Objects to display

And then shall Ages be
Within its wide Eternity;
All Kingdoms stand,
Howe'r remote, yet nigh at hand;
The Skies, and what beyond them ly,
Exposed unto evry Ey.

Nor shall we then invent
Nor alter Things; but with content 50
All in their places see,
As doth the Glorious Deity;
Within the Scope of whose Great Mind,
We all in their tru Nature find.

Hosanna

No more shall Walls, no more shall Walls confine
That glorious Soul which in my Flesh doth shine:
No more shall Walls of Clay or Mud
Nor Ceilings made of Wood,
Nor Crystal Windows, bound my Sight,
But rather shall admit Delight.
The Skies that seem to bound
My Joys and Treasures,
Or more endearing Pleasures
Themselvs becom a Ground: 10
While from the Center to the utmost Sphere
My Goods are multiplied evry where.

The Deity, the Deity to me
Doth All things giv, and make me clearly see
The Moon and Stars, the Air and Sun
Into my Chamber com:
The Seas and Rivers hither flow,
Yea, here the Trees of *Eden* grow,
The Fowls and Fishes stand,
Kings and their Thrones, 20
As 'twere, at my Command;
God's Wealth, His Holy Ones,

The Ages too, and Angels all conspire:
While I, that I the Center am, admire.

No more, No more shall Clouds eclyps my Treasures,
Nor viler Shades obscure my highest Pleasures;
No more shall earthen Husks confine
My Blessings which do shine
Within the Skies, or els *abov:*
Both Worlds one Heven made by Lov, 30
In common happy I
With Angels walk
And there my Joys espy;
With God himself I talk;
Wondring with Ravishment all Things to see
Such *Reall* Joys, so truly *Mine,* to be.

No more shall Trunks & Dishes be my Store,
Nor Ropes of Pearl, nor Chains of Golden Ore;
As if such Beings yet were not,
They all shall be forgot. 40
No such in Eden did appear,
No such in Heven: Heven here
Would be, were those remov'd;
The Sons of Men
Liv in Jerusalem,
Had they not Baubles lov'd.
These Clouds dispers'd, the Hevens clear I see.
Wealth new-invented, *mine* shall never be.

Transcendent Objects doth my God provide,
In such convenient Order all contriv'd, 50
That All things in their proper place
My Soul doth best embrace,
Extends its Arms beyond the Seas,
Abov the Hevens its self can pleas,
With God enthron'd may reign:
Like sprightly Streams
My Thoughts on Things remain;
Or els like vital Beams
They reach to, shine on, quicken Things, and make
Them truly Usefull; while I *All* partake. 60

For Me the World created was by Lov;
For Me the Skies, the Seas, the Sun, do mov;

The Earth for Me doth stable stand;
For Me each fruitful Land
For Me the very Angels God made *His*
And *my* Companions in Bliss:
His Laws command all Men
That they lov Me,
Under a Penalty
Severe, in case they miss: 70
His Laws require His Creatures all to prais
His Name, and when they do't be most my Joys.

Amendment

1

That all things should be mine;
This makes his Bounty most Divine.
But that they all more Rich should be,
And far more Brightly shine,
As usd by Me:
It ravisheth my Soul to see the End,
To which this Work so Wonderfull doth tend.

2

That we should make the Skies
More Glorious far before thine Eys,
Then Thou didst make them, and even Thee 10
Far more thy Works to prize,
As usd they be,
Then as they're made; is a Stupendious Work,
Wherin thy Wisdom Mightily doth lurk.

3

Thy Greatness, and thy Love,
Thy Power, in this, my Joy doth move,
Thy Goodness and Felicitie,
In this Exprest abov
All Praise, I see:
While thy Great Godhead over all doth reign, 20
And such an End in such a sort attain.

4

What Bound may we Assign
O God to any Work of thine!

Their Endlessness discovers Thee
In all to be Divine;
A Deitie,
That wilt for evermore Exceed the End
Of all that Creatures Wit can comprehend.

5

Am I a Glorious Spring
Of Joys and Riches to my King? 30
Are Men made Gods! And may they see
So Wonderfull a Thing
As God in me!
And is my Soul a Mirror that must Shine
Even like the Sun, and be far more Divine?

6

Thy Soul, O God, doth prize
The Seas, the Earth, our Souls, the Skies,
As we return the same to Thee;
They more delight thine Eys,
And sweeter be, 40
As unto Thee we Offer up the same,
Then as to us, from Thee at first they came.

7

O how doth Sacred Lov
His Gifts refine, Exalt, Improve!
Our Love to Creatures makes them be
In thine Esteem above
Themselvs to Thee!
O here his Goodness evermore admire
He made our Souls to make his Creatures Higher.

Love

I

O Nectar! O Delicious Stream!
O ravishing and only Pleasure! Where
Shall such another Theme
Inspire my Tongue with Joys, or pleas mine Ear!
Abridgement of Delights!
And Queen of Sights!

O Mine of Rarities! O Kingdom Wide!
O more! O Caus of all! O Glorious Bride!
    O God! O Bride of God! O King!
    O Soul and Crown of evry Thing! *10*

2

    Did not I covet to behold
Som Endless Monarch, that did always live
        In Palaces of Gold
Willing all Kingdoms Realms and Crowns to give
        Unto my Soul! Whose Lov
            A Spring might prov
Of Endless Glories, Honors, friendships, Pleasures,
Joys, Praises, Beauties and Celestial Treasures!
    Lo, now I see there 's such a King,
    The fountain Head of evry Thing! *20*

3

    Did my Ambition ever Dream
Of such a Lord, of such a Love! Did I
        Expect so Sweet a Stream
As this at any time! Could any Ey
        Believ it? Why all Power
            Is used here
Joys down from Heaven on my Head to shower
And Jove beyond the Fiction doth appear
    Once more in Golden Rain to come.
    To Danae's Pleasing Fruitfull Womb. *30*

4

    His Ganimede! His Life! His Joy!
Or he comes down to me, or takes me up
        That I might be his Boy,
And fill, and taste, and give, and Drink the Cup.
        But these (tho great) are all
            Too short and small,
Too Weak and feeble Pictures to Express
The true Mysterious Depths of Blessedness.
    I am his Image, and his Friend.
    His Son, Bride, Glory, Temple, End. *40*

Richard Crashaw

Richard Crashaw was born in 1612 (or early 1613) in London, the son of William Crashaw, preacher at Temple Church, a learned man strongly disposed towards Puritanism and against Catholicism. By 1626, when William Crashaw died, Richard had already lost his mother and a beloved stepmother. He was left to the guardianship of the law. In 1629 he was admitted to the Charterhouse, and in 1631 to Pembroke College, Cambridge. In 1634 he received his B.A.; and in 1635 he was elected Fellow of Peterhouse, center of the Laudian movement in Cambridge. By 1639 he was ordained, and was appointed Curate and later Catechist to the Church of Little Saint Mary's, connected with the college. There he lived piously according to the rules of Little Gidding, the Anglican community with which he had been intimate since his first years at Cambridge. He left Cambridge in 1643, though he was not formally ejected by the Puritans until 1644.

In February 1643–44 he was in Leyden, in great spiritual distress. The next two years of his biography are uncertain. He may have returned to England; possibly he joined the Court at Oxford. By 1646 he had already been converted to Catholicism and had taken up residence in Paris, where he was familiar with the members of the exiled Court of Queen Henrietta Maria. Recommended to the Pope by the Queen, he set out for Rome in 1646. He waited a year, however, before being appointed to the retinue of the Cardinal Palotto. The Cardinal appointed him to a minor post at the Cathedral of Loreto, where

Crashaw remained the last few months of his life. He died on August 21, 1649.

The Epigrammatum Sacrorum Liber, *Crashaw's Latin epigrams, many of them written when he was probably very young, appeared in 1634.* Steps to the Temple, Sacred Poems, With Other Delights of the Muses *was published in 1646; the* Delights *contains his secular poems, most of them probably written before 1635. A second edition with changes and considerable additions was issued in 1648. In 1652,* Carmen Deo Nostro *was published in Paris; it consisted largely of the 1648 edition with some few but important additions.*

The text follows the Clarendon Press edition, prepared by L. C. Martin.

FROM

Steps to the Temple

from DIVINE EPIGRAMS

The sicke implore St. Peter's *shadow*

Under thy shadow may I lurke a while,
Death's busie search I'le easily beguile:
Thy shadow *Peter*, must shew me the Sun,
My light's thy shadowes shadow, or 'tis done.

To the Infant Martyrs

Goe smiling soules, your new built Cages breake,
In Heav'n you'l learne to sing ere here to speake,
Nor let the milky fonts that bath your thirst,
Bee your delay;
The place that calls you hence, is at the worst
Milke all the way.

Divine Epigrams: The epigrams, published in the 1646 edition of *Steps to the Temple*, are substantially English versions of some of the Latin epigrams published in the *Epigrammatum Sacrorum Liber* of 1634. Modelled on the Jesuit epigrams of the Counter-Reformation, they are less important in themselves than as indications of the witty style of Crashaw's later works.

To our Lord, upon the Water made Wine

Thou water turn'st to Wine (faire friend of Life)
Thy foe to crosse the sweet Arts of thy Reigne
Distills from thence the Teares of wrath and strife,
And so turnes wine to Water backe againe.

Upon our Saviours Tombe wherein never man was laid

How Life and Death in Thee
Agree?
Thou had'st a virgin Wombe
And Tombe.
A *Joseph* did betroth
Them both.

Sospetto d'Herode

LIBRO PRIMO

Argomento

Casting the times with their strong signes,
Death's Master his owne death divines.
Strugling for helpe, his best hope is
Herod's *suspition may heale his.*
Therefore he sends a fiend to wake
The sleeping Tyrant's fond mistake;
Who feares (in vaine) that he whose Birth
Meanes Heav'n, should meddle with his Earth.

Sospetto d'Herode: Crashaw's poem is a translation of the first canto of Marino's sacred epic *La Strage degli Innocenti* (1610) in four books on the theme of the Slaughter of the Innocents. Crashaw translated only the first of the four cantos of Marino's epic; in theme the canto is comparable to the consultation of the princes of Hell in Book II of *Paradise Lost.* Though Crashaw follows the facts of Marino's poem, in style he is already writing in his own voice. Mario Praz sees the poem as a "kind of apprenticeship for Crashaw." ("The Flaming Heart: Richard Crashaw and the Baroque," *The Flaming Heart*, Garden City, N.Y.: Anchor Books, 1958, p. 232.)

1

Muse, now the servant of soft Loves no more,
Hate is thy Theame, and *Herod,* whose unblest
Hand (ô what dares not jealous Greatnesse?) tore
A thousand sweet Babes from their Mothers Brest:
The Bloomes of Martyrdome. O be a Dore
Of language to my infant Lips, yee best
  Of Confessours: whose Throates answering his swords,
  Gave forth your Blood for breath, spoke soules for words.

2

Great *Anthony! Spains* well-beseeming pride,
Thou mighty branch of Emperours and Kings. 10
The Beauties of whose dawne what eye may bide,
Which with the Sun himselfe weigh's equall wings.
Mappe of Heroick worth! whom farre and wide
To the beleeving world Fame boldly sings:
  Deigne thou to weare this humble Wreath that bowes,
  To be the sacred Honour of thy Browes.

3

Nor needs my Muse a blush, or these bright Flowers
Other then what their owne blest beauties bring.
They were the smiling sons of those sweet Bowers,
That drinke the deaw of Life, whose deathlesse spring, 20
Nor *Sirian* flame, nor *Borean* frost deflowers:
From whence Heav'n-labouring Bees with busie wing,
  Suck hidden sweets, which well digested proves
  Immortall Hony for the Hive of Loves.

4

Thou, whose strong hand with so transcendent worth,
Holds high the reine of faire *Parthenope,*
That neither *Rome,* nor *Athens* can bring forth
A Name in noble deedes Rivall to thee!
Thy Fames full noise, makes proud the patient Earth,
Farre more then matter for my Muse and mee. 30
  The *Tyrrhene* Seas, and shores sound all the same,
  And in their murmures keepe thy mighty Name.

5

Below the Botome of the great Abysse,
There where one Center reconciles all things;

The worlds profound Heart pants; There placed is
Mischifes old Master, close about him clings
A curl'd knot of embracing Snakes, that kisse
His correspondent cheekes: these loathsome strings
  Hold the perverse Prince in eternall Ties
  Fast bound, since first he forfeited the skies, *40*

6

The Judge of Torments, and the King of Teares:
Hee fills a burnisht Throne of quenchlesse fire:
And for his old faire Roabes of Light, hee weares
A gloomy Mantle of darke flames, the Tire
That crownes his hated head on high appeares;
Where seav'n tall Hornes (his Empires pride) aspire.
  And to make up Hells Majesty, each Horne
  Seav'n crested *Hydra's* horribly adorne.

7

His Eyes, the sullen dens of Death and Night,
Startle the dull Ayre with a dismall red: *50*
Such his fell glances as the fatall Light
Of staring Comets, that looke Kingdomes dead.
From his black nostrills, and blew lips, in spight
Of Hells owne stinke, a worser stench is spread.
  His breath Hells lightning is: and each deepe grone
  Disdaines to thinke that Heav'n Thunders alone.

8

His flaming Eyes dire exhalation,
Unto a dreadfull pile gives fiery Breath;
Whose unconsum'd consumption preys upon
The never-dying Life, of a long Death. *60*
In this sad House of slow Destruction,
(His shop of flames) hee fryes himselfe, beneath
  A masse of woes, his Teeth for Torment gnash,
  While his steele sides sound with his Tayles strong lash.

9

Three Rigourous Virgins waiting still behind,
Assist the Throne of th' Iron-Sceptred King.
With whips of Thornes and knotty vipers twin'd
They rouse him, when his ranke Thoughts need a sting.
Their lockes are beds of uncomb'd snakes that wind
About their shady browes in wanton Rings. *70*

Thus reignes the wrathfull King, and while he reignes
His Scepter and himselfe both he disdaines.

10

Disdainefull wretch! how hath one bold sinne cost
Thee all the Beauties of thy once bright Eyes?
How hath one blacke Eclipse cancell'd, and crost
The glories that did guild thee in thy Rise?
Proud Morning of a perverse Day! how lost
Art thou unto thy selfe, thou too selfe-wise
Narcissus? foolish *Phaeton*? who for all
Thy high-aym'd hopes, gaind'st but a flaming fall. *80*

11

From Death's sad shades, to the Life-breathing Ayre,
This mortall Enemy to mankinds good,
Lifts his malignant Eyes, wasted with care,
To become beautifull in humane blood.
Where *Jordan* melts his Chrystall, to make faire
The fields of *Palestine*, with so pure a flood,
There does he fixe his Eyes: and there detect
New matter, to make good his great suspect.

12

He calls to mind th'old quarrell, and what sparke
Set the contending Sons of Heav'n on fire: *90*
Oft in his deepe thought he revolves the darke
Sibills divining leaves: hee does enquire
Into th'old Prophesies, trembling to marke
How many present prodigies conspire,
To crowne their past predictions, both hee layes
Together, in his pondrous mind both weighes.

13

Heavens Golden-winged Herald, late hee saw
To a poore *Galilean* virgin sent:
How low the Bright Youth bow'd, and with what awe
Immortall flowers to her faire hand present. *100*
Hee saw th'old *Hebrewes* wombe, neglect the Law
Of Age and Barennesse, and her Babe prevent
His Birth, by his Devotion, who began
Betimes to be a Saint, before a Man.

14

Hee saw rich Nectar thawes, release the rigour
Of th'Icy North, from frost-bount *Atlas* hands
His Adamantine fetters fall: greene vigour
Gladding the *Scythian* Rocks, and *Libian* sands.
Hee saw a vernall smile, sweetly disfigure
Winters sad face, and through the flowry lands 110
  Of faire *Engaddi* hony-sweating Fountaines
  With *Manna*, Milk, and Balm, new broach the Mountaines.

15

Hee saw how in that blest Day-bearing Night,
The Heav'n-rebuked shades made hast away;
How bright a Dawne of Angels with new Light
Amaz'd the midnight world, and made a Day
Of which the Morning knew not: Mad with spight
Hee markt how the poore Shepheards ran to pay
  Their simple Tribute to the Babe, whose Birth
  Was the great businesse both of Heav'n and Earth. 120

16

Hee saw a threefold Sun, with rich encrease,
Make proud the Ruby portalls of the East.
Hee saw the Temple sacred to sweet Peace,
Adore her Princes Birth, flat on her Brest.
Hee saw the falling Idols, all confesse
A comming Deity. Hee saw the Nest
  Of pois'nous and unnaturall loves, Earth-nurst;
  Toucht with the worlds true *Antidote* to burst.

17

He saw Heav'n blossome with a new-borne light,
On which, as on a glorious stranger gaz'd 130
The Golden eyes of Night: whose Beame made bright
The way to *Beth'lem*, and as boldly blaz'd,
(Nor askt leave of the Sun) by Day as Night.
By whom (as Heav'ns illustrious Hand-maid) rais'd
  Three Kings (or what is more) three Wise men went
  Westward to find the worlds true *Orient*.

18

Strucke with these great concurrences of things,
Symptomes so deadly, unto Death and him;

Faine would hee have forgot what fatall strings,
Eternally bind each rebellious limbe. *140*
Hee shooke himselfe, and spread his spatious wings:
Which like two Bosom'd sailes embrace the dimme
Aire, with a dismall shade, but all in vaine,
Of sturdy Adamant is his strong chaine.

19

While thus Heav'ns highest counsails, by the low
Footsteps of their Effects, hee trac'd too well,
Hee tost his troubled eyes, Embers that glow
Now with new Rage, and wax too hot for Hell.
With his foule clawes hee fenc'd his furrowed Brow,
And gave a gastly shreeke, whose horrid yell *150*
Ran trembling through the hollow vaults of Night,
The while his twisted Tayle hee gnaw'd for spight.

20

Yet on the other side, faine would he start
Above his feares, and thinke it cannot be.
Hee studies Scripture, strives to sound the heart,
And feele the pulse of every Prophecy.
Hee knowes (but knowes not how, or by what Art)
The Heav'n expecting Ages, hope to see
A mighty Babe, whose pure, unspotted Birth,
From a chast Virgin wombe, should blesse the Earth. *160*

21

But these vast Mysteries his senses smother,
And Reason (for what's Faith to him?) devoure.
How she that is a maid should prove a Mother,
Yet keepe inviolate her virgin flower;
How Gods eternall Sonne should be mans Brother,
Poseth his proudest Intellectuall power.
How a pure Spirit should incarnate bee,
And life it selfe weare Deaths fraile Livery.

22

That the Great Angell-blinding light should shrinke
His blaze, to shine in a poore Shepheards eye. *170*
That the unmeasur'd God so low should sinke,
As Pris'ner in a few poore Rags to lye.
That from his Mothers Brest hee milke should drinke,
Who feeds with Nectar Heav'ns faire family.

That a vile Manger his low Bed should prove,
Who in a Throne of stars Thunders above.

23

That hee whom the Sun serves, should faintly peepe
Through clouds of Infant flesh: that hee the old
Eternall Word should bee a Child, and weepe.
That hee who made the fire, should feare the cold; *180*
That Heav'ns high Majesty his Court should keepe
In a clay-cottage, by each blast control'd.
That Glories selfe should serve our Griefs, & feares:
And free Eternity, submit to yeares.

24

And further, that the Lawes eternall Giver,
Should bleed in his owne lawes obedience:
And to the circumcising Knife deliver
Himselfe, the forfeit of his slaves offence.
That the unblemisht Lambe, blessed for ever,
Should take the marke of sin, and paine of sence. *190*
These are the knotty Riddles, whose darke doubt
Intangles his lost Thoughts, past getting out.

25

While new Thoughts boyl'd in his enraged Brest,
His gloomy Bosomes darkest Character,
Was in his shady forehead seen exprest.
The forehead's shade in Griefes expression there,
Is what in signe of joy among the blest
The faces lightning, or a smile is here.
Those stings of care that his strong Heart opprest,
A desperate, *Oh mee,* drew from his deepe Brest. *200*

26

Oh mee! (thus bellow'd hee) *oh mee!* what great
Portents before mine eyes their Powers advance?
And serves my purer sight, onely to beat
Downe my proud Thought, and leave it in a Trance?
Frowne I; and can great Nature keep her seat?
And the gay starrs lead on their Golden dance?
Can his attempts above still prosp'rous be,
Auspicious still, in spight of Hell and me?

27

Hee has my Heaven (what would he more?) whose bright
And radiant Scepter this bold hand should beare. *210*
And for the never-fading fields of Light
My faire Inheritance, hee confines me here,
To this darke House of shades, horrour, and Night,
To draw a long-liv'd Death, where all my cheere
Is the solemnity my sorrow weares,
That Mankinds Torment waits upon my Teares.

28

Darke, dusty Man, he needs would single forth,
To make the partner of his owne pure ray:
And should we Powers of Heav'n, Spirits of worth
Bow our bright Heads, before a King of clay? *220*
It shall not be, said I, and clombe the *North,*
Where never wing of *Angell* yet made way
What though I mist my blow? yet I strooke high,
And to dare something, is some victory.

29

Is hee not satisfied? meanes he to wrest
Hell from me too, and sack my Territories?
Vile humane Nature means he now t'invest
(O my despight!) with his divinest Glories?
And rising with rich spoiles upon his Brest,
With his faire Triumphs fill all future stories? *230*
Must the bright armes of Heav'n, rebuke these eyes?
Mocke me, and dazle my darke Mysteries?

30

Art thou not *Lucifer*? hee to whom the droves
Of Stars, that guild the Morne in charge were given?
The nimblest of the lightning-winged Loves?
The fairest, and the first-borne smile of Heav'n?
Looke in what Pompe the Mistresse Planet moves
Rev'rently circled by the lesser seaven,
Such, and so rich, the flames that from thine eyes,
Oprest the common-people of the skyes. *240*

31

Ah wretch! what bootes thee to cast back thy eyes,
Where dawning hope no beame of comfort showes?

While the reflection of thy forepast joyes,
Renders thee double to thy present woes.
Rather make up to thy new miseries,
And meet the mischiefe that upon thee growes.
 If Hell must mourne, Heav'n sure shall sympathize
 What force cannot effect, fraud shall devise.

32

And yet whose force feare I? have I so lost
My selfe? my strength too with my innocence? *250*
Come try who dares, *Heav'n, Earth,* what ere dost boast,
A borrowed being, make thy bold defence.
Come thy Creator too, what though it cost
Mee yet a second fall? wee'd try our strengths.
 Heav'n saw us struggle once, as brave a fight
 Earth now should see, and tremble at the sight.

33

Thus spoke th'impatient Prince, and made a pause,
His foule Hags rais'd their heads, & clapt their hands.
And all the Powers of Hell in full applause
Flourisht their Snakes, and tost their flaming brands. *260*
Wee (said the horrid sisters) wait thy lawes,
Th'obsequious handmaids of thy high commands.
 Be it thy part, Hells mighty Lord, to lay
 On us thy dread commands, ours to obey.

34

What thy *Alecto*, what these hands can doe,
Thou mad'st bold proofe upon the brow of Heav'n,
Nor should'st thou bate in pride, because that now,
To these thy sooty Kingdomes thou art driven.
Let Heav'ns Lord chide above lowder then thou
In language of his Thunder, thou art even *270*
 With him below: here thou art Lord alone
 Boundlesse and absolute: Hell is thine owne.

35

If usuall wit, and strength will doe no good,
Vertues of stone, nor herbes: use stronger charmes,
Anger, and love, best hookes of humane blood.
If all faile wee'l put on our proudest Armes,
And pouring on Heav'ns face the Seas huge flood
Quench his curl'd fires, wee'l wake with our Alarmes

Ruine, where e're she sleepes at Natures feet;
And crush the world till his wide corners meet. 280

36

Reply'd the proud King, O my Crownes Defence?
Stay of my strong hopes, you of whose brave worth,
The frighted stars tooke faint experience,
When 'gainst the Thunders mouth wee marched forth:
Still you are prodigal of your Love's expence
In our great projects, both 'gainst Heav'n and Earth.
I thanke you all, but one must single out,
Cruelty, she alone shall cure my doubt.

37

Fourth of the cursed knot of Hags is shee,
Or rather all the other three in one; 290
Hells shop of slaughter shee do's oversee,
And still assist the Execution.
But chiefly there do's shee delight to be,
Where Hells capacious Cauldron is set on:
And while the black soules boile in their owne gore,
To hold them down, and looke that none seethe o're.

38

Thrice howl'd the Caves of Night, and thrice the sound,
Thundring upon the bankes of those black lakes
Rung, through the hollow vaults of Hell profound:
At last her listning Eares the noise o'retakes, 300
Shee lifts her sooty lampes, and looking round
A gen'rall hisse, from the whole Tire of snakes
Rebounding, through Hells inmost Cavernes came,
In answer to her formidable Name.

39

Mongst all the Palaces in Hells command,
No one so mercilesse as this of hers.
The Adamantine Doors, for ever stand
Impenetrable, both to prai'rs and Teares,
The walls inexorable steele, no hand
Of *Time*, or Teeth of hungry *Ruine* feares. 310
Their ugly ornaments are the bloody staines,
Of ragged limbs, torne sculls, & dasht out Braines.

40

There has the purple *Vengeance* a proud seat,
Whose ever-brandisht Sword is sheath'd in blood.
About her *Hate, Wrath, Warre,* and *Slaughter* sweat;
Bathing their hot limbs in life's pretious flood.
There rude impetuous Rage do's storme, and fret:
And there, as Master of this murd'ring brood,
  Swinging a huge Sith stands impartiall *Death.*
  With endlesse businesse almost out of Breath. *320*

41

For Hangings and for Curtaines, all along
The walls, (abominable ornaments!)
Are tooles of wrath, Anvills of Torments hung;
Fell Executioners of foule intents,
Nailes, hammers, hatchets sharpe, and halters strong,
Swords, Speares, with all the fatall Instruments
  Of sin, and Death, twice dipt in the dire staines
  Of Brothers mutuall blood, and Fathers braines.

42

The Tables furnisht with a cursed Feast,
Which *Harpyes,* with leane *Famine* feed upon, *330*
Unfill'd for ever. Here among the rest,
Inhumane *Erisi-cthon* too makes one;
Tantalus, Atreus, Progne, here are guests:
Wolvish *Lycaon* here a place hath won.
  The cup they drinke in is *Medusa's* scull,
  Which mixt with gall & blood they quaffe brim full.

43

The foule Queens most abhorred Maids of Honour
Medæa, Jezabell, many a meager Witch
With *Circe, Scylla,* stand to wait upon her.
But her best huswifes are the *Parcæ,* which *340*
Still worke for her, and have their wages from her.
They prick a bleeding heart at every stitch.
  Her cruell cloathes of costly threds they weave,
  Which short-cut lives of murdred *Infants* leave.

44

The house is hers'd about with a black wood,
Which nods with many a heavy headed tree.

Each flowers a pregnant poyson, try'd and good,
Each herbe a Plague. The winds sighes timed-bee
By a black Fount, which weeps into a flood.
Through the thick shades obscurely might you see 350
Minotaures, Cyclopses, with a darke drove
Of *Dragons, Hydraes, Sphinxes,* fill the Grove.

45

Here *Diomed's* Horses, *Phereus* dogs appeare,
With the fierce Lyons of *Therodamas.*
Busiris ha's his bloody Altar here,
Here *Sylla* his severest prison has.
The *Lestrigonians* here their Table reare;
Here strong *Procrustes* plants his Bed of Brasse.
Here cruell *Scyron* boasts his bloody rockes,
And hatefull *Schinis* his so feared Oakes. 360

46

What ever Schemes of Blood, fantastick frames
Of Death *Mezentius,* or *Geryon* drew;
Phalaris, Ochus, Ezelinus, names
Mighty in mischiefe, with dread *Nero* too,
Here are they all, Here all the swords or flames
Assyrian Tyrants, or *Egyptian* knew.
Such was the House, so furnisht was the Hall,
Whence the fourth *Fury,* answer'd *Pluto's* call.

47

Scarce to this Monster could the shady King,
The horrid summe of his intentions tell; 370
But shee (swift as the momentary wing
Of lightning, or the words he spoke) left Hell.
Shee rose, and with her to our world did bring,
Pale proofe of her fell presence. Th'aire too well
With a chang'd countenance witnest the sight,
And poore fowles intercepted in their flight.

48

Heav'n saw her rise, and saw Hell in the sight.
The field's faire Eyes saw her, and saw no more,
But shut their flowry lids for ever. Night,
And Winter strow her way; yet, such a sore 380
Is shee to Nature, that a generall fright,
An universall palsie spreading o're

The face of things, from her dire eyes had run,
Had not her thick Snakes hid them from the Sun.

49

Now had the Night's companion from her den,
Where all the busie day shee close doth ly,
With her soft wing, wipt from the browes of men
Day's sweat, and by a gentle Tyranny,
And sweet oppression, kindly cheating them
Of all their cares, tam'd the rebellious eye *390*
Of sorrow, with a soft and downy hand,
Sealing all brests in a *Lethæan* band.

50

When the *Erinnys* her black pineons spread,
And came to *Bethlem*, where the cruell King
Had now retyr'd himselfe, and borrowed
His Brest a while from care's unquiet sting.
Such as at *Thebes* dire feast shee shew'd her head,
Her sulphur-breathed Torches brandishing,
Such to the frighted Palace now shee comes,
And with soft feet searches the silent roomes. *400*

51

By *Herod* leige to Cesar now was borne
The Scepter, which of old great *David* swaid.
Whose right by *David's* linage so long worne,
Himselfe a stranger to, his owne had made:
And from the head of *Judahs* house quite torne
The Crowne, for which upon their necks he laid
A sad yoake, under which they sigh'd in vaine,
And looking on their lost state sigh'd againe.

52

Up, through the spatious Pallace passed she,
To where the Kings proudly-reposed head *410*
(If any can be soft to *Tyranny*
And selfe-tormenting sin) had a soft bed.
She thinkes not fit such he her face should see,
As it is seene by Hell; and seene with dread.
To change her faces stile she doth devise,
And in a pale Ghost's shape to spare his Eyes.

53

Her selfe a while she layes aside, and makes
Ready to personate a mortall part.
Joseph the Kings dead Brothers shape she takes,
What he by Nature was, is she by Art. 420
She comes toth' King and with her cold hand slakes
His Spirits, the Sparkes of Life, and chills his heart,
Lifes forge; fain'd is her voice, and false too, be
Her words, sleep'st thou fond man? sleep'st thou? (said she)

54

So sleeps a Pilot, whose poore Barke is prest
With many a mercylesse o're mastring wave;
For whom (as dead) the wrathfull winds contest,
Which of them deep'st shall digge her watry Grave.
Why dost thou let thy brave soule lye supprest,
In Death-like slumbers; while thy dangers crave 430
A waking eye and hand? looke up and see
The fates ripe, in their great conspiracy.

55

Know'st thou not how of th' Hebrewes royall stemme
(That old dry stocke) a despair'd branch is sprung
A most strange Babe! who here conceal'd by them
In a neglected stable lies, among
Beasts and base straw: Already is the streame
Quite turn'd: th' ingratefull Rebells this their young
Master (with voyce free as the Trumpe of *Fame*)
Their new King, and thy Successour proclaime. 440

56

What busy motions, what wild Engines stand
On tiptoe in their giddy Braynes? th' have fire
Already in their Bosomes; and their hand
Already reaches at a sword: They hire
Poysons to speed thee; yet through all the Land
What one comes to reveale what they conspire?
Goe now, make much of these; wage still their wars
And bring home on thy Brest more thanklesse scarrs.

57

Why did I spend my life, and spill my Blood,
That thy firme hand for ever might sustaine *450*
A well-pois'd Scepter? does it now seeme good
Thy Brothers blood be-spilt life spent in vaine?
'Gainst thy owne sons and Brothers thou hast stood
In Armes, when lesser cause was to complaine:
And now crosse Fates a watch about thee keepe,
Can'st thou be carelesse now? now can'st thou sleep?

58

Where art thou man? what cowardly mistake
Of thy great selfe, hath stolne King *Herod* from thee?
O call thy selfe home to thy selfe, wake, wake,
And fence the hanging sword Heav'n throws upon thee. *460*
Redeeme a worthy wrath, rouse thee, and shake
Thy selfe into a shape that may become thee.
Be *Herod*, and thou shalt not misse from mee
Immortall stings to thy great thoughts, and thee.

59

So said, her richest snake, which to her wrist
For a beseeming bracelet shee had ty'd
(A speciall Worme it was as ever kist
The foamy lips of *Cerberus*) shee apply'd
To the Kings Heart, the Snake no sooner hist,
But vertue heard it, and away shee hy'd, *470*
Dire flames diffuse themselves through every veine,
This done, Home to her Hell shee hy'd amaine.

60

Hee wakes, and with him (ne're to sleepe) new feares:
His Sweat-bedewed Bed had now betrai'd him,
To a vast field of thornes, ten thousand Speares
All pointed in his heart seem'd to invade him:
So mighty were th'amazing Characters
With which his feeling Dreame had thus dismay'd him,
Hee his owne fancy-framed foes defies:
In rage, *My armes, give me my armes,* hee cryes. *480*

61

As when a Pile of food-preparing fire,
The breath of artificiall lungs embraves,

The Caldron-prison'd waters streight conspire,
And beat the hot Brasse with rebellious waves:
He murmures, and rebukes their bold desire;
Th'impatient liquor, frets, and foames, and raves;
  Till his o'reflowing pride suppresse the flame,
  Whence all his high spirits, and hot courage came.

62

So boyles the fired *Herods* blood-swolne brest,
Not to be slakt but by a Sea of blood. 490
His faithlesse Crowne he feeles loose on his Crest,
Which on false Tyrants head ne're firmly stood.
The worme of jealous envy and unrest,
To which his gnaw'd heart is the growing food
  Makes him impatient of the lingring light.
  Hate the sweet peace of all-composing Night.

63

A Thousand Prophecies that talke strange things,
Had sowne of old these doubts in his deepe brest.
And now of late came tributary Kings,
Bringing him nothing but new feares from th'East, *500*
More deepe suspicions, and more deadly stings,
With which his feav'rous cares their cold increast.
  And now his dream (Hels firebrand) stil more bright,
  Shew'd him his feares, and kill'd him with the sight.

64

No sooner therefore shall the Morning see
(Night hangs yet heavy on the lids of Day)
But all his Counsellours must summon'd bee,
To meet their troubled Lord without delay.
Heralds and Messengers immediately
Are sent about, who poasting every way *510*
  To th'heads and Officers of every band;
  Declare who sends, and what is his command.

65

Why art thou troubled *Herod*? what vaine feare
Thy blood-revolving Brest to rage doth move?
Heavens King, who doffs himselfe weake flesh to weare,
Comes not to rule in wrath, but serve in love.
Nor would he this thy fear'd Crown from three Teare,
But give thee a better with himselfe above.

Poore jealousie! why should he wish to prey
Upon thy Crowne, who gives his owne away? *520*

66

Make to thy reason man; and mocke thy doubts,
Looke how below thy feares their causes are;
Thou art a Souldier *Herod;* send thy Scouts
See how hee's furnish't for so fear'd a warre.
What armour does he weare? A few thin clouts.
His Trumpets? tender cryes, his men to dare
So much? rude Shepheards. What his steeds? alas
Poore Beasts! a slow Oxe, and a simple Asse.

Il fine del libro primo

On Mr. G. Herberts Booke Intituled the Temple of Sacred Poems, Sent to a Gentlewoman

Know you faire, on what you looke;
Divinest love lyes in this booke:
Expecting fire from your eyes,
To kindle this his sacrifice.
When your hands unty these strings,
Thinke you have an Angell by th' wings.
One that gladly will bee nigh,
To waite upon each morning sigh.
To flutter in the balmy aire,
Of your well-perfumed prayer. *10*
These white plumes of his heele lend you,
Which every day to heaven will send you:
To take acquaintance of the *spheare*,
And all the smooth faced kindred there.
And though *Herberts* name doe owe
These devotions, fairest; know
That while I lay them on the shrine
Of your white hand, they are mine.

FROM

The Delights of the Muses

Musicks Duell

Now Westward *Sol* had spent the richest Beames
Of Noons high Glory, when hard by the streams
Of *Tiber,* on the sceane of a greene plat,
Under protection of an Oake; there sate
A sweet Lutes-master: in whose gentle aires
Hee lost the Dayes heat, and his owne hot cares.
  Close in the covert of the leaves there stood
A Nightingale, come from the neighbouring wood:
(The sweet inhabitant of each glad Tree,
Their Muse, their *Syren,* harmlesse *Syren* shee) *10*
There stood she listning, and did entertaine
The Musicks soft report: and mold the same
In her owne murmures, that what ever mood
His curious fingers lent, her voyce made good:
The man perceiv'd his Rivall, and her Art,
Dispos'd to give the light-foot Lady sport
Awakes his Lute, and 'gainst the fight to come
Informes it, in a sweet *Præludium*
Of closer straines, and ere the warre begin,
Hee lightly skirmishes on every string *20*
Charg'd with a flying touch: and streightway shee
Carves out her dainty voyce as readily,
Into a thousand sweet distinguish'd Tones,
And reckons up in soft divisions,
Quicke volumes of wild Notes; to let him know
By that shrill taste, shee could doe something too.
  His nimble hands instinct then taught each string
A capring cheerefullnesse; and made them sing

The Delights of the Muses: First published, with its own title, as part of *Steps to the Temple* of 1646.
Musicks Duell: The poem is a free translation of a Latin prolusion of the Jesuit *Famianus Strada;* Crashaw, however, uses only fourteen lines of his original. For an interesting devotional interpretation see William G. Madsen, "A Reading of 'Musicks Duell,'" *Studies in Honor of John Wilcox,* A. D. Wallace, W. D. Ross, eds. (Detroit: Wayne State University Press, 1958), pp. 39–50.

To their owne dance; now negligently rash
Hee throwes his Arme, and with a long drawne dash 30
Blends all together; then distinctly tripps
From this to that; then quicke returning skipps
And snatches this againe, and pauses there.
Shee measures every measure, every where
Meets art with art; sometimes as if in doubt
Not perfect yet, and fearing to bee out
Trayles her playne Ditty in one long-spun note,
Through the sleeke passage of her open throat:
A cleare unwrinckled song, then doth shee point it
With tender accents, and severely joynt it 40
By short diminutives, that being rear'd
In controverting warbles evenly shar'd,
With her sweet selfe shee wrangles; Hee amazed
That from so small a channell should be rais'd
The torrent of a voyce, whose melody
Could melt into such sweet variety
Straines higher yet; that tickled with rare art
The tatling strings (each breathing in his part)
Most kindly doe fall out; the grumbling Base
In surly groanes disdaines the Trebles Grace. 50
The high-perch't treble chirps at this, and chides,
Untill his finger (Moderatour) hides
And closes the sweet quarrell, rowsing all
Hoarce, shrill, at once; as when the Trumpets call
Hot Mars to th' Harvest of Deaths field, and woo
Mens hearts into their hands; this lesson too
Shee gives him backe; her supple Brest thrills out
Sharpe Aires, and staggers in a warbling doubt
Of dallying sweetnesse, hovers ore her skill,
And folds in wav'd notes with a trembling bill, 60
The plyant Series of her slippery song.
Then starts shee suddenly into a Throng
Of short thicke sobs, whose thundring volleyes float,
And roule themselves over her lubricke throat
In panting murmurs, still'd out of her Breast
That ever-bubling spring; the sugred Nest
Of her delicious soule, that there does lye
Bathing in streames of liquid Melodie;
Musicks best seed-plot, whence in ripend Aires
A Golden-headed Harvest fairely reares 70
His Honey-dropping tops, plow'd by her breath
Which there reciprocally laboureth

In that sweet soyle. It seemes a holy quire
Founded to th' Name of great *Apollo's* lyre
Whose sylver-roofe rings with the sprightly notes
Of sweet-lipp'd Angell-Imps, that swill their throats
In creame of Morning *Helicon*, and then
Preferre soft Anthems to the Eares of men,
To woo them from their Beds, still murmuring
That men can sleepe while they their Mattens sing: 80
(Most divine service) whose so early lay,
Prevents the Eye-lidds of the blushing day.
There might you heare her kindle her soft voyce
In the close murmur of a sparkling noyse.
And lay the ground-worke of her hopefull song,
Still keeping in the forward streame, so long
Till a sweet whirle-wind (striving to gett out)
Heaves her soft Bosome, wanders round about,
And makes a pretty Earthquake in her Breast,
Till the fledg'd Notes at length forsake their Nest; 90
Fluttering in wanton shoales, and to the Sky
Wing'd with their owne wild Eccho's pratling fly.
Shee opes the floodgate, and lets loose a Tide
Of streaming sweetnesse, which in state doth ride
On the wav'd backe of every swelling straine,
Rising and falling in a pompous traine.
And while shee thus discharges a shrill peale
Of flashing Aires; shee qualifies their zeale
With the coole Epode of a graver Noat,
Thus high, thus low, as if her silver throat 100
Would reach the brasen voyce of warr's hoarce Bird;
Her little soule is ravisht: and so pour'd
Into loose extasies, that shee is plac't
Above her selfe, Musicks *Enthusiast*.
  Shame now and anger mixt a double staine
In the Musitians face; yet once againe
(Mistresse) I come; now reach a straine my Lute
Above her mocke, or bee for ever mute.
Or tune a song of victory to mee,
Or to thy selfe, sing thine owne Obsequie; 110
So said, his hands sprightly as fire hee flings,
And with a quavering coynesse tasts the strings.
The sweet-lip't sisters musically frighted,
Singing their feares are fearfully delighted.
Trembling as when *Appollo's* golden haires
Are fan'd and frizled, in the wanton ayres

Of his owne breath: which marryed to his lyre
Doth tune the *Sphæares*, and make Heavens selfe looke
higher.
From this to that, from that to this hee flyes
Feeles Musicks pulse in all her Arteryes, *120*
Caught in a net which there *Appollo* spreads,
His fingers struggle with the vocall threads,
Following those little rills, hee sinkes into
A Sea of *Helicon;* his hand does goe
Those parts of sweetnesse which with *Nectar* drop,
Softer then that which pants in *Hebe's* cup.
The humourous strings expound his learned touch,
By various Glosses; now they seeme to grutch,
And murmur in a buzzing dinne, then gingle
In shrill tongu'd accents: striving to bee single. *130*
Every smooth turne, every delicious stroake
Gives life to some new Grace; thus doth h'invoke
Sweetnesse by all her Names; thus, bravely thus
(Fraught with a fury so harmonious)
The Lutes light *Genius* now does proudly rise,
Heav'd on the surges of swolne Rapsodyes.
Whose flourish (Meteor-like) doth curle the aire
With flash of high-borne fancyes: here and there
Dancing in lofty measures, and anon
Creeps on the soft touch of a tender tone: *140*
Whose trembling murmurs melting in wild aires
Runs to and fro, complaining his sweet cares
Because those pretious mysteryes that dwell,
In musick's ravish't soule hee dare not tell,
But whisper to the world: thus doe they vary
Each string his Note, as if they meant to carry
Their Masters blest soule (snatcht out at his Eares
By a strong Extasy) through all the sphæares
Of Musicks heaven; and seat it there on high
In th' *Empyræum* of pure Harmony. *150*
At length (after so long, so loud a strife
Of all the strings, still breathing the best life
Of blest variety attending on
His fingers fairest revolution
In many a sweet rise, many as sweet a fall)
A full-mouth *Diapason* swallowes all.
This done, hee lists what shee would say to this,
And shee although her Breath's late exercise
Had dealt too roughly with her tender throate,

Yet summons all her sweet powers for a Noate 160
Alas! in vaine! for while (sweet soule) shee tryes
To measure all those wild diversities
Of chatt'ring stringes, by the small size of one
Poore simple voyce, rais'd in a Naturall Tone;
Shee failes, and failing grieves, and grieving dyes.
Shee dyes; and leaves her life the Victors prise,
Falling upon his Lute; ô fit to have
(That liv'd so sweetly) dead, so sweet a Grave!

Wishes
To his (supposed) Mistresse

Who ere shee bee,
That not impossible shee
That shall command my heart and mee;

Where ere shee lye,
Lock't up from mortall Eye,
In shady leaves of Destiny:

Till that ripe Birth
Of studied fate stand forth,
And teach her faire steps to our Earth;

Till that Divine 10
Idæa, take a shrine
Of Chrystall flesh, through which to shine:

Meet you her my wishes,
Bespeake her to my blisses,
And bee yee call'd my absent kisses.

I wish her Beauty,
That owes not all his Duty
To gaudy Tire, or glistring shoo-ty.

Something more than
Taffata or Tissew can, 20
Or rampant feather, or rich fan.

More then the spoyle
Of shop, or silkewormes Toyle
Or a bought blush, or a set smile.

A face thats best
By its owne beauty drest,
And can alone commend the rest.

A face made up
Out of no other shop,
Then what natures white hand sets ope. *30*

A cheeke where Youth,
And Blood, with Pen of Truth
Write, what the Reader sweetly ru'th.

A Cheeke where growes
More then a Morning Rose:
Which to no Boxe his being owes.

Lipps, where all Day
A lovers kisse may play,
Yet carry nothing thence away.

Lookes that oppresse *40*
Their richest Tires but dresse
And cloath their simplest Nakednesse.

Eyes, that displaces
The Neighbour Diamond, and out faces
That Sunshine by their owne sweet Graces.

Tresses that weare
Jewells, but to declare
How much themselves more pretious are.

Whose native Ray,
Can tame the wanton Day *50*
Of Gems, that in their bright shades play.

Each Ruby there,
Or Pearle that dare appeare,
Bee its owne blush, bee its owne Teare.

A well tam'd Heart,
For whose more noble smart,
Love may bee long chusing a Dart.

Eyes, that bestow
Full quivers on loves Bow;
Yet pay lesse Arrowes then they owe. 60

Smiles, that can warme
The blood, yet teach a charme,
That Chastity shall take no harme.

Blushes, that bin
The burnish of no sin,
Nor flames of ought too hot within.

Joyes, that confesse,
Vertue their Mistresse,
And have no other head to dresse.

Feares, fond and flight, 70
As the coy Brides, when Night
First does the longing lover right.

Teares, quickly fled,
And vaine, as those are shed
For a dying Maydenhead.

Dayes, that need borrow,
No part of their good Morrow,
From a fore spent night of sorrow.

Dayes, that in spight
Of Darkenesse, by the Light 80
Of a cleere mind are Day all Night.

Nights, sweet as they,
Made short by lovers play,
Yet long by th'absence of the Day.

Life, that dares send
A challenge to his end,
And when it comes say *Welcome Friend.*

Sydnæan showers
Of sweet discourse, whose powers
Can Crowne old Winters head with flowers, *90*

Soft silken Houres,
Open sunnes; shady Bowers,
Bove all; Nothing within that lowres.

What ere Delight
Can make Dayes forehead bright;
Or give Downe to the Wings of Night.

In her whole frame,
Have Nature all the Name,
Art and ornament the shame.

Her flattery, *100*
Picture and Poesy,
Her counsell her owne vertue bee.

I wish, her store
Of worth, may leave her poore
Of wishes; And I wish—No more.

Now if Time knowes
That her whose radiant Browes,
Weave them a Garland of my vowes;

Her whose just Bayes,
My future hopes can raise, *110*
A trophie to her present praise;

Her that dares bee,
What these Lines wish to see:
I seeke no further, it is shee.

'Tis shee, and heere
Lo I uncloath and cleare,
My wishes cloudy Character.

May shee enjoy it,
Whose merit dare apply it,
But Modesty dares still deny it. *120*

Such worth as this is,
Shall fixe my flying wishes,
And determine them to kisses.

Let her full Glory,
My fancyes, fly before yee,
Bee ye my fictions; But her story.

FROM

Carmen Deo Nostro

To The Name Above Every Name, The Name of Jesus
A Hymn

I Sing the NAME which None can say
But touch't with An interiour RAY:
The Name of our New PEACE; our Good:
Our Blisse: & Supernaturall Blood:
The Name of All our Lives & Loves.
Hearken, And Help, ye holy Doves!
The high-born Brood of Day; you bright
Candidates of blissefull Light,
The HEIRS Elect of Love; whose Names belong
Unto The everlasting life of Song; *10*
All ye wise SOULES, who in the wealthy Brest
Of This unbounded NAME build your warm Nest.
Awake, My glory. SOUL, (if such thou be,
And That fair WORD at all referr to Thee)
    Awake & sing
    And be All Wing;

Carmen Deo Nostro, Te Decet Hymnus, Sacred Poems Collected, Corrected: published in Paris in 1652. The poems following represent both considerably enlarged versions of earlier originals and some new poems.
To The Name . . . A Hymn: This poem was first published in 1648 under the title "On the name of Jesus." For an interesting analysis of the poem as a meditation, see Louis Martz, *The Poetry of Meditation* (New Haven: Yale University Press, 1954), Appendix I: "Thus it appears that in this poem the art of meditation has provided the fundamental unity of structure necessary to control the daring adventures of the baroque imagination."

Bring hither thy whole SELF; & let me see
What of thy Parent HEAVN yet speakes in thee.
O thou art Poore
Of noble POWRES, I see, *20*
And full of nothing else but empty ME,
Narrow, & low, & infinitely lesse
Then this GREAT mornings mighty Busynes.
One little WORLD or two
(Alas) will never doe.
We must have store.
Goe, SOUL, out of thy Self, & seek for More.
Goe & request
Great NATURE for the KEY of her huge Chest
Of Heavns, the self involving Sett of Sphears *30*
(Which dull mortality more Feeles then heares)
Then rouse the nest
Of nimble ART, & traverse round
The Aiery Shop of soul-appeasing Sound:
And beat a summons in the Same
All-soveraign Name
To warn each severall kind
And shape of sweetnes, Be they such
As sigh with supple wind
Or answer Artfull Touch, *40*
That they convene & come away
To wait at the love-crowned Doores of
This Illustrious DAY.
Shall we dare This, my Soul? we'l doe't and bring
No Other note for't, but the Name we sing
Wake LUTE & HARP
And every sweet-lipp't Thing
That talkes with tunefull string;
Start into life, And leap with me
Into a hasty Fitt-tun'd Harmony. *50*
Nor must you think it much
T'obey my bolder touch;
I have Authority in LOVE's name to take you
And to the worke of Love this morning wake you
Wake; In the Name
Of HIM who never sleeps, All Things that Are,
Or, what's the same,
Are Musicall;
Answer my Call
And come along; *60*

Help me to meditate mine Immortall Song.
Come, ye soft ministers of sweet sad mirth,
Bring All your houshold stuffe of Heavn on earth;
O you, my Soul's most certain Wings,
Complaining Pipes, & prattling Strings,
  Bring All the Store
Of SWEETS you have; And murmur that you have no
    more.
  Come, nere to part,
  NATURE & ART!
  Come; & come strong, 70
To the conspiracy of our Spatious song.
  Bring All the Powres of Praise
Your Provinces of well-united WORLDS can raise;
Bring All your LUTES & HARPS of HEAVN & EARTH;
What e're cooperates to The comon mirthe
  Vessells of vocall Joyes,
Or You, more noble Architects of Intellectuall Noise,
Cymballs of Heav'n, or Humane sphears,
Solliciters of SOULES or EARES;
  And when you'are come, with All 80
That you can bring or we can call;
  O may you fix
  For ever here, & mix
  Your selves into the long
And everlasting series of a deathlesse SONG;
Mix All your many WORLDS, Above,
And loose them into ONE of Love,
  Chear thee my HEART!
  For Thou too hast thy Part
  And Place in the Great Throng 90
Of This unbounded All-imbracing SONG.
  Powres of my Soul, be Proud!
  And speake lowd
To All the dear-bought Nations This Redeeming Name,
And in the wealth of one Rich WORD proclaim
New Similes to Nature.
  May it be no wrong
Blest Heavns, to you, & your Superiour song,
That we, dark Sons of Dust & Sorrow,
  A while Dare borrow 100
The Name of Your Delights & our Desires,
And fitt it to so farr inferior LYRES.
Our Murmurs have their Musick too,

Ye mighty ORBES, as well as you,
    Nor yeilds the noblest Nest
Of warbling SERAPHIM to the eares of LOVE,
A choicer Lesson then the joyfull BREST
    Of a poor panting Turtle-Dove.
And we, low Wormes have leave to doe
The Same bright Busynes (ye Third HEAVENS) with
        you. *110*
Gentle SPIRITS, doe not complain.
    We will have care
    To keep it fair,
And send it back to you again.
Come, lovely NAME! Appeare from forth the Bright
    Regions of peacefull Light
Look from thine own Illustrious Home,
Fair KING of NAMES, & come.
Leave All thy native Glories in their Gorgeous Nest,
And give thy Self a while The gracious Guest *120*
Of humble Soules, that seek to find
    The hidden Sweets
    Which man's heart meets
When Thou art Master of the Mind.
Come, lovely Name; life of our hope!
Lo we hold our HEARTS wide ope!
Unlock thy Cabinet of DAY
Dearest Sweet, & come away.
    Lo how the thirsty Lands
Gasp for thy Golden Showres! with long stretch't
        Hands *130*
    Lo how the laboring EARTH
    That hopes to be
    All Heaven by THEE,
    Leapes at thy Birth.
The'attending WORLD, to wait thy Rise,
    First turn'd to eyes;
And then, not knowing what to doe;
Turn'd Them to TEARES, & spent Them too.
Come ROYALL Name, & pay the expence
Of All this Pretious Patience. *140*
    O come away
And kill the DEATH of This Delay.
O see, so many WORLDS of barren yeares
Melted & measur'd out in Seas of TEARES.
O see, The WEARY liddes of wakefull Hope

(Love's Eastern windowes) All wide ope
With Curtains drawn,
To catch The Day-break of Thy Dawn.
O dawn, at last, long look't for Day!
Take thine own wings, & come away. *150*
Lo, where Aloft it comes! It comes, Among
The Conduct of Adoring Spirits, that throng
Like diligent Bees, And swarm about it.
O they are wise;
And know what Sweetes are suck't from out it.
It is the Hive,
By which they thrive,
Where All their Hoard of Hony lyes.
Lo where it comes, upon The snowy Dove's
Soft Back; And brings a Bosom big with Loves. *160*
Welcome to our dark world, Thou
Womb of Day!
Unfold thy fair Conceptions; And display
The Birth of our Bright Joyes.
O thou compacted
Body of Blessings: spirit of Soules extracted!
O dissipate thy spicy Powres
(Clowd of condensed sweets) & break upon us
In balmy showrs;
O fill our senses, And take from us *170*
All force of so Prophane a Fallacy
To think ought sweet but that which smells of Thee.
Fair, flowry Name; In none but Thee
And Thy Nectareall Fragrancy,
Hourly there meetes
An universall Synod of All sweets;
By whom it is defined Thus
That no Perfume
For ever shall presume
To passe for Odoriferous, *180*
But such alone whose sacred Pedigree
Can prove it Self some kin (sweet name) to Thee.
Sweet Name, in Thy each Syllable
A Thousand Blest Arabias dwell;
A Thousand Hills of Frankincense;
Mountains of myrrh, & Beds of spices,
And ten Thousand Paradises
The soul that tasts thee takes from thence.
How many unknown Worlds there are

O Comforts, which Thou hast in keeping! *190*
How many Thousand Mercyes there
In Pitty's soft lap ly a sleeping!
Happy he who has the art
    To awake them,
    And to take them
Home, & lodge them in his HEART.
O that it were as it was wont to be!
When thy old Freinds of Fire, All full of Thee,
Fought against Frowns with smiles; gave Glorious
        chase
To Persecutions; And against the Face *200*
Of DEATH & feircest Dangers, durst with Brave
And sober pace march on to meet A GRAVE.
On their Bold BRESTS about the world they bore thee
And to the Teeth of Hell stood up to teach thee,
In Center of their inmost Soules they wore thee,
Where Rackes & Torments striv'd, in vain, to reach
        thee.
    Little, alas, thought They
Who tore the Fair Brests of thy Freinds,
    Their Fury but made way
For Thee; And serv'd therein Thy glorious ends. *210*
What did Their weapons but with wider pores
Inlarge thy flaming-brested Lovers
    More freely to transpire
    That impatient Fire
The Heart that hides Thee hardly covers.
What did their Weapons but sett wide the Doores
For Thee: Fair, purple Doores, of love's devising;
The Ruby windowes which inrich't the EAST
Of Thy so oft repeated Rising.
Each wound of Theirs was Thy new Morning; *220*
And reinthron'd thee in thy Rosy Nest,
With blush of thine own Blood thy day adorning,
It was the witt of love o'reflowd the Bounds
Of WRATH, & made thee way through All Those
        WOUNDS.
Wellcome dear, All-Adored Name!
    For sure there is no Knee
    That knowes not THEE
Or if there be such sonns of shame,
    Alas what will they doe
    When stubborn Rocks shall bow *230*

And Hills hang down their Heavn-saluting Heads
To seek for humble Beds
Of Dust, where in the Bashfull shades of night
Next to their own low NOTHING they may ly,
And couch before the dazeling light of thy dread
majesty.
They that by Love's mild Dictate now
Will not adore thee,
Shall Then with just Confusion, bow
And break before thee.

In The Holy Nativity of Our Lord God a Hymn Sung as by the Shepheards

THE HYMN

Chorus

Come we shepheards whose blest Sight
Hath mett love's Noon in Nature's night;
Come lift we up our loftyer Song
And wake the SUN that lyes too long.

To all our world of well-stoln joy
He slept; and dream't of no such thing.
While we found out Heavn's fairer ey
And kis't the Cradle of our KING.
Tell him He rises now, too late
To show us ought worth looking at. *10*

Tell him we now can show Him more
Then He e're show'd to mortall Sight;
Then he Himselfe e're saw before;
Which to be seen needes not His light.
Tell him, Tityrus, where th'hast been
Tell him, Thyrsis, what th'hast seen.

Tityrus. Gloomy night embrac't the Place
Where The Noble Infant lay.

In The Holy . . . Shepheards: **This poem when first published in 1646 as "A Hymne of the Nativity" lacked the choric repetitions of the later version.**

The BABE look't up and shew'd his Face;
 In spite of Darknes, it was DAY. 20
It was THY day, SWEET! and did rise
Not from the EAST, but from thine EYES.

Chorus It was THY day, Sweet

Thyrs. WINTER chidde aloud; and sent
 The angry North to wage his warres.
The North forgott his feirce Intent;
 And left perfumes in stead of scarres.
By those sweet eyes' persuasive powrs
Where he mean't frost, he scatter'd flowrs.

Chorus By those sweet eyes' 30

Both. We saw thee in thy baulmy Nest,
 Young dawn of our æternall DAY!
We saw thine eyes break from their EASTE
 And chase the trembling shades away.
We saw thee; and we blest the sight
We saw thee by thine own sweet light.

Tity. Poor WORLD (said I.) what wilt thou doe
 To entertain this starry STRANGER?
Is this the best thou can'st bestow?
 A cold, and not too cleanly, manger? 40
Contend, ye powres of heav'n and earth.
To fitt a bed for this huge birthe.

Chorus Contend ye powers

Thyr. Proud world, said I; cease your contest
 And let the MIGHTY BABE alone.
The Phænix builds the Phænix's nest.
 Love's architecture is his own.
The BABE whose birth embraves this morn.
Made his own bed e're he was born.

Chorus The BABE whose.

Tit. I saw the curl'd drops, soft and slow,
 Come hovering o're the place's head;

Offring their whitest sheets of snow
  To furnish the fair INFANT's bed
Forbear, said I; be not too bold.
Your fleece is white But t'is too cold.

Chorus Forbear, sayd I

Thyr. I saw the obsequious SERAPHIMS
  Their rosy fleece of fire bestow.
For well they now can spare their wings 60
  Since HEAVN itself lyes here below.
Well done, said I: but are your sure
Your down so warm, will passe for pure?

Chorus Well done sayd I

Tit. No no. your King's not yet to seeke
  Where to repose his Royall HEAD
See see, how soon his new-bloom'd CHEEK
  Twixt's mother's brests is gone to bed.
Sweet choise, said we! no way but so
Not to ly cold, yet sleep in snow. 70

Chorus Sweet choise, said we.

Both. We saw thee in thy baulmy nest,
  Bright dawn of our æternall Day!
We saw thine eyes break from their EAST
  And chase the trembling shades away.
We saw thee: and we blest the sight.
We saw thee, by thine own sweet light.

Chorus We saw thee, etc.

Full Chorus

Wellcome, all WONDERS in one sight!
  Æternity shutt in a span. 80
Sommer in Winter. Day in Night.
  Heaven in earth, and GOD in MAN.
Great little one! whose all-embracing birth
Lifts earth to heaven, stoopes heav'n to earth.

WELLCOME. Though nor to gold nor silk.
  To more than Caesar's birthright is;

Two sister-seas of Virgin-Milk,
 With many a rarely-temper'd kisse
That breathes at once both MAID and MOTHER,
Warmes in the one, cooles in the other. 90

WELLCOME, though not to those gay flyes.
 Guilded ith' Beames of earthly kings;
Slippery soules in smiling eyes;
 But to poor Shepheards, home-spun things:
Whose Wealth's their flock, whose witt, to be
 Well read in their simplicity.
Yet when young April's husband showrs
 Shall blesse the fruitfull Maja's bed
We'l bring the First-born of her flowrs
 To kisse thy FEET and crown thy HEAD. 100
To thee, dread lamb! whose love must keep
 The shepheards, more then they the sheep.
To THEE, meek Majesty! soft KING
 Of simple GRACES and sweet LOVES.
Each of us his lamb will bring
 Each his pair of sylver Doves;
Till burnt at last in fire of Thy fair eyes,
 Our selves become our own best SACRIFICE.

In The Glorious Epiphanie of Our Lord God, a Hymn Sung as by The Three Kings

(1. KINGE)

Bright BABE! Whose awfull beautyes make
The morn incurr a sweet mistake;
(2.) For whom the'officious heavns devise
To disinheritt the sun's rise,
(3.) Delicately to displace
The Day, & plant it fairer in thy face;
[1.] O thou born KING of loves,
 [2.] Of lights,
 [3.] Of joyes!

In The Glorious . . . Kings: Originally published in 1648 with some variations as "A Hymne for the Epiphanie." For a careful analysis of the hymn as a definition of the *via negativa*, based on Dionysius, see Ruth Wallerstein, *Richard Crashaw* (Madison: University of Wisconsin Press, 1959), pp. 143 ff.

(*Cho.*) Look up, sweet BABE, look up & see 10
For love of Thee
Thus farr from home
The EAST is come
To seek her self in thy sweet Eyes
(1.) We, who strangely went astray,
Lost in a bright
Meridian night,
(2.) A Darkenes made of too much day,
(3.) Becken'd from farr
By thy fair starr, 20
Lo at last have found our way.
(*Cho.*) To THEE, thou DAY of night! thou east of west!
Lo we at last have found the way.
To thee, the world's great universal east.
The Generall & indifferent DAY.
(1.) All-circling point. All centring sphear.
The world's one, round, Æternall year.
(2.) Whose full & all-unwrinkled face
Nor sinks nor swells with time or place;
(3.) But every where & every while 30
Is One Consistent solid smile;
(1.) Not vext & tost
(2.) 'Twixt spring & frost,
(3.) Nor by alternate shredds of light
Sordidly shifting hands with shades & night.
(*Cho.*) O little all! in thy embrace
The world lyes warm, & likes his place.
Nor does his full Globe fail to be
Kist on Both his cheeks by Thee.
Time is too narrow for thy YEAR 40
Nor makes the whole WORLD thy half-sphear.
(1.) To Thee, to Thee
From him we flee
(2.) From HIM, whom by a more illustrious ly,
The blindnes of the world did call the eye;
(3.) To HIM, who by These mortall clouds hast made
Thy self our sun, though thine own shade.
(1.) Farewell, the world's false light.
Farewell, the white
Ægypt! a long farewell to thee 50
Bright IDOL; black IDOLATRY.
The dire face of interior DARKNES, kis't

And courted in the pompous mask of a more specious
mist.
(2.) Farewell, farewell
The proud & misplac't gates of hell,
Pertch't, in the morning's way
And double-guilded as the doores of DAY.
The deep hypocrisy of DEATH & NIGHT
More desperately dark, Because more bright.
(3.) Welcome, the world's sure Way! *60*
HEAVN's wholsom ray.
(*Cho.*) Wellcome to us; and we
(SWEET) to our selves, in THEE.
(1.) The deathles HEIR of all thy FATHER's day!
(2.) Decently Born.
Embosom'd in a much more Rosy MORN,
The Blushes of thy All-unblemish't mother.
(3.) No more that other
Aurora shall sett ope
Her ruby casements, or hereafter hope *70*
From mortall eyes
To meet Religious welcomes at her rise.
(*Cho.*) We (Pretious ones!) in you have won
A gentler MORN, a juster sun.
(1.) His superficiall Beames sun-burn't our skin;
(2.) But left within
(3.) The night & winter still of death & sin.
(*Cho.*) Thy softer yet more certaine DARTS
Spare our eyes, but peirce our HARTS.
(1.) Therefore with His proud persian spoiles *80*
(2.) We court thy more concerning smiles.
(3.) Therfore with his Disgrace
We guild the humble cheek of this chast place;
(*Cho.*) And at thy FEET powr forth his FACE.
(1.) The doating nations now no more
Shall any day but THINE adore.
(2.) Nor (much lesse) shall they leave these eyes
For cheap Ægyptian Deityes.
(3.) In whatsoe're more Sacred shape *90*
Of Ram, He-goat, or reverend ape,
Those beauteous ravishers opprest so sore
The too-hard-tempted nations.
(1.) Never more
By wanton heyfer shall be worn

(2.) A Garland, or a guilded horn.
The altar-stall'd ox, fatt OSYRIS now
With his fair sister cow,
(3.) Shall kick the clouds no more; But lean & tame,
(*Cho.*) See his horn'd face, & dy for shame. *100*
And MITHRA now shall be no name.
(1.) No longer shall the immodest lust
Of Adulterous GODLES dust
(2.) Fly in the face of heav'n; As if it were
The poor world's Fault that he is fair.
(3.) Nor with perverse loves & Religious RAPES
Revenge thy Bountyes in their beauteous shapes;
And punish Best Things worst; Because they stood
Guilty of being much for them too Good.
[1.] Proud sons of death! that durst compell *110*
Heav'n it self to find them hell;
[2.] And by strange witt of madnes wrest
From this world's EAST the other's WEST.
[3.] All-Idolizing wormes! that thus could crowd
And urge Their sun into thy cloud;
Forcing his sometimes eclips'd face to be
A long deliquium to the light of thee.
[*Cho.*] Alas with how much heavyer shade
The shamefac't lamp hung down his head
For that one eclipse he made *120*
Then all those he suffered!
[1.] For this he look't so bigg; & every morn
With a red face confes't this scorn.
Or hiding his vex't cheeks in a hir'd mist
Kept them from being so unkindly kis't.
[2.] It was for this the day did rise
So oft with blubber'd eyes.
For this the evening wept; and we ne're knew
But call'd it deaw.
[3.] This dayly wrong *130*
Silenc't the morning-sons, & damp't their song
[*Cho.*] Nor was't our deafnes, but our sins, that thus
Long made th'Harmonious orbes all mute to us
[1.] Time has a day in store
When this so proudly poor
And self-oppressed spark, that has so long
By the love-sick world bin made
Not so much their sun as SHADE,
Weary of this Glorious wrong

From them & from himself shall flee *140*
For shelter to the shadow of thy TREE;
[*Cho.*] Proud to have gain'd this pretious losse
And chang'd his false crown for thy CROSSE.
[2.] That dark Day's clear doom shall define
Whose is the Master FIRE, which sun should shine.
That sable Judgment-seat shall by new lawes
Decide & settle the Great cause
Of controverted light,
[*Cho.*] And natur's wrongs rejoyce to doe thee Right.
[3.] That forfeiture of noon to night shall pay *150*
All the idolatrous thefts done by this night of day;
And the Great Penitent presse his own pale lipps
With an elaborate love-eclipse
To which the low world's lawes
Shall lend no cause
[*Cho.*] Save those domestick which he borrowes
From our sins & his own sorrowes.
[1.] Three sad hour's sackcloth then shall show to us
His penance, as our fault, conspicuous.
[2.] And he more needfully & nobly prove *160*
The nation's terror now then erst their love.
[3.] Their hated loves changd into wholsom feares,
[*Cho.*] The shutting of his eye shall open Theirs.
[1.] As by a fair-ey'd fallacy of day
Miss-ledde before they lost their way,
So shall they, by the seasonable fright
Of an unseasonable night,
Loosing it once again, stumble'on true LIGHT
[2.] And as before his too-bright eye
Was Their more blind idolatry, *170*
So his officious blindnes now shall be
Their black, but faithfull perspective of thee;
[3.] His new prodigious night,
Their new & admirable light;
The supernaturall DAWN of Thy pure day.
While wondring they
(The happy converts now of him
Whom they compell'd before to be their sin)
Shall henceforth see
To kisse him only as their rod *180*
Whom they so long courted as GOD,
[*Cho.*] And their best use of him they worship't be
To learn of Him at lest, to worship Thee.

[1.] It was their Weaknes woo'd his beauty;
But it shall be
Their wisdome now, as well as duty,
To'injoy his Blott; & as a large black letter
Use it to spell Thy beautyes better;
And make the night it self their torch to thee.
[2.] By the oblique ambush of this close night 190
Couch't in that conscious shade
The right-ey'd Areopagite
Shall with a vigorous guesse invade
And catche thy quick reflex; and sharply see
On this dark Ground
To descant THEE.
[3.] O prize of the rich SPIRIT! with what feirce chase
Of his strong soul, shall he
Leap at thy lofty FACE,
And seize the swift Flash in rebound 200
From this obsequious cloud;
Once call'd a sun;
Till dearly thus undone,
[*Cho.*] Till thus triumphantly tam'd (o ye two
Twinne SUNNES!) & taught now to negotiate you.
[1.] Thus shall that reverend child of light,
[2.] By being scholler first of that new night,
Come forth Great master of the mystick day;
[3.] And teach obscure MANKIND a more close way
By the frugall negative light 210
Of a most wise & well-abused Night
To read more legible thine originall Ray,
[*Cho.*] And make our Darknes serve THY day;
Maintaining t'wixt thy world & ours
A commerce of contrary powres,
A mutuall trade
'Twixt sun & SHADE,
By confederat BLACK & WHITE
Borrowing day & lending night.
[1.] Thus we, who when with all the noble powres 220
That (at thy cost) are call'd, not vainly, ours
We vow to make brave way
Upwards, & presse on for the pure intelligentiall Prey;
[2.] At lest to play
The amorous Spyes
And peep & proffer at thy sparkling Throne;

[3.] In stead of bringing in the blissfull PRIZE
And fastening on Thine eyes,
Forfeit our own
And nothing gain 230
But more Ambitious losse, at lest of brain;
[*Cho.*] Now by abased liddes shall learn to be
Eagles; and shutt our eyes that we may see.

The Close.

Therfore to THEE & thine Auspitious ray
(Dread sweet!) lo thus
At lest by us,
The delegated EYE of DAY
Does first his Scepter, then HIMSELF in solemne Tribute pay.
Thus he undresses
His sacred unshorn tresses; 240
At thy adored FEET, thus, he layes down
[1.] His gorgeous tire
Of flame & fire,
[2.] His glittering ROBE, [3.] his sparkling CROWN,
[1.] His GOLD, [2.] his MIRRH, [3.] his FRANKINCENCE,
[*Cho.*] To which He now has no pretence.
For being show'd by this day's light, how farr
He is from sun enough to make THY starr,
His best ambition now, is but to be
Somthing a bright SHADOW [sweet] of thee. 250
Or on heavn's azure forhead high to stand
Thy golden index; with a duteous Hand
Pointing us Home to our own sun
The world's & his HYPERION.

Sainte Mary Magdalene or The Weeper

Loe where a WOUNDED HEART with Bleeding EYES conspire.
Is she a FLAMING Fountain or a Weeping fire!

Sainte . . . Weeper: With some variations, the poem was first published in 1646 as "The Weeper." For a commentary on the poem see Mario Praz, pp. 218–232.

I

Hail, sister springs!
Parents of sylver-footed rills!
Ever bubling things!
Thawing crystall! snowy hills,
Still spending, never spent! I mean
Thy fair eyes, sweet MAGDALENE!

II

Heavens thy fair eyes be;
Heavens of ever-falling starres.
'Tis seed-time still with thee
And starres thou sow'st, whose harvest
dares 10
Promise the earth to counter shine
Whatever makes heavn's forhead fine.

III

But we'are deceived all.
Starres indeed they are too true;
For they but seem to fall,
As Heavn's other spangles doe.
It is not for our earth & us
To shine in Things so pretious.

IV

Upwards thou dost weep.
Heavn's bosome drinks the gentle stream. 20
Where th'milky rivers creep,
Thine floates above; & is the cream.
Waters above th' Heavns, what they be
We' are taught best by thy TEARES & thee.

V

Every morn from hence
A brisk Cherub somthing sippes
Whose sacred influence
Addes sweetnes to his sweetest Lippes.
Then to his musick. And his song
Tasts of this Breakfast all day long. 30

VI

Not in the evening's eyes
When they Red with weeping are
For the Sun that dyes,
Sitts sorrow with a face so fair,
No where but here did ever meet
Sweetnesse so sad, sadnesse so sweet.

VII

When sorrow would be seen
In her brightest majesty
(For she is a Queen)
Then is she drest by none but thee. *40*
Then, & only then, she weares
Her proudest pearles; I mean, thy TEARES.

VIII

The deaw no more will weep
The primrose's pale cheek to deck,
The deaw no more will sleep
Nuzzel'd in the lilly's neck;
Much reather would it be thy TEAR,
And leave them Both to tremble here.

IX

There's no need at all
That the balsom-sweating bough *50*
So coyly should let fall
His med'cinable teares; for now
Nature hath learn't to'extract a deaw
More soveraign & sweet from you.

X

Yet let the poore drops weep
(Weeping is the ease of woe)
Softly let them creep,
Sad that they are vanquish't so.
They, though to others no releife,
Balsom maybe, for their own greife. *60*

XI

Such the maiden gemme
By the purpling vine put on,

Peeps from her parent stemme
And blushes at the bridegroome sun.
This watry Blossom of thy eyn,
Ripe, will make the richer wine.

XII

When some new bright Guest
Takes up among the starres a room,
And Heavn will make a feast,
Angels with crystall violls come 70
And draw from these full eyes of thine
Their master's Water: their own Wine.

XIII

Golden though he be,
Golden Tagus murmures tho;
Were his way by thee,
Content & quiet he would goe.
So much more rich would he esteem
Thy sylver, then his golden stream.

XIV

Well does the May that lyes
Smiling in thy cheeks, confesse 80
The April in thine eyes.
Mutuall sweetnesse they expresse.
No April ere lent kinder showres,
Nor May return'd more faithfull flowres.

XV

O cheeks! Bedds of chast loves
By your own showres seasonably dash't
Eyes! nests of milky doves
In your own wells decently washt,
O wit of love! that thus could place
Fountain & Garden in one face. 90

XVI

O sweet Contest; of woes
With loves, of teares with smiles disputing!
O fair, & Freindly Foes,
Each other kissing & confuting!
While rain & sunshine, Cheekes & Eyes
Close in kind contrarietyes.

XVII

But can these fair Flouds be
Freinds with the bosom fires that fill thee
Can so great flames agree
Æternall Teares should thus distill thee! *100*
O flouds, o fires! o suns ô showres!
Mixt & made freinds by love's sweet powres.

XVIII

Twas his well-pointed dart
That digg'd these wells, & drest this Vine;
And taught the wounded HEART
The way into these weeping Eyn.
Vain loves avant! bold hands forbear!
The lamb hath dipp't his white foot here.

XIX

And now where're he strayes,
Among the Galilean mountaines, *110*
Or more unwellcome wayes,
He's follow'd by two faithfull fountaines;
Two walking baths; two weeping motions;
Portable, & compendious oceans.

XX

O Thou, thy lord's fair store!
In thy so rich & rare expenses,
Even when he show'd most poor,
He might provoke the wealth of Princes.
What Prince's wanton'st pride e're could
Wash with Sylver, wipe with Gold. *120*

XXI

Who is that King, but he
Who calls't his Crown to be call'd thine,
That thus can boast to be
Waited on by a wandring mine,
A voluntary mint, that strowes
Warm sylver shoures where're he goes!

XXII

O pretious Prodigall!
Fair spend-thrift of thy self! thy measure

(Mercilesse love!) is all.
Even to the last Pearle in thy treasure. *130*
All places, Times, & objects be
Thy teare's sweet opportunity.

XXIII

Does the day-starre rise?
Still thy starres doe fall & fall
Does day close his eyes?
Still the FOUNTAIN weeps for all.
Let night or day doe what they will,
Thou hast thy task; thou weepest still.

XXIV

Does thy song lull the air?
Thy falling teares keep faith full time. *140*
Does thy sweet-breath'd praire
Up in clouds of incense climb?
Still at each sigh, that is, each stop,
A bead, that is, A TEAR, does drop.

XXV

At these thy weeping gates,
(Watching their watry motion)
Each winged moment waits,
Takes his TEAR, & gets him gone.
By thine Ey's tinct enobled thus
Time layes him up; he's pretious. *150*

XXVI

Not, so long she lived,
Shall thy tomb report of thee;
But, so long she grieved,
Thus must we date thy memory.
Others by moments, months, & yeares
Measure their ages; thou, by TEARES.

XXVII

So doe perfumes expire.
So sigh tormented sweets, opprest
With proud unpittying fire.
Such Teares the suffring Rose that's vext *160*
With ungentle flames does shed,
Sweating in a too warm bed.

XXVIII

Say, ye bright brothers,
The fugitive sons of those fair Eyes
Your fruitfull mothers!
What make you here? what hopes can tice
You to be born? what cause can borrow
You from Those nests of noble sorrow?

XXIX

Whither away so fast?
For sure the sordid earth *170*
Your Sweetnes cannot tast
Nor does the dust deserve your birth.
Sweet, whither hast you then? o say
Why you trip so fast away?

XXX

We goe not to seek,
The darlings of Auroras bed,
The rose's modest Cheek
Nor the violet's humble head.
Though the Feild's eyes too WEEPERS be
Because they want such TEARES as we. *180*

XXXI

Much lesse mean we to trace
The Fortune of inferior gemmes,
Preferr'd to some proud face
Or pertch't upon fear'd Diadems.
Crown'd Heads are toyes. We goe to meet
A worthy object, our lord's FEET.

A Hymn to The Name and Honor of The Admirable Sainte Teresa, Foundresse of the Reformation of the Discalced Carmelites, both men & Women; A Woman for Angelicall heigth of speculation, for Masculine courage of performance, more than a woman.
who
Yet a child, out ran maturity, and durst plott a Martyrdome;

THE HYMNE

Love, thou art Absolute sole lord
Of Life & Death. To prove the word,
Wee'l now appeal to none of all
Those thy old Souldiers, Great & tall,
Ripe Men of Martyrdom, that could reach down
With strong armes, their triumphant crown;
Such as could with lusty breath
Speak lowd into the face of death
Their Great Lord's glorious name, to none
Of those whose spatious Bosomes spread a throne *10*
For Love at larg to fill: spare blood & sweat;
And see him take a private seat,
Making his mansion in the mild
And milky soul of a soft child.
  Scarse has she learn't to lisp the name
Of Martyr; yet she thinks it shame
Life should so long play with that breath
Which spent can buy so brave a death.
She never undertook to know
What death with love should have to doe; *20*
Nor has she e're yet understood
Why to show love, she should shed blood
Yet though she cannot tell you why,
She can Love, & she can Dy.
  Scarse has she Blood enough to make
A guilty sword blush for her sake;
Yet has she'a Heart dares hope to prove

A Hymn . . . Teresa: Originally published in 1646 as "In memory of the Vertuous and Learned Lady Madre de Teresa that sought an early Martyrdome."

How much lesse strong is DEATH then LOVE.
Be love but there; let poor six yeares
Be pos'd with the maturest Feares *30*
Man trembles at, you straight shall find
LOVE knowes no nonage, nor the MIND.
'Tis LOVE, not YEARES or LIMBS that can
Make the Martyr, or the man.
LOVE touch't her HEART, & lo it beates
High, & burnes with such brave heates;
Such thirsts to dy, as dares drink up,
A thousand cold deaths in one cup.
Good reason. For she breathes All fire.
Her weake brest heaves with strong desire *40*
Of what she may with fruitles wishes
Seek for amongst her MOTHER's kisses.
Since 'tis not to be had at home
She'l travail to a Martyrdom.
No home for hers confesses she
But where she may a Martyr be.
She'l to the Moores; And trade with them,
For this unvalued Diadem.
She'l offer them her dearest Breath,
With CHRIST's Name in't, in change for death. *50*
Sh'el bargain with them; & will give
Them GOD; teach them how to live
In him: or, if they this deny,
For him she'l teach them how to DY.
So shall she leave amongst them sown
Her LORD's Blood; or at lest her own.
FAREWEL then, all the world! Adieu.
TERESA is no more for you.
Farewell, all pleasures, sports, & joyes,
(Never till now esteemed toyes) *60*
Farewell what ever deare may bee,
MOTHER's armes or FATHER's knee
Farewell house, & farewell home!
SHE's for the Moores, & MARTYRDOM.
SWEET, not so fast! lo thy fair Spouse
Whom thou seekst with so swift vowes,
Calls thee back, & bidds thee come
T'embrace a milder MARTYRDOM.
Blest powres forbid, Thy tender life
Should bleed upon a barborous knife; *70*
Or some base hand have power to race

Thy Brest's chast cabinet, & uncase
A soul kept there so sweet, ô no;
Wise heavn will never have it so
THOU art love's victime; & must dy
A death more mysticall & high.
Into love's armes thou shalt let fall
A still-surviving funerall.
His is the DART must make the DEATH
Whose stroke shall tast thy hallow'd breath; *80*
A Dart thrice dip't in that rich flame
Which writes thy spouse's radiant Name
Upon the roof of Heav'n; where ay
It shines, & with a soveraign ray
Beates bright upon the burning faces
Of soules which in that name's sweet graces
Find everlasting smiles. So rare,
So spirituall, pure, & fair
Must be th'immortall instrument
Upon whose choice point shall be sent *90*
A life so lov'd; And that there be
Fitt executioners for Thee,
The fair'st & first-born sons of fire
Blest SERAPHIM, shall leave their quire
And turn love's souldiers, upon THEE
To exercise their archerie.
O how oft shalt thou complain
Of a sweet & subtle PAIN.
Of intolerable JOYES;
Of a DEATH, in which who dyes *100*
Loves his death, and dyes again.
And would for ever so be slain.
And lives, & dyes; and knowes not why
To live, But that he thus may never leave to DY.
How kindly will thy gentle HEART
Kisse the sweetly-killing DART!
And close in his embraces keep
Those delicious Wounds, that weep
Balsom to heal themselves with. Thus
When These thy DEATHS, so numerous, *110*
Shall all at last dy into one,
And melt thy Soul's sweet mansion;
Like a soft lump of incense, hasted
By too hott a fire, & wasted
Into perfuming clouds, so fast

Shalt thou exhale to Heavn at last
In a resolving SIGH, and then
O what? Ask not the Tongues of men.
Angells cannot tell, suffice,
Thy selfe shall feel thine own full joyes *120*
And hold them fast for ever. There
So soon as thou shalt first appear,
The MOON of maiden starrs, thy white
MISTRESSE, attended by such bright
Soules as thy shining self, shall come
And in her first rankes make thee room;
Where 'mongst her snowy family
Immortall wellcomes wait for thee.
O what delight, when reveal'd LIFE shall stand
And teach thy lipps heav'n with his hand; *130*
On which thou now maist to thy wishes
Heap up thy consecrated kisses.
What joyes shall seize thy soul, when she
Bending her blessed eyes on thee
(Those second Smiles of Heav'n) shall dart
Her mild rayes through thy melting heart!
Angels, thy old freinds, there shall greet thee
Glad at their own home now to meet thee.
All thy good WORKES which went before
And waited for thee, at the door, *140*
Shall own thee there; and all in one
Weave a constellation
Of CROWNS, with which the KING thy spouse
Shall build up thy triumphant browes.
All thy old woes shall now smile on thee
And thy paines sitt bright upon thee
All thy sorrows here shall shine,
All thy SUFFRINGS be divine.
TEARES shall take comfort, & turn gemms
And WRONGS repent to Diademms. *150*
Ev'n thy DEATHS shall live; & new
Dresse the soul that erst they slew.
Thy wounds shall blush to such bright scarres
As keep account of the LAMB's warres.
Those rare WORKES where thou shalt leave writt,
Love's noble history, with witt
Taught thee by none but him, while here
They feed our soules, shall cloth THINE there.
Each heavnly word by whose hid flame

Our hard Hearts shall strike fire, the same 160
Shall flourish on thy browes. & be
Both fire to us & flame to thee;
Whose light shall live bright in thy FACE
By glory, in our hearts by grace.
Thou shalt look round about, & see
Thousands of crown'd Soules throng to be
Themselves thy crown. Sons of thy vowes
The virgin-births with which thy soveraign spouse
Made fruitfull thy fair soul, goe now
And with them all about thee bow 170
To Him, put on (hee'l say) put on
(My rosy love) That thy rich zone
Sparkling with the sacred flames
Of thousand soules, whose happy names
Heav'n keeps upon thy score. (Thy bright
Life brought them first to kisse the light
That kindled them to starrs.) and so
Thou with the LAMB, thy lord, shalt goe;
And whereso'ere he setts his white
Stepps, walk with HIM those wayes of light 180
Which who in death would live to see,
Must learn in life to dy like thee.

An Apologie for The Fore-going Hymne as having been writt when the author was yet among the protestantes.

Thus have I back again to thy bright name
(Fair floud of holy fires!) transfus'd the flame
I took from reading thee, tis to thy wrong
I know, that in my weak & worthlesse song
Thou here art sett to shine where thy full day
Scarse dawnes. O pardon if I dare to say

An Apologie . . . Hymne: Originally published in 1646 under the title "An Apologie for the precedent Hymne." Crashaw's changing titles are indicative of his changing religious convictions and the freedom that publication in Paris gave him.

Thine own dear bookes are guilty. For from thence
I learn't to know that love is eloquence.
That hopefull maxime gave me hart to try
If, what to other tongues is tun'd so high, *10*
Thy praise might not speak English too; forbid
(By all thy mysteryes that here ly hidde)
Forbid it, mighty Love! let no fond Hate
Of names & wordes, so farr præjudicate.
Souls are not SPANIARDS too, one freindly floud
Of BAPTISM blends them all into a blood.
CHRIST'S faith makes but one body of all soules
And love's that body's soul, no law controwlls
Our free traffique for heav'n, we may maintaine
Peace, sure, with piety, though it come from SPAIN. *20*
What soul so e're, in any language, can
Speak heav'n like her's is my souls country-man.
O 'tis not spanish, but 'tis heav'n she speaks!
'Tis heav'n that lyes in ambush there, & breaks
From thence into the wondring reader's brest;
Who feels his warm HEART hatch'd into a nest
Of little EAGLES & young loves, whose high
Flights scorn the lazy dust, & things that dy.
There are enow, whose draughts (as deep as hell)
Drink up al SPAIN in sack. Let my soul swell *30*
With thee, strong wine of love! let others swimme
In puddles; we will pledge this SERAPHIM
Bowles full of richer blood then blush of grape
Was ever guilty of, Change we too 'our shape
(My soul,) Some drink from men to beasts, o then
Drink we till we prove more, not lesse, then men,
And turn not beasts, but Angels. Let the king
Me ever into these his cellars bring
Where flowes such wine as we can have of none
But HIM who trod the wine-presse all alone *40*
Wine of youth, life, & the sweet Deaths of love;
Wine of immortall mixture; which can prove
It's Tincture from the rosy nectar; wine
That can exalt weak EARTH; & so refine
Our dust, that at one draught, mortality
May drink it self up, and forget to dy.

The Flaming Heart
Upon The Book and
Picture of the seraphicall saint Teresa,
(as she is usually expressed
with a Seraphim biside her.)

Well meaning readers! you that come as freinds
And catch the pretious name this peice pretends;
Make not too much hast to'admire
That fair-cheek't fallacy of fire.
That is a SERAPHIM, they say
And this the great TERESIA.
Readers, be rul'd by me; and make
Here a well-plac't and wise mistake
You must transpose the picture quite,
And spell it wrong to read it right; *10*
Read HIM for her, and her for him;
And call the SAINT the SERAPHIM.
  Painter, what didst thou understand
To put her dart into his hand!
See, even the yeares and size of him
Showes this the mother SERAPHIM.
This is the mistress flame; and duteous he
Her happy fire-works, here, come down to see.
O most poor-spirited of men!
Had thy cold Pencil kist her PEN *20*
Thou couldst not so unkindly err
To show us This faint shade for HER
Why man, this speakes pure mortall frame;
And mockes with female FROST love's manly flame.
One would suspect thou meant'st to paint
Some weak, inferiour, woman saint.
But had thy pale-fac't purple took
Fire from the burning cheeks of that bright Booke
Thou wouldst on her have heap't up all
That could be found SERAPHICALL; *30*
What e're this youth of fire weares fair,
Rosy fingers, radiant hair,
Glowing cheek, and glistering wings,
All those fair and flagrant things,

The Flaming . . . her: Lines 1–84 of this poem were first published in 1648 with the title "The Flaming Heart."

But before all, that fiery DART
Had fill'd the Hand of this great HEART.
  Doe then as equall right requires,
Since HIS the blushes be, and her's the fires,
Resume and rectify thy rude design;
Undresse thy Seraphim into MINE. *40*
Redeem this injury of thy art;
Give HIM the vail, give her the dart.
  Give Him the vail; that he may cover
The Red cheeks of a rivall'd lover.
Asham'd that our world, now, can show
Nests of new Seraphims here below.
  Give her the DART for it is she
(Fair youth) shootes both thy shaft and THEE.
Say, all ye wise and well-peirc't hearts
That live and dy amidst her darts, *50*
What is't your tastfull spirits doe prove
In that rare life of Her, and love?
Say and bear wittnes. Sends she not
A SERAPHIM at every shott?
What magazins of immortall ARMES there shine!
Heavn's great artillery in each love-spun line.
Give then the dart to her who gives the flame;
Give him the veil, who kindly takes the shame.
  But if it be the frequent fate
Of worst faults to be fortunate; *60*
If all's praescription; and proud wrong
Hearkens not to an humble song;
For all the gallantry of him,
Give me the suff'ring SERAPHIM,
His be the bravery of all those Bright things,
The glowing cheekes, the glistering wings;
The Rosy hand, the radiant DART;
Leave HER alone THE FLAMING HEART.
  Leave her that; and thou shalt leave her
Not one loose shaft but love's whole quiver. *70*
For in love's feild was never found
A nobler weapon than a WOUND.
Love's passives are his activ'st part.
The wounded is the wounding heart.
O HEART! the aequall poise of lov'es both parts
Bigge alike with wounds and darts.
Live in these conquering leaves; live all the same;
And walk through all tongues one triumphant FLAME

Live here, great HEART; and love and dy and kill;
And bleed and wound; and yeild and conquer still. 80
Let this immortall life wherere it comes
Walk in a crowd of loves and MARTYRDOMES.
Let mystick DEATHS wait on't; and wise soules be
The love-slain wittnesses of this life of thee.
O sweet incendiary! shew here thy art,
Upon this carcasse of a hard, cold, hart,
Let all thy scatter'd shafts of light, that play
Among the leaves of thy larg BOOKS of day,
Combin'd against this BREST at once break in
And take away from me my self and sin, 90
This gratious Robbery shall thy bounty be;
And my best fortunes such fair spoiles of me.
O thou undanted daughter of desires!
By all thy dowr of LIGHTS and FIRES;
By all the eagle in thee, all the dove;
By all thy lives and deaths of love;
By thy larg draughts of intellectuall day,
And by thy thrists of love more large then they;
By all thy brim-fill'd Bowles of feirce desire
By thy last Morning's draught of liquid fire; 100
By the full kingdome of that finall kisse
That seiz'd thy parting Soul, and seal'd thee his;
By all the heav'ns thou hast in him
(Fair sister of the SERAPHIM!
By all of HIM we have in THEE;
Leave nothing of my SELF in me.
Let me so read thy life, that I
Unto all life of mine may dy.

Prayer.

An Ode, Which Was Præfixed to a little Prayer-book given to a young Gentle-Woman

Lo here a little volume, but great Book!
A nest of new-born sweets;
Whose native fires disdaining

Prayer: An earlier version was published as "On a prayer booke sent to Mrs. M. R." in 1646.

To ly thus folded, & complaining
Of these ignoble sheets,
Affect more comly bands
(Fair one) from thy kind hands
And confidently look
To find the rest
Of a rich binding in your BREST 10
It is, in one choise handfull, heavenn; & all
Heavn's Royall host; incamp't thus small
To prove that true, schooles use to tell,
Ten thousand Angels in one point can dwell.
It is love's great artillery
Which here contracts it self, & comes to ly
Close couch't in your white bosom: & from thence
As from a snowy fortresse of defence,
Against your ghostly foes to take your part,
And fortify the hold of your chast heart. 20
It is an armory of light
Let constant use but keep it bright,
You'l find it yeilds
To holy hands & humble hearts
More swords & sheilds
Then sin hath snares, or Hell hath darts.
Only be sure
The hands be pure
That hold these weapons; & the eyes
Those of turtles, chast & true; 30
Wakefull & wise;
Here is a freind shall fight for you,
Hold but this book before your heart
Let prayer alone to play his part,
But ô the heart
That studyes this high ART
Must be a sure house-keeper;
And yet no sleeper.
Dear soul, be strong.
MERCY will come e're long 40
And bring his bosom fraught with blessings,
Flowers of never fading graces
To make immortall dressings
For worthy soules, whose wise embraces
Store up themselves for HIM, who is alone
The SPOUSE of Virgins & the Virgin's son.
But if the noble BRIDEGROOM, when he come,

Shall find the loytering HEART from home;
Leaving her chast aboad
To gadde abroad *50*
Among the gay mates of the god of flyes;
To take her pleasure & to play
And keep the devill's holyday;
To dance ith' sunshine of some smiling
But beguiling
Spheares of sweet & sugred Lyes,
Some slippery Pair
Of false, perhaps as fair,
Flattering but forswearing eyes;
Doubtlesse some other heart *60*
Will gett the start
Mean while, & stepping in before
Will take possession of that sacred store
Of hidden sweets & holy joyes.
WORDS which are not heard with EARES
(Those tumultuous shops of noise)
Effectuall wispers, whose still voice
The soul it selfe more feeles then heares;
Amorous languishments; luminous trances;
SIGHTS which are not seen with eyes; *70*
Spirituall & soul-peircing glances
Whose pure & subtil lightning flyes
Home to the heart, & setts the house on fire
And melts it down in sweet desire
Yet does not stay
To ask the windows leave to passe that way;
Delicious DEATHS; soft exalations
Of soul; dear & divine annihilations;
A thousand unknown rites
Of joyes & rarefy'd delights; *80*
A hundred thousand goods, glories, & graces.
And many a mystick thing
Which the divine embraces
Of the deare spouse of spirits with them will bring
For which it is no shame
That dull mortality must not know a name.
Of all this store
Of blessings & ten thousand more
(If when he come
He find the Heart from home) *90*
Doubtlesse he will unload

Himself some other where,
And poure abroad
His pretious sweets
On the fair soul whom first he meets.
O fair, ô fortunate; O riche, ô dear!
O happy & thrice happy she
Selected dove
Who ere she be
Whose early love *100*
With winged vowes
Makes hast to meet her morning spouse
And close with his immortall kisses.
Happy indeed, who never misses
To improve that pretious hour,
And every day
Seize her sweet prey
All fresh & fragrant as he rises
Dropping with a baulmy Showr
A delicious dew of spices; *110*
O let the blissfull heart hold fast
Her heavnly arm-full, she shall tast
At once ten thousand paradises;
She shall have power
To rifle & deflour
The rich & roseall spring of those rare sweets
Which with a swelling bosome there she meets
Boundles & infinite
Bottomles treasures
Of pure inebriating pleasures. *120*
Happy proof! she shal discover
What joy, what blisse,
How many Heav'ns at once it is
To have her GOD become her LOVER.

Hope

Hope whose weak beeing ruin'd is
Alike if it succeed or if it misse!

Hope: In the 1646 edition of *Steps to the Temple*, this poem and the following one, "M. Crashaws Answer For Hope," were incorporated as one poem, in alternating stanzas of ten lines assigned to Cowley and Crashaw, and entitled "On Hope, By way of Question and Answer, betweene A. Cowley, and R. Crashaw."

Whom ill or good does equally confound
And both the hornes of fate's dilemma wound.
Vain shadow; that dost vanish quite.
Both at full noon & perfect night!
The starres have not a possibility
Of blessing Thee.
If things then from their end we happy call,
'Tis hope is the most hopelesse thing of all. 10
Hope, thou bold Taster of delight!
Who instead of doing so, devourst it quite.
Thou bringst us an estate, yet leav'st us poor
By clogging it with legacyes before.
The joyes which we intire should wed
Come deflour'd-virgins to our bed.
Good fortunes without gain imported be
Such mighty custom's paid to Thee.
For joy like wine kep't close, does better tast;
If it take air before his spirits wast. 20
Hope fortun's cheating lottery
Where for one prize, an hundred blankes there be.
Fond archer, hope. Who tak'st thine aime so farr
That still or short or wide thine arrowes are
Thinne empty cloud which th'ey deceives
With shapes that our own fancy gives.
A cloud which gilt & painted now appeares
But must drop presently in teares
When thy false beames o're reason's light prevail,
By Ignes Fatui for north starres we sail. 30
Brother of fear more gayly clad.
The merryer fool oth two, yet quite as mad.
Sire of repentance, child of fond desire
That blow'st the chymick & the lover's fire.
Still leading them insensibly'on
With the strong witchcraft of Anon.
By thee the one does changing nature through
Her endlesse labyrinth's pursue,
And th'other chases woman; while she goes
More wayes & turnes then hunted nature knowes. 40

M. Crashaws Answer For Hope

Dear hope! earth's dowry, & heavn's debt!
The entity of those that are not yet.
Subtlest, but surest beeing! Thou by whom
Our nothing has a definition!
Substantiall shade! whose sweet allay
Blends both the noones of night & day.
Fates cannot find out a capacity
Of hurting thee.
From Thee their lean dilemma, with blunt horn,
Shrinkes, as the sick moon from the wholsome morn. *10*
Rich hope! love's legacy, under lock
Of faith! still spending, & still growing stock!
Our crown-land lyes above yet each meal brings
A seemly portion for the sonnes of kings.
Nor will the virgin joyes we wed
Come lesse unbroken to our bed,
Because that from the bridall cheek of blisse
Thou steal'st us down a distant kisse.
Hope's chast stealth harmes no more joye's maidenhead
Then spousall rites prejudge the marriage bed. *20*
Fair hope! our earlyer heav'n by thee
Young time is taster to eternity
Thy generous wine with age growes strong, not sowre.
Nor does it kill thy fruit, to smell thy flowre.
Thy golden, growing, head never hangs down
Till in the lappe of loves full noone
It falls; and dyes! o no, it melts away
As does the dawn into the day.
As lumpes of sugar loose themselves; and twine
Their supple essence with the soul of wine. *30*
Fortune? alas, above the world's low warres
Hope walks; & kickes the curld heads of conspiring starres.
Her keel cutts not the waves where These winds stirr
Fortune's whole lottery is one blank to her.
Her shafts, and shee fly farr above,
And forrage in the fields of light and love.

M. Crashaws . . . Hope: See the note on the preceding poem, "Hope."

Sweet hope! kind cheat! fair fallacy by thee
We are not WHERE nor What we be,
But WHAT & WHERE we would be. Thus art thou
Our absent PRESENCE, and our future Now.
  Faith's sister! nurse of fair desire! *40*
Fear's antidote! a wise & well-stay'd fire!
Temper twixt chill despair, & torrid joy!
Queen Regent in yonge love's minority!
    Though the vext chymick vainly chases
    His fugitive gold through all her faces;
Though love's more feirce, more fruitlesse, fires assay
    One face more fugitive then all they;
True hope's a glorious hunter & her chase,
The GOD of nature in the feilds of grace. *50*

VIVE JESU.

Bibliography

GENERAL

ALLEN, DON CAMERON. *Image and Meaning: Metaphoric Traditions in Renaissance Poetry.* Baltimore: Johns Hopkins Press, 1960.

BUSH, DOUGLAS. *English Literature in the Earlier Seventeenth Century 1600–1660.* Oxford: Clarendon Press, 1945.

DAVIES, GODFREY. *Early Stuarts 1603–1660.* Oxford: Clarendon Press, 1937.

FREEMAN, ROSEMARY. *English Emblem Books.* London: Chatto & Windus, 1948.

FRYE, NORTHROP. *Anatomy of Criticism.* Princeton: Princeton University Press, 1957.

GRIERSON, H. J. C. *Cross-Currents in 17th Century English Literature.* New York: Harper Torchbooks, 1958. (First published in 1929.)

HALLER, WILLIAM. *Rise of Puritanism.* New York: Columbia University Press, 1938.

HARDISON, O. B. *The Enduring Monument: A Study in the Idea of Praise in Renaissance Literary Theory and Practice.* Chapel Hill: University of North Carolina Press, 1962.

HOLLANDER, JOHN. *Untuning of The Sky: Ideas of Music in English Poetry 1500–1700.* Princeton: Princeton University Press, 1961.

KEAST, WILLIAM, ed. *Seventeenth Century English Poetry: Modern Essays in Criticism.* New York: Galaxy Books, 1962.

MAHOOD, M. M. *Poetry and Humanism.* London: Jonathan Cape, 1950.

MARTZ, LOUIS L. *The Poetry of Meditation.* New Haven: Yale University Press, 1954.

MORE, P. E., and F. L. CROSS. *Anglicanism: The Thought and Practice of the Church of England.* London: S.P.C.K., 1935.

NICOLSON, MARJORIE HOPE. *The Breaking of the Circle: Studies in the Effect of the New Science upon 17th Century Poetry.* Evanston, Ill.: Northwestern University Press, 1950.

ROSS, MALCOLM M. *Poetry and Dogma: Transfiguration of Eucharistic*

Symbols in Seventeenth Century English Poetry. New Brunswick: Rutgers University Press, 1954.

WALLERSTEIN, RUTH. *Studies in Seventeenth-Century Poetic.* Madison: University of Wisconsin Press, 1950.

METAPHYSICAL POETRY

ALVAREZ, A. *The School of Donne.* New York: Pantheon Books, 1961.

BENNETT, JOAN. *Four Metaphysical Poets. Donne. Herbert. Vaughan. Crashaw.* New York: Vintage Books, 1960. (First published in 1934.)

DUNCAN, JOSEPH E. *Revival of Metaphysical Poetry: The History of a Style, 1800 to the Present.* Minneapolis: University of Minnesota Press, 1959.

ELIOT, T. S. *Homage to John Dryden.* London: Hogarth Press, 1924.

———. *Selected Essays.* London: Faber & Faber, 1934.

ELLRODT, ROBERT. *Les poetes metaphysiques Anglais.* Paris: Librairie José Corti, 1960, 3 vols.

ESCH, ARNO. *Englische Religiose lyrik des 17. Jahrhunderts: studien zu Donne, Herbert, Crashaw, Vaughan.* Tubingen: Max Niemeyer Verlag, 1950.

GRIERSON, H. J. C. Introductory essay to: *Metaphysical Lyrics and Poems of the Seventeenth-Century from Donne to Butler.* New York: Galaxy Books, 1959. (First published in 1921.)

HUSAIN, ITRAT. *The Mystical Element in the Metaphysical Poets of the Seventeenth Century.* London: Oliver & Boyd, 1948.

LEISHMAN, J. B. *The Metaphysical Poets.* Oxford: Clarendon Press, 1934.

MAZZEO, JOSEPH A. *Renaissance and Seventeenth Century Studies.* New York: Columbia University Press, 1964.

DE MOURGUES, ODETTE. *Metaphysical, Baroque and Precieux Poetry.* Oxford: Clarendon Press, 1953.

PRAZ, MARIO. *Studies in Seventeenth-Century Imagery.* London: Warburg Institute, 1939, 2 vols.

SHARP, ROBERT L. *From Donne to Dryden: The Revolt Against Metaphysical Poetry.* Chapel Hill: University of North Carolina Press, 1940.

SPENCER, THEODORE, and MARK VAN DOREN. *Studies in Metaphysical Poetry.* New York: Columbia University Press, 1939.

TUVE, ROSEMOND. *Elizabethan and Metaphysical Imagery.* Chicago: University of Chicago Press, 1947.

WALTON, GEOFFREY. *Metaphysical to Augustan: Studies in Tone and Sensibility in the Seventeenth Century.* London: Bowes & Bowes, 1955.

WARNKE, FRANK J., ed., *European Metaphysical Poetry*. New Haven: Yale University Press, 1961.

WHITE, HELEN C. *The Metaphysical Poets: A Study in Religious Experience*. New York: Collier Books, 1962. (First published in 1936.)

WILLIAMSON, GEORGE. *The Donne Tradition*. Cambridge: Harvard University Press, 1930.

JOHN DONNE

Texts:

GARDNER, HELEN, ed. *John Donne: The Divine Poems*. Oxford: Clarendon Press, 1952.

———. *The Elegies and the Songs and Sonnets of John Donne*. Oxford: Clarendon Press, 1965.

GRIERSON, H. J. C., ed. *The Poems of John Donne*. Oxford: Clarendon Press, 1912, 2 vols.

MANLEY, FRANK, ed. *John Donne: The Anniversaries*. Baltimore: Johns Hopkins Press, 1963.

REDPATH, THEODORE, ed. *The Songs and Sonets of John Donne*, an Editio Minor. London: Methuen, 1956.

Critical Works:

ANDREASON, N. J. C. "Theme and Structure in Donne's *Satyres*," *Studies in English Literature*, III (1963), 59–75.

COFFIN, CHARLES M. *John Donne and the New Philosophy*. New York: Columbia University Press, 1958. (First published in 1937.)

GARDNER, HELEN, ed. *John Donne: A Collection of Critical Essays*. Englewood Cliffs, N. J.: Spectrum Books, 1962.

HUNT, CLAY. *Donne's Poetry: Essays in Literary Analysis*. New Haven: Yale University Press, 1954.

LEISHMAN, J. B. *The Monarch of Wit*. London: Hutchinson's University Library, 1951.

SIMPSON, EVELYN M. *A Study of the Prose Works of John Donne*, 2nd ed. Oxford: Clarendon Press, 1948. (First published in 1924.)

SPENCER, THEODORE, ed. *A Garland for John Donne 1631–1931*. Oxford: Oxford University Press, 1931.

WILLIAMSON, GEORGE. "The Design of Donne's *Anniversaries*," *MP*, *LX* (1963), 183–191.

See also:

Listings under *Metaphysical Poetry*.

GEORGE HERBERT

Text:

HUTCHINSON, F. E., ed. *The Works of George Herbert.* Oxford: Clarendon Press, 1941.

Critical Works:

BOTTRALL, MARGARET. *George Herbert.* London: John Murray, 1954.

BOWERS, FREDSON. "Herbert's Sequential Imagery: 'The Temper,'" *MP,* LIX (February, 1962), 202–213.

COLIE, ROSALIE. "Logos in *The Temple,* George Herbert and the Shape of Content," *Journal of the Warburg and Courtauld Institutes,* XXVI (1963), 327–342.

OSTRIKER, ALICIA. "Song and Speech in the Metrics of George Herbert," *PMLA,* LXXX (March, 1965), 62–68.

SUMMERS, JOSEPH. *George Herbert, his Religion and Art.* Cambridge: Harvard University Press, 1954.

TUVE, ROSEMOND. *A Reading of George Herbert.* Chicago: University of Chicago Press, 1952.

———. "Sacred 'Parody' of Love Poetry, and Herbert," *Studies in the Renaissance* (New York: Renaissance Society of America, 1961), vol. VIII, 249–290.

See also:

Listings under *Metaphysical Poetry* and *General Bibliography,* particularly Freeman, Martz, White.

HENRY VAUGHAN

Texts:

FOGLE, FRENCH, ed. *Complete Poetry of Henry Vaughan.* New York: Anchor Books, 1964.

MARTIN, L. C., ed. *The Works of Henry Vaughan,* 2nd ed. Oxford: Clarendon Press, 1957.

Critical Works:

DURR, R. A. *On the Mystical Poetry of Henry Vaughan.* Cambridge: Harvard University Press, 1962.

GARNER, ROSS. *Henry Vaughan: Experience and the Tradition.* Chicago: University of Chicago Press, 1959.

HOLMES, ELIZABETH. *Henry Vaughan and the Hermetic Philosophy.* Oxford: Blackwell, 1932.

HUTCHINSON, F. E. *Henry Vaughan: A Life and Interpretation.* Oxford: Clarendon Press, 1947.

KERMODE, F. "The Private Imagery of Henry Vaughan," *RES*, I (1950), 206–225.

MARTZ, LOUIS. *The Paradise Within: Studies in Vaughan, Traherne and Milton.* New Haven: Yale University Press, 1964.

PETTET, E. C. *Of Paradise and Light.* Cambridge: Harvard University Press, 1960.

See also:

Listings under *General Bibliography* and *Metaphysical Poetry*, especially Martz, White, Mahood, Allen.

THOMAS TRAHERNE

Text:

MARGOLIOUTH, H. M., ed. *Thomas Traherne, Centuries, Poems, and Thanksgivings.* Oxford: Clarendon Press, 1958, 2 vols.

Critical Works:

COLIE, ROSALIE L. "Traherne and the Infinite," *HLQ*, XXI (1957), 69–82.

MARTZ, LOUIS. *The Paradise Within: Studies in Vaughan, Traherne and Milton.* New Haven: Yale University Press, 1964.

SALTER, K. W. *Thomas Traherne: Mystic and Poet.* New York: Barnes & Noble, 1964.

WADE, GLADYS I. *Thomas Traherne: A Critical Biography.* Princeton: Princeton University Press, 1944.

See also:

Leishman; Mahood; White.

RICHARD CRASHAW

Text:

MARTIN, L. C., ed. *Poems English, Latin and Greek of Richard Crashaw,* 2nd ed. Oxford: Clarendon Press, 1957.

Critical Works:

MADSEN, WILLIAM G. "A Reading of 'Musicks Duell,' " *Studies in Honor of John Wilcox,* A. D. Wallace and W. O. Ross, eds. (Detroit: Wayne State University Press, 1958), 39–50.

PETTOELLO, LAURA. "A Current Misconception Concerning the Influence of Marino's Poetry on Crashaw's," *MLR,* LII (July, 1957), 321–328.

PRAZ, MARIO. "The Flaming Heart," in *The Flaming Heart: Essays on Crashaw, Macchiavelli and Other Studies.* Garden City, N. Y.: Anchor Books, 1958.

RICKEY, MARY ELLEN. *Rhyme and Meaning in Crashaw*. Lexington: University of Kentucky Press, 1961.

WALLERSTEIN, RUTH C. *Richard Crashaw: A Study in Style and Poetic Development*. Madison: University of Wisconsin Press, 1959. (First published in 1935.)

WARREN, AUSTIN. *Richard Crashaw: A Study in Baroque Sensibility*. Ann Arbor: University of Michigan Press, 1957. (First published in 1939.)

WILLIAMS, GEORGE WALTON. *Image and Symbol in the Sacred Poetry of Richard Crashaw*. Columbia: University of South Carolina Press, 1963.

See also:

Listings under *Metaphysical Poetry* and *General Bibliography*, especially Freeman, Keast, Martz, White.

Index of Titles and First Lines

ABOUT THE EDITOR

MIRIAM K. STARKMAN, Professor of English at Queens College of The City University of New York, received her B.A. from Brooklyn College and her M.A. and Ph.D. from Columbia University. She has been a Fulbright Professor in Israel and has received a Guggenheim Fellowship for a book on seventeenth-century poetry. Professor Starkman is the author of Swift's Satire on Learning in A Tale of a Tub, *editor of* Gulliver's Travels and Other Writings, *and is a frequent contributor to various scholarly journals.*

A NOTE ON THE TYPE

The text of this book was set on the Linotype in a new face called Primer, designed by Rudolph Ruzicka, earlier responsible for the design of Fairfield and Fairfield Medium, Linotype faces whose virtues have for some time now been accorded wide recognition.

The complete range of sizes of Primer was first made available in 1954, although the pilot size of 12 point was ready as early as 1951. The design of the face makes general reference to Linotype Century (long a serviceable type, totally lacking in manner or frills of any kind) but brilliantly corrects the characterless quality of that face.

The book was designed by Betty Anderson and was composed, printed, and bound by H. Wolff, New York.